# GENERATION Q

# GENERATION Q

gays, lesbians, and bisexuals born around
1969's Stonewall riots tell their stories
of growing up in the age of information

edited by
## Robin Bernstein
and
## Seth Clark Silberman

ALYSON PUBLICATIONS
LOS ANGELES

Manufactured in the United States of America.
Printed on acid-free paper.

This trade paperback original is published by Alyson Publications Inc.
P.O. Box 4371, Los Angeles, California 90078.
Distribution in the United Kingdom by Turnaround Publisher Services Ltd.,
27 Horsell Road, London N5 1XL, England.

First edition: September 1996

5  4  3  2  1

ISBN 1-55583-356-X


Library of Congress Cataloging-in-Publication Data

Generation Q : gays, lesbians, and bisexuals born around 1969's Stonewall riots tell their stories of growing up in the age of information / edited by Robin Bernstein and Seth Clark Silberman. — 1st ed.
    ISBN 1-55583-356-X
    1. Gay youth—United States—Attitudes. 2. Gays—United States—Identity.
3. Lesbian youth—United States—Attitudes. 4. Lesbians—United States—
Identity. 5. Bisexuals—United States—Attitudes. I. Bernstein, Robin, 1969–    .
II. Silberman, Seth Clark, 1968–    .
HQ76.3.U5G45 1996                                        96-9860
306.76'6—dc20                                            CIP

For Andy, Florence, Joanne, and Michael Bernstein,
and in memory of Leonard Bernstein.
—*R.B.*

For Craig and my family.
—*S.C.S.*

# Contents

# CONTENTS

## My Real Love Was Pop Culture

## A Difficult Floating Garden

## Face-to-Face With Fears and Strange Knowledges

## CONTENTS

### My Swollen Little Libido

### A Hand Curls Into a Fist

### A Fag, a Dyke, a Gender-Switch Queer

# Acknowledgments

The editors would like to thank Evelyn Torton Beck, Kenneth Cameron, Diane DiMassa, Michael Dumas, Lisa Furst, Patti Gillespie, Susan Leonardi, Michael Lowenthal, Lee Lynch, Carla Peterson, Richard Schneider Jr., Margaret Seymour, Stacy A. Sheehan, Mark Sullivan, Maya Townsend, Julie Trevelyan, Alistair Williamson, and Bruce Wright for their invaluable help. Thanks are also due to the panelists and moderators at the terrific panels on editing anthologies at OutWrite '92 and '95: Mi Ok Bruining, Loraine Hutchins, John Preston, Assoto Saint, Jo Schneiderman, and Judith Stein. We especially thank Lesléa Newman for her constant support, advice, wisdom, and kindness.

# Introduction

A forty-year-old gay man is leading a support group for queer teens. Today, he tries to spark discussion about gay celebrities. "How about Melissa Etheridge?" he says to a fifteen-year-old lesbian. "She must be a great role model, right?"

"No," says the girl. "I don't like her music."

"But she's out, she's proud, she's a rock star!" says the man. "She *must* be a role model."

"*You're not listening to me,*" says the girl. "*I don't like her music.*"

As the post-Stonewall generation comes out, we often find a chasm between our experiences and perspectives and those of the lesbians, gay men, bisexuals, and transgendered people who came before us. We are members of the so-called Generation X: We grew up with Reagan and Bush as presidents and a declining economy; much more often than previous generations, we were latchkey kids, children of dual-career, divorced, separated, or alternative families. We are stereotyped as politically apathetic, consumeristic, alienated, irreverent, and media savvy.

As young lesbians, gay men, bisexuals, and transgendered people, however, we differ from not only our gay forebears but also our straight peers. We are not just "X" but "Q"—*Queer,* a word embraced by our generation.

As members of Generation Q, we were born after or shortly before the Stonewall riots of 1969, which marked the beginning of the modern gay rights movement, and we came out during the eighties and nineties. The first three sections of this book explore our origins: our families, the communities in which we grew up, and our universal wet nurse—pop culture.

Anna Myers-Parrelli writes in "Significant Others: A Queer Autobiography":

> Coming out to my parents had not followed the scripts I had studied in the history books—*our* history books, the ones I had relied upon to guide me through my closet doors. When a lesbian comes out, the books read, parents are supposed to faint/cry/scream/disown you/deny/argue. But all mine said was, "So?" If my coming out was not following the course that other lesbians before me had charted, I wondered, then how much of the rest of my life would their experiences apply to?

The essays in this book draw a fresh map with new terrain, new boundaries, and new directions. Our communities are changing—they are becoming stronger and more visible. A deep closet has become more unthinkable. Certainly the closet has not been eradicated, but few members of Generation Q imagine a closeted life as a reasonable long-term option. The closet has become a temporary convenience, a practical safety measure, a tool to use in particular circumstances, a toy to play with, rather than a constant, coercive presence.

As the closet becomes less rigid, more permeable, and less central, so too does the initial act of coming out. But if coming out is no longer necessarily the primary rite of passage for queer youth, what is? Many of the men and women in this anthology would probably answer, "AIDS. Taking the test. Losing a love. Becoming an activist."

Generation Q is the first with no memory of sex before AIDS. We came out in the mid-eighties or later, after Rock Hudson became ill and AIDS hit the mainstream media. For us, sex, love, queerness, and AIDS have been inextricably linked from the very beginning. The section "A Difficult Floating Garden" focuses on our experiences of love—but AIDS is a conspicuous presence for almost all the men and women in that section.

Our generation been stereotyped as hypersexual; for many of us, however, sex has become a site of fear and tension. We originally conceived the fifth section of this book as the "sex" portion. The pieces that congregated there, however, were grim and bitter—hardly sex-positive fare. Thus, we titled that section "Face-to-Face With Fears and Strange Knowledges."

With AIDS a constant presence from the moment we come out, it is no wonder that the sexually triumphant and joyful essays in this book have more to do with reading and watching sex—that is, totally safe activities—than with actual sexual contact. The sixth section, "My Swollen Little Libido," explores our use of pornography and other eroticized gazing.

While our generation has been accused of "having it easy," we have endured a serious wave of hate crimes and other forms of violence against us. The seventh section, "A Hand Curls Into a Fist," addresses the violence present in our lives and our responses to it.

Some characteristics of our generation are so pervasive that we could not create a separate section for them. Activism, for example, has become a given in many of our lives, particularly during the college years. The essayists in this collection include a "survivor" of ACT UP and Queer Nation, a Lesbian Avenger, and a riot grrrl. In this way, Generation Q contradicts the stereotype of Generation X's political apathy.

"It is a truism," write Kris Franklin and Sarah E. Chinn, "that AIDS activism brought lesbians and gay men back into political and social contact with one another." This contact has spread beyond the immediate field of AIDS activism; before the plague, for example, a forty-year-old gay man would have been less likely to provide organized support to a fifteen-year-old lesbian.

Indeed, partially because AIDS activism has enabled gay men and lesbians to form loving—and sometimes sexual—relationships with one another, the bisexual movement has gained great momentum over the past ten years. Generation Q is the first to come out into a world in which a bi identity is a clear, definite option, celebrated in magazines and anthologies. While biphobia still exists, such bigotry meets with increasing challenge; to young ears, epithets such as "fence-sitter" can seem like relics of another era.

Generation Q's respect for bisexuality has led some of our elders to believe that for our generation, queerness and bisexuality are synonymous. This is not true, however—whereas a bisexual identity can be as fixed and rigid as any other, queerness is about resisting categorization. Queerness, the FRINGE Manifesto asserts, is "twisted and disgusting, beautiful and glamorous, extreme and alive."

The final section of this book, "A Fag, a Dyke, a Gender-Switch Queer" explores Generation Q's adoption of this powerful and problematic identity. Queerness, it turns out, both unites and divides us. The word *queer* breaks down boundaries among microcommunities (lesbians, gay men, bisexuals, transgendered people, fags, dykes, perverts) and gives us a united queer community that can certainly be more powerful than disorganized, individual factions.

At the same time, however, the diversity within that macrocommunity makes us less likely to feel instant kinship with people who share our labels: A fifteen-year-old lesbian does not necessarily identify with Melissa Etheridge simply because they share a sexual orientation. As *queer* stretches to include more people and as the meanings of words such as *lesbian* become less fixed, it becomes harder to know what the hell we do mean, who the fuck we are fucking. It becomes easier to find people sort of like us, but harder to find and connect with people very similar to us. The glorification of a queer macrocommunity can make us feel guilty if, for example, lesbians want space with other lesbians. Or it can gloss over differences among us to the point where we don't even know for whom, exactly, we're lonely for. We fail to imagine what we could enjoy and accomplish within our microcommunities. By slurring our differences, queerness can also mask the ways in which we are able to oppress one another.

Self-contradiction and resistance to categorization form the heart of queerness. Such persistent paradoxes do not emerge from a void; rather, they reflect Generation Q's contradictory inheritance from pre-Stonewall eras and from Stonewall itself.

The Legend of the Stonewall Rebellion tells us that a group of black and Latino drag queens, saddened and angered by the recent death of Judy Garland, attacked police with bricks as the cops raided the Stonewall Inn bar. Like any good myth the legend is perhaps based more on romantic cultural stereotypes—gay men distraught over Judy's death, fierce black and Latino drag queens with nothing to lose—than on actual events. What really happened at the Stonewall Inn that night is both contestable and possibly irrelevant, as Justin Chin argues in the final essay of this anthology, "Q-Punk Grammar."

## INTRODUCTION

Our contemporary movement, therefore, is built on and fueled by a self-contradictory, unverifiable, and possibly irrelevant mythology. Generation Q exists within contradictions. We have inherited a joyous, visible, powerful, accessible, diverse culture; astonishing support networks; and previously unimaginable freedoms. We have also inherited, in Chin's words, "a virus, a wrecked community, memorials, the NAMES Quilt, clinical trials, and the AIDS industry as a viable and 'noble' career choice." We have inherited the Christian religious right and a backlash against feminism, multiculturalism, affirmative action, and civil rights. And we are still not safe on the streets in broad daylight.

Before Stonewall, a fifteen-year-old lesbian could not have joined a queer teens' support group and conversed with a forty-year-old gay man about out celebrities. Today, miraculously, it is possible, but the girl and the man still don't necessarily understand each other. And when they walk out the door together, they still face enormous risks. Everything, and nothing, has changed.

Robin Bernstein and Seth Clark Silberman
March 1996

*Prologue*

# A Birth at Stonewall
## by Hedda Lettuce

On a sweltering night in June 1969, a young woman was getting off work. She was pregnant. Extremely pregnant. And her name was Mary. She scrubbed floors on her callused hands and knees to make ends meet. Her usual route home was along Christopher Street. Oh, she loved that block. Such a peaceful block. The trees, the light traffic, the handsome men. Poor, poor, dim-witted Mary, she didn't realize that these men were cruising one another, looking for that special piece of meat that would help pass the time.

But peaceful was the last thing Christopher Street was this night. Underneath the men's cruisy exteriors lay anger, fear, and frustration from years of oppression, police brutality, and bad hair. On this sticky night in June, this would change forever. The gay liberation movement would be born. And something else. Someone else.

As Mary got closer to Sheridan Square, she saw all this commotion, all this activity, all these police. Something Mary wasn't accustomed to seeing. And being the nosy person she was, she couldn't help taking a closer look.

Maybe it was the heat. Or maybe it was because Judy was being placed in the ground, leaving poor Liza an orphan. Or maybe the queers had just had it and it was time for them to stand up for their rights. Whatever the reason, the battle of Stonewall had begun.

In a matter of moments, this pregnant broad was right in the thick of it. Like a deer caught in headlights, she couldn't believe what she was seeing. Hard-looking women throwing parking meters at the police. *What could be going on?* Mary thought to herself. Before Mary could make out what was happening, one of these hard-looking gals ran up to her and cried, "Come on girl, help us out here!" And placed an empty beer bottle in her hand. "Help out with what?" Mary asked.

At that moment there was a gust of wind, and Mary thought she heard angels singing, but they sounded like the Munchkins from *The Wizard of Oz*. Then this yellow orb, this glowing bubble, floated toward Mary. Inside the bubble was not Glinda, the good witch, but Judy Garland herself! Not the perky young Judy, but the tired, old, haggard Judy, piss-drunk as usual. She stopped a few feet in front of Mary and slurred, "Listen lady, I've got to make this brief. There's a riot going on, in case you haven't noticed. This is why you have to throw that bottle." And she showed Mary snapshots of all the pain gays and lesbians have suffered throughout the ages. It was special, like a Kodak moment. Then Judy burped, the bubble burst, and she was gone.

Disgusted by what Judy showed her, Mary cast her bottle into the fray, striking a cop right between his bulbous eyes. Way to go, Mary!

This angered the cop, and he ran over to Mary, billy club in hand, and whacked her right in her pregnant stomach. *Tsk, tsk, tsk.* Maybe he thought she was a potbellied drag queen. Mary fell to the ground, reeling in pain. But before the cop could lay another blow on Mary, he was knocked unconscious by a parking meter. As Mary caught her breath, she felt another pain, sharper than before. And she noticed that she was sitting in a puddle. "Holy shit," she cried as a flock of white doves flew overhead. "My water broke! I'm having my baby!"

All seemed lost. Who would care about some pregnant broad lying on the pavement, screaming? Those fags probably thought it was a cheap attention-getting gag. Another media whore trying to steal focus from one of the most important events in gay history. Typical.

Then, out of the crowd like a vision descending upon her, this black queen with daisies in her hair and crimson lips knelt before her and exclaimed, "My name is Marsha P. Johnson. Now push, Mary, push." Before Mary knew it she was cradling her baby in her arms. Mary watched in amazement as Marsha took the broken bottle she was going to throw at the cops and cut the umbilical cord. Then this angelic drag-queen midwife kissed the baby's forehead and disappeared into the angry mob.

# A BIRTH AT STONEWALL

Mary looked down at her child, saw the lipstick stain on his forehead, and knew this child was destined for glamour. And that glamorous baby was *me!* Flash forward to today. Here I am. And don't I look fabulous? I do still have that dent in my forehead where that billy club hit my mother's stomach. But I cover it with Dermablend. Look how far this movement's come since my birth. We have...ah... We've got... We have... We have the Gay Games! And we can be in the military if we don't tell anyone, and lesbians are chic, and Steven Spielberg made a movie about drag queens, and gay sex is legal in almost half the states, and we're here, and it's not raining. You've come a long way, baby.

*Family Photographs*

# On Raising the Issue
## by Erika Kleinman

I used to chase girls when I was in second grade. I used to chase them on the playground, and they would run away, squealing. Much like the boys who participated in the same activity, I wouldn't have known what to do if I'd actually caught one. But I did want the girls to notice me.

Most of the other girls chased boys. One blue-eyed boy in particular was the favorite. Groups of girls would chase him up to the tire swing, down around the tetherball poles, and across the soccer field, until he was cornered in the basketball court. Then they would tickle or spank him. He would scream and laugh.

I could see this from where I was usually standing in line to play tetherball with Laura Quintero, the object of my crush. She was tetherball champion. I was terrible at sports. Laura Quintero would look at me, ask, "Ready?" I would say yes, and then she would gracefully throw the ball in the air and smack it with considerable force. I would stand there, watching her strong brown arms reach back to hit the ball each time it passed while I stood on the other side, mesmerized. I wasn't a tomboy, but I sure did like them.

Blue-eyed boy caught on to the fact that I was the only girl in class who didn't chase him. "Why don't you chase me?" he asked me once while the rest of the class was watching show-and-tell. He sounded pouty.

"I don't know," I said. "Maybe I don't feel like it."

"All the other girls chase me. Why don't you chase me?"

"I don't know," I said again.

"I think you're pretty," he said. He kissed my arm. I moved my arm away.

"Quit it, or I'll tell," I said. He was starting to annoy me.

"I'm going to chase you at recess." He gave me a winning smile.

"I'm playing tetherball at recess," I said.

I did too. I waited faithfully to totally lose to tomboy Laura. I was disappointed when Laura, who had short black hair that she frequently flipped out of her face by whipping her head back in a boyish manner, let her hair grow long and adorned her braids with ribbons. She started wearing dresses. And she mysteriously stopped playing sports.

I mysteriously stopped chasing girls too. When I was in the fourth grade, people started calling me "lezzie." I wasn't really sure what a lezzie was, but it didn't sound good. On the school bus I asked my friend Sara what a lezzie was, exactly. Sara, being quite worldly, enlightened me. "A lezzie is a girl who humps another girl."

"What do you mean, 'hump'?"

Sara rolled her eyes. "Humping," she said, "is when a guy puts his thing in a woman's thing."

"Oh," I said. "My mom told me that's called making love."

Sara shrugged. "My mom says it's called humping."

I pondered this new information. "But if a guy puts his thing in a woman's thing, then what do lezzies do?"

"They have a fake one," she said. "My mom has one too."

"Is your mom a lezzie?" My eyes widened with alarm.

"No, dummy," she said. "She has one for when she's by herself."

"Well," I said, "I think lezzies are gross." I watched Sara's face for a reaction.

"The Bible says it's gross," she replied, looking out the window.

**\* \* \***

"Lezzies are gross!" I informed my mother. I said it like any nine-year-old girl might say it: with exaggerated prissiness and simulated nausea, my eyes squeezed shut with the horror of it all.

"That's not very nice to say," my mother responded. She looked at me. "Why? Why are they gross?" She asked it as if she wanted to know the answer.

"Because, Mom. They just are. They do gross things."

"Why is loving someone gross?"

I was getting irritated. She wasn't cooperating. "I don't know. Girls are supposed to be with boys."

"Well," my mother said, laughing, "I think people can be with whoever they want. It's not up to you." Then she told me that she knew some lesbians from when she was a stewardess—and some gay men too. She said that before she married my dad, she had a gay male roommate, Petey-Poo.

"Petey-Poo? Why did you call him that?"

"Because," she said. "That's what he wanted us to call him."

Even though I didn't know I was gay yet, I felt better.

I felt like if I accidentally maybe turned out to be a lesbian, my mom wouldn't think I was gross.

It was conversations like these that kept my relationship with my mother intact through my teenage years. We had our arguments—mostly about my bad haircuts and consistent failure in gym class and the occasional bad friend—but there was always at the core something very tender and strong at the same time. Something I could count on.

* * *

In middle school and high school, I felt and was regarded as "different" by friends and teachers. I was never really picked on, because I had a talent for verbal retaliation. I couldn't say that I was popular. I never felt that I was part of the crowd, and I didn't like high school dances. I couldn't dance, for one thing. And, unlike my female friends, I didn't hope that any particular Mr. Dreamboat would ask me to dance. I had a few boyfriends. I even got naked with a few of them. But that was even more boring than after-school dances.

The entire universe started to make sense when I was fifteen. I met a girl in high school. We began flirting rituals similar to those of our heterosexual colleagues, meaning we wrote silly little notes back and forth, exchanged awkward romantic sexual innuendos, and spent our spare time daydreaming about each other. We went out on "dates," waiting feverishly to make or take the first move. We held hands during *When Harry Met Sally*, and later we admitted shyly that our sweaty, interlaced hands was the most erotic thing we had ever felt. And when we made love, months later, it was exciting, passionate, clumsy, and disappointing all at the same time. After all, this was new.

But unlike our heterosexual colleagues, we were afraid. We were afraid of this thing that bound us together. While other couples clung to each other, we were afraid to hold hands while walking down the halls. While other couples enjoyed public make-out sessions, we were afraid to kiss between classes. We were afraid of the inevitable rumors that buzzed around the classrooms.

"They're dykes! Have you seen the way they touch each other's faces? And they're always together." One time some girls screamed out the school bus window, "Dykes!" During one of our more daring moments, we held hands on the school bus—underneath our coats, of course. We didn't want to embarrass or offend. Two girls sitting near us pointed at our conspicuous lumpy jackets and shuddered. "Those dykes make me fucking sick," one of them said loudly, not caring who heard.

Although these attitudes were intimidating and hurtful, I felt that they were, for the most part, exaggerated and derived from ignorance. Queer visibility in the news had increased over the past five years owing to the ever-increasing AIDS epidemic and through Queer Nation actions, but most of the kids with whom I went to school had never actually met a proud gay person. There was a small blurb in our health class textbook that stated mysteriously, "Homosexuality is not a mental illness." Then what *is* homosexuality? No one said, "Homosexuality is loving someone of the same gender. Homosexuals are an oppressed group. Historically, gays and lesbians have spent lifetimes hiding their lives and loves from the public. Homosexual teenagers are more likely to experience depression, drug and alcohol addiction, attempted suicide, and suicide. One in ten people is gay, so chances are, there are two or three homos in your classroom right now."

The more I began to notice that gays and lesbians just weren't being represented, the more I wondered why I wasn't doing something about it. My girlfriend and I had been going to a support group for lesbian youth downtown, and I was starting to feel more confident.

"We should just tell everyone we're gay," I told her in the girls' bathroom. There was no one else in there.

"Yeah, right," she said, glancing at the doorway.

"I'm serious."

She laughed tensely. "No," she said. "They wouldn't be able to handle it."

\* \* \*

Later that same day, I came out to my mother. We had always been very close, and I felt burdened by this secret I was keeping from her.

"Let me guess," she said. "You're seeing Helena."

"Yep," I said.

She patted me on the shoulder. Although we were intellectually and emotionally close, she wasn't really one for affection. "It's OK," she said, walking away. *Good,* I thought. *She says it's OK.*

So why did I feel so alone inside?

**\* \* \***

The next day, I tried to tell my mother about the essay I was writing in class about *Huckleberry Finn.* "How come the white person always gets to be the hero? It's like that's the theme this year: Strong White Person sticks up for Poor Black Person. First it was *To Kill a Mockingbird,* then it was *Twelve Angry Men.* As if cool white people are the only reason the black civil rights movement got anywhere. Why don't they assign books that deal with racism from a person of color's point of view?" She wasn't looking at me. "You're not listening to me," I said, pouting.

"Well, I guess I can't listen to you every single minute, Erika." She said it in a mean way.

"What's wrong?" I asked her.

"Nothing," she said, turning on the television.

This cold treatment went on for a couple of days, and I was very confused. *She's not homophobic,* I kept telling myself. *She's an atheist. Only religious people have problems with having a gay kid, right?*

I decided that she needed to know that everything was the same. I bought three carnations and put them in a vase in the living room along with a note that read, "To my mother, with understanding and reassurance that I will always be me, irritating and all." When she came upstairs after she read the note, she threw herself on me, sobbing, "What did I do wrong? What did I do wrong?" I was terrified. Who was the parent here? I patted her on the shoulder. I told her she hadn't done anything wrong.

Then I did the worst thing I could have done. I told her I would try to be straight. She looked at me. She couldn't help it; she was hopeful. Now her daughter could live the good life, settle down, have children, be free from danger. She wouldn't have to worry about what the neighbors might say, what someone might do, what someone might be angry enough to do to her daughter.

"Really?" she asked meekly. She was really going to buy this. My liberal, freethinking, intelligent, atheist mother was willing to totally accept that her daughter would "try to be straight."

I think my mother was processing. She was educated enough to know that I probably wouldn't turn straight. The issue never came up. And inevitably, after three uneventful months as a straight girl, I said, "Mom, I'm really gay, and you can tell anyone you want."

"Anyone I *want?*" She looked at me, as if questioning my sanity. She didn't even want to tell my thirteen-year-old brother. "He couldn't handle it," she said.

"Well, we've got to tell Dad," I said.

"Erika thinks she's gay," my mother said to my father, who had just walked in the door.

He looked at me. "Figured that," he said, not smiling.

**\* \* \***

My mom said she didn't want Helena and me to hold hands in the house. "I'm not ready yet," she told me. I had just started going to Queer Nation. I was becoming indignant, and her little rules bugged me.

"Mother, it doesn't have anything to do with you," I said.

"Yes, it does," she said calmly. "You're my kid."

"But I'm not your baby," I replied. "I'm a big girl."

She stood in the doorway, one hand on her hip. A familiar pose. "Why are you doing this to me?" she asked.

"Mom." I tried to sound gentle. "I'm not doing it to you. I'm just doing it."

**\* \* \***

My dad asked me if I were really a lesbian. "Are you sure?" he asked.

"Yeah," I said. "I mean, I guess so."

"It's not an easy life," he said. "People might not be nice to you all the time." It sounded like one of the numerous veiled warnings I had received as a child: It may look fun, but you'll skin your knees.

I shrugged. "I guess there's nothing I can do about that except try to change their minds."

"Well." He looked sad. "If you're sure." He patted my hand. "I love you no matter what," he said. His fingertips were rough and dry. His hand felt warm.

"Yeah, I love you too," I said. "No matter what."

"OK," he said, squeezing my hand.

\*\*\*

My mother was never one for saving articles. She always read the paper, but she wasn't the type of mom who would go to any great lengths to cut out articles of interest.

That is why I was surprised at the growing number of articles my mother was saving for me. "Look," she said, thrusting yet another article into my semi-extended hand. "Two skinheads beat up a gay man on Capitol Hill yesterday. The man is in the hospital. And that gay rights bill they were trying to pass failed in the House last week."

"Mother," I said emphatically, "will you stop? You're depressing me!"

She looked confused. "I'm just trying to warn you."

I handed her the article. "I don't need your warnings, Mom. I need your support."

"It is a difficult path that you're choosing, and I can't be there all the time for you."

"I can take care of myself. I don't want you to accompany me through the streets of Seattle, I just want you to be my mom. I mean, like you used to be."

"I want you to be prepared, Erika." I hoped she wouldn't cry again. "And I don't want anyone to do anything mean to my kid."

"They won't," I said. I felt like she was the little girl and I was the mother who promised that everything in the whole wide world would be fine, just fine.

"How the hell do you know?" she said, snapping back into her motherly role. "You can't control the world."

"I know. But I'm trying to see what I can do to change it."

\*\*\*

My parents didn't want me to tell my brother. "Oh, my God, Mom, like he doesn't already know."

"Nobody has told him anything," she said.

"Nobody has to." I put my hand on her shoulder. "Look, Mom. Ronnie got mad at me last week, and he called me a fucking dyke."

"That's why we can't tell him yet."

"Why? Just because he's immature and doesn't know anything about it?"

"Yes."

"I think those are perfect reasons to tell him."

She was getting irritated. "Fine, fine. Do what you want." Her eyes said, *Where's my real daughter?*

My eyes replied, *She's right here.*

**\* \* \***

I told my brother I wanted to talk to him. "Ron, I have to tell you. Your sister is a lez."

He nodded, glancing at the floor. "That's what I thought."

"You can tell anyone you want to."

"Shit, no! I'm not telling nobody!"

"Why not?" I asked.

"I don't want people coming up to me and saying, 'Your sister's a lez!' "

"If you tell them first, they won't have the chance."

He shook his head. "No way."

"It's up to you. I just want you to know that I'm not ashamed of it."

"That's cool," he said. He looked like he was done talking.

"Ronnie."

"What?"

"I also want you to know that I won't hide it. Not from you, not from your friends, not from anybody."

He put his head in his hands. "Aw, shit," he said.

**\* \* \***

My girlfriend and I ended our relationship. Like most people who date in high school, we discovered that we were growing in different directions and that maybe we didn't like each other that much after all. I was becoming very active politically with Queer Nation, and she was uncomfortable with that. I wanted to confront homophobia in high school; she didn't want to hold hands in public. After her parents had discovered a love letter in her bedroom, they kicked her out of the house. My mother had just started going to PFLAG meetings. My ex-girlfriend's parents sent her pamphlets from Exodus International and Homosexuals Anonymous, a twelve-step program that teaches gays to hate themselves. My father told a coworker that his homophobic comments were a direct attack on his daughter.

My ex-girlfriend didn't want to "shove our sexuality in people's faces." I was tired of others shoving their hateful and ignorant attitudes in my face. I wanted to be openly gay. I wanted all of my classmates to know that I was a lesbian. I wanted them to know that every time they told an antigay joke, every time they called someone a faggot or a queer, they were hurting someone. I wanted to increase dyke visibility at Mountlake Terrace High School.

I started by telling anyone who asked. Even if they didn't really mean to ask.

"Contemporary Living" was a required class about "social and financial issues," such as how to balance your checkbook, how to win friends and influence people, how to deal with pesky drug dealers, how to date. On the first day of class, the teacher said, "Boys on one side of the room, girls on the other. Talk about what attracts you to the opposite sex. I want a list in fifteen minutes."

I looked at her. "Teacher?"

"Yes?"

"I'm a lesbian. Where do you want me to go?"

She grew concerned. "Well Erika, you certainly don't have to participate if you don't feel comfortable."

I considered that option. My choices were: Do what you're told or don't be included. "I know what let's do," I said pleasantly. "Why don't I stay with the boys? I'm sure we have more in common."

"That's up to you," she said, heading toward the girls.

I sat with the boys. They were embarrassed. One boy said he liked girls who wore lots of makeup. "I don't like a lot of makeup," I said.

"Neither do I," said another boy.

"Also," I said, "I like hairy armpits. And hairy legs."

"I like a girl with a tan," said one boy. "And I like hard bodies."

"Tans are nice," I said. "But what about their minds? Don't we have to say something about what's in there?"

Afterward, we read our list out loud to the class. Our list was the only one that had "intellectual girl" on it. It also listed "women who wear men's cologne." No one looked at me. Not even the teacher.

\*\*\*

A Queer Nation Conversation: Part I
Scene 1:
*(DAY/INTERIOR)*
*A shopping mall without any particular character. Several "dykes" and "fags" are standing around in same-gender pairs. Most of the couples are kissing intensely and groping each other. They are all wearing brightly-colored stickers that say things such as FUCK YOUR GENDER, ASSIMILATE MY BIG OL' STRAP-ON DILDO, and, of course, DYKE and FAG. Various conservatively dressed passersby, including children, alternately stare and try not to stare. A LEATHER-CLAD DYKE (hereafter "ME") holds hands with her AFFECTION PARTNER (hereafter "AP"). Enter IGNORANT LADY.*

ME: Hi. We are Queer Nation of Seattle. We'd just like to say that we are everywhere…

IGNORANT LADY [*looking directly at* ME]: You people make me sick. Why don't you just go back into your disgusting closets and get out of our lives!

ME: Because, Ma'am, lesbians and gays are discriminated against in this country every day. If I go to a shopping mall and hold hands with my girlfriend, everyone stares. So we are giving everyone a good look.

[*AP kisses* ME *chastely on the cheek.* IGNORANT LADY *looks at* AP's *sticker, which reads,* DYKES TAKE OVER THE WORLD.]

IGNORANT LADY: Just look at that. You are here to recruit. You people should be shot.

AP: I'm sorry you feel that way about your brother and sister human beings.

IGNORANT LADY: You're not human beings. You're deviants.

[*Exit* IGNORANT LADY. *From backstage, teenage boys scream in unison,* "Faggots and dykes go home!" *A* FLAMER, *turning in the direction of the voices, shouts,* "We are home, little boys!"]

\*\*\*

A Queer Nation Conversation: Part II

I thought we were the first ones. We at Queer Nation were the cutting edge of the gay, lesbian, bisexual and transgendered civil rights movement. Then I met a fifty-year-old homosexual at one of the Queer Nation actions. "Why do you have to use those words?" he asked. " 'Queer,' 'fag,' 'dyke.' Those are not words you should be calling yourselves. Those are words of hatred." His voice shook as he spoke.

"We're reclaiming those words," I said, but I was ashamed. I had never been hurt by these words. I had never been afraid to be called a dyke or a queer. I had never been bashed or even intimidated by someone who really hated me for being gay.

"Those words will always have come from an evil place." He walked away. *Wait,* I wanted to say. *Wait. Tell me what it was like for you. Tell me how you had to lie or how you refused to lie. Tell me how they tried to push you down. Tell me if you ever let them. Tell me how they told you to go to hell, to the hospital, to an island, to another planet. Tell me how they beat you down with those evil words, with evil smirks, with their fists, with weapons.*

*Then tell me how you survived.*

\*\*\*

My knowledge of the history of the gay and lesbian community came in bits and pieces. Gay and lesbian history was absent from the school curriculum. The organizations I joined were more concerned with where we were going next. Let's have a kiss-in at Northgate Mall! Let's go protest the Billy Graham convention! What's Stonewall? "Oh, some queers rioted against gay-bashers in New York in the sixties." It was like an ingredient to some mysterious recipe. I finally started thinking, "What are we cooking here? How long has this been going on? How much do we have left to do?"

\*\*\*

My parents begged me not to do it. "You're putting yourself in danger," my father said.

"I'm putting myself in danger by not doing it."

"Erika," my mother said, "they wouldn't be able to handle it. Why do you always have to raise the issue?"

"Mom, I want to do this. I want to bring Nikki to school. I want to walk around campus holding hands. I want to show everyone that I'm not afraid. And then I want them to ask me questions."

My dad shrugged. "Maybe she's right."

I looked at my mother. "You raised me to be this way, Mom. You taught me to stand up for myself, and that's what I'm doing. I'm not going to let them shove me back into the closet."

**\* \* \***

I took Nikki to school. We held hands during "priority period," which was the fifteen minutes before classes started. We were supposed to be studying or talking to teachers or something. Mostly people sat around or drank coffee and tried to recover from hangovers. So we had a captive audience. We put our arms around each other. Someone said, "Oh, my God, she's a dyke!" I turned and waved. Then priority period was over. We kissed good-bye, and Nikki went home. And I went to class. I didn't expect any trouble.

And I didn't get any. It was my junior year. I still had another year left. I did get quite a few questions and comments. "Why are you a lesbian? Have you ever had a boyfriend? What do you guys do, anyway?" Several students approached me with issues of their own. "My uncle/brother/sister/father/mother/grandmother/cousin is gay. I really appreciate what you did." Some students told me that they thought they might be gay. One even asked me if *she* was gay. Some students told me they thought it was "cool." Many teachers openly supported me.

The administration was a little less supportive. I was called into the vice principal's office. "Erika, we have a rule here," said Mr. Vice Principal, "about public displays of affection." He seemed embarrassed.

"What I did," I said, "was a lot tamer than what your average heterosexual couple does between classes."

"Yes...well. We discourage that behavior as well."

"Do you call your students out of class to reprimand them?"

"Occasionally," he lied.

"I think you are uncomfortable with the fact that we are lesbians."

"It is true," he said, looking at Mrs. Principal, "that the nature of your relationship is a little more distracting to the students here."

"I don't think I was interfering with anyone's education. I think I was enhancing it."

He smiled briefly and stood up. "We just need to make sure that you understand our rule against public displays of affection."

"I understand that it is enforced arbitrarily," I said. I remained seated.

"Well," he said, gesturing toward the door, "I guess that will be all, then."

"Do you think I'm your only gay student, Mr. Vice Principal?" I didn't ask that. But I should have. Instead I said, "Whatever," and walked out the door and out of the school. And when I got to my car, I cried.

\* \* \*

When I got home my mother asked me how it went. I told her everyone acted maturely except for the administration. I told her how the kids were more surprised and curious rather than hostile.

"I feel like I made a difference today, Mom."

"Good," she said. "I'm proud of you, I guess."

"I know," I said.

She sighed, shaking her head. "Why couldn't I have a normal child?"

"Normal?" I smiled like a little angel. "That would be boring."

"Boring might be nice. I've never had a chance to experience it." She smiled at me. I threw my arms around her and kissed her head.

# Conversation Piece
## by M. Paz Galupo

CLEAN HANDS. My straight friends think they are too strong-willed to be queer. They think sleeping with a woman is like a nose piercing. To them, it's a fashion statement they are above making. Too transparent. Way too trendy. To them, the image just isn't worth the pain associated with creation. It hurts when a 16-gauge needle first enters, then exits the flesh. Their eyes water to think about it. A silver-plated post rotated three times daily. Proper care a must. Clean hands. Triple-protection antibiotic. All this, and you are left with an undeniable hole. A ruby marks its place. My straight friends think lesbianism is like that ruby nose ring. A conversation piece. They think one day I'll look down and mistake the ruby for a pimple. I'll scratch at it. Pick it. It'll ooze pus. Maybe I'll try to let it heal over. My straight friends think being queer is too vogue. They think I've been taken in by the fad that they resist. They think they are stronger than I am because of it. To them, my queerness is a weakness. Mine and theirs both. I don't question their fondness of me. They love me, my quirkiness, even my queerness. They need me. Without my friendship they would seem closed-minded.

STIGMA. It has been much easier to accept myself as a lesbian than as a divorced woman. I choke on the word *divorced* because I equate it with failure. There is no other direction in it. My mother imagines my coming-out to be stigma-ridden in that same way. As if it takes a lot of courage to admit. As if shame is involved. She pronounces the word "lesbian" with care. Tentatively, as if she were learning a foreign language.

After saying the word "lesbian," studying its meaning, its relation to her daughter, my mother wanted to talk. To consult her friends by phone. To whisper it to my cousins at family gatherings. My father finally took her aside and explained that it wasn't her place to go telling the world. The world wasn't ready for it. The world didn't want to know. When his gentle reasoning didn't persuade her, he yelled. He yelled at the top of his lungs on his way out of the kitchen. "I can't believe that you are announcing to everyone that our daughter is *fucking another woman!*" When I picture that scene—my mother standing behind the kitchen counter cutting the fat off a chicken, my father walking across the tile floor in his golden-toed dress socks, discussing my sexuality—I feel young again. I feel safe.

THIRD VISIT TO THE QUEER BAR. "So are you latent or what?" A question posed to me by a friend of my girlfriend's. I guess I didn't answer quickly enough. She continued, "I just wondered what your story was. I asked someone once about you...because of the way you smile...I always seem to fall for women with children."

I told her that before coming out, I tried to intellectualize myself into being a lesbian. I didn't really know any at the time, but I imagined a lesbian's life to be an easier one somehow. I tried to imagine myself physically entwined with another woman. I didn't imagine anything like the lovemaking I now enjoy. I imagined arms and legs bending in painful contortions. I imagined beautiful, big-haired, big-breasted women, but I couldn't imagine what to do with them. I rubbed my legs together to my husband's *Hustler's Busty Beauties* and decided that I just wasn't attracted to women. I haven't yet met a woman (gay or straight) who mirrors those models. And if I did, I'd have the same reaction. I'm just not all that attracted to your everyday straight woman. Not even the beautiful ones. I like butchy women. The butchier, the better. There's something about the way they stand with their hands on their hips. Something in the pull of the shoulders, the strength of the gaze. It turns my mouth to cotton, my labia to silk. It's a chemical thing. Something that, years back when I was busy imagining lesbianism, I just didn't get. If you have to intellectualize yourself into being a lesbian, you're missing the point.

CHOCOLATE ECLAIRS. My ex-husband thinks a lesbian's life is a decadent one. He says this with admiration. He imagines me indulgent and throws in my love for sushi as proof. He imagines that I dine on chocolate eclairs and smoke clove cigarettes. "Being a lesbian is like living beyond your means," he says. He thinks he is drawing parallels between our lives, because he is perpetually broke.

My ex-husband sees lesbianism as a luxury, but I disagree. I don't see my lesbianism as a lavish reward following a long workweek. Maybe it could have seemed that way at first. As if I had done the marriage and childbearing part, met societal expectations, and then decided to be true to myself. But it is far more than a bedroom issue. To my ex-husband and my straight counterparts, the luxury lies inside the bedroom. And I admit that sex goes on in my bedroom. I admit that sex is good. But I've never heard a straight person refer to his or her sex life as a luxury. It may be taboo in conversation. It may be limited to the darkest hours and the most remote bedrooms. But even to the most tight-lipped straight person, sex is a fact. For them, sex is, at worst, a given. For me, sex becomes, at best, an extravagance.

LESBIAN FORM. My girlfriend is ten years older than I am. She wants me to be a lesbian the hard way. Her way. My lesbian form is all wrong. She thinks I admire men too much. She scolds me, as if I were a child sitting too close to the television and she is afraid I might fall in. My thirty-something friends hold fast to a separatist ideal that I do not share. An ideal they think I'll adopt in time, as if it were a natural part of every lesbian's evolution. I see it as a test. It's like the test in my recurring dream. I've studied. I know all the answers. But when it comes time to take the test, the words lift off the page and rearrange themselves. The letters settle randomly into stories that make me giggle and lull me to sleep.

I admit I feel self-righteous. I feel I've evolved past the separatist existence they never created but cling to anyway. I don't want to have to do things their way. I want what I don't have, what they don't want to imagine. I can't believe in a lesbian's predestined separatism any more than I can believe that I love all the wrong people because the planet Venus was in Virgo on the day I was born. Maybe I do love all the wrong people. No maybe about it. Sometimes believing can be a dead end worse than failed love.

SALIVA. Being lesbian, it seems, isn't enough. I haven't figured out exactly how to be the right amount. But I have learned that definite quantities of lesbianism exist. Among my lesbian elders I am not lesbian enough. Too young and too coddled. Among everyone else, I am most definitely too lesbian. Too young. Too coddled. My straight friends call themselves "hets." I hadn't even heard the term until they spat it at me. They strain the word like saliva through their teeth. They say, "you people dismiss us as hets, as *bre-e-eders.*" They educate me about this injustice. I laugh because I am the only mother among them. At the local gay-friendly restaurant, they insist the wait staff snubs them for being straight. They boycott the place.

Everyone has an agenda for my lesbianism. I'm politically minded. I can see the good in this. I can say "sexism" and "homophobia" three times fast. Everyone wants to imagine their lives to be hard. It's hard to be straight in the nineties. I listen. I agree. I was straight once. I know that there is a lot to be said for heterosexual privilege. A lot to be said for being taken seriously, for being acknowledged, for being left alone.

COHORT EFFECT. I don't know many lesbians my own age. My girlfriend and our friends are in their late thirties. They stump me with the titles to bad seventies music. To them, I'm a baby, not yet a proven lesbian. Not enough years or lovers behind me. They bet on whether I'll cut it, whether I'll return to men.

I guess my coming-out was too simple. Not enough grappling or self-doubt. I just never expected anyone to act differently than they have. I kept my lesbianism a secret from my family for an agonizing week. My boss was one of the first to know. I told him of my intentions to sleep with a woman before it ever happened. My coming-out was too easy. It makes the most-seasoned lesbians suspicious. How can they be sure I am a true lesbian? I was never properly initiated with hate mail from my mother (as my girlfriend was). My mother called to say thank you for the So-Your-Daughter-Is-a-Lesbian book I sent her. I think she even read it. I haven't had to worry about my ex-husband's using my sexuality in order to get custody of our daughter. I know that I am lucky, even for my generation. But luck is a crazy thing. Everyone stands around and wonders whether you deserve it after all.

# Shiftings
## by Forrest Tyler Stevens

*For my father's father, Bill Curtain*

My grandfather died in the 1940s—of a heart attack—in San Francisco. I know these three facts about Bill Curtain, my father's father, because my mother, like many women of her generation, ministered to the emotional needs of others, if not to her own. She offered these facts to me as a way to assuage my father's anger toward me, his hatred of me, his loathing for my love for men. I in turn arranged the rough-cut pieces of my mother's story of my grandfather's life in front of me to suggest a life *I* might have had.

If there were a photo in front of you, it would be white-bordered (black-and-white but really grays), a photo of a handsome young man in a white cotton T-shirt standing against a shiny, then-new car. He wears cotton pants and has a thin waist and strong biceps. The shade of gray suggests that the pants are probably blue. The white, ragged border of the photo is stamped with a truncated date: '44. The young man looks back at the camera and out of the photo, but he doesn't smile broadly, only slightly. He stares cross-armed into the camera.

My grandfather died at the age of thirty-three. I know this because it was a fact of his past that my father offered me growing up, a boy in south-central Missouri. My father, in solemn cheer, offered it as a parable, said that he was told only that his father died of a heart attack. That I should be happy that I have a father. He didn't even know the city where he died. Dad informed me with a nod of the head that Christ was the same age when he died. And I should be happy that I have a father. We sat at our metal-and-Formica kitchen table, at the back of a small brown kitchen with a hot Franklin stove next to the wall, and talked about Christ and my granddad. The head of Christ sat in a homemade wooden frame ministering in browns and golds over the table.

My grandparents divorced shortly after my father was born, no particular reason ever offered by my boozy grandmother, even in her drunken states. She got tight-lipped about it. My father wondered what his father was like. He didn't know. I should be happy that I have a father. My mother sat tight-lipped about it.

At the kitchen table, listening to my mother and her friends talk over coffee and cigarettes, I thought of boys I liked. I can list the boys I had crushes on between 1973 and 1981: Danny, Gary, Steve, Kevin, David, Matthew, Bart. I invited each of them for a sleepover at my house at one time or another. Some my mother liked, some she didn't. I forgot what age I was when she thought that the sleepovers should stop.

Mom claims—my grandmother's dead, there's no verification of the claim—that my grandfather died of a heart attack in San Francisco. This was a fact offered to her by my boozy grandmother one drunken night after my father flew into a rage about her taste for vodka. Bill and my grandmother divorced shortly after she got pregnant and they were wed—no reason offered. My father was the only child of that union. In a car on the interstate out of Denver, my mother offered this fact and my grandmother's innuendo as an explanation for my father's rage and anger, his near-murderous hatred.

Did my grandfather sleep with men? I'm only beginning to accept that as a child and a gay teen I lived in my grandfather's life, couched in the anger and violence flowing from my father. His rage at my grandfather's death in San Francisco echoes shame and desire; the recognitions of identifications with and desires for a father he didn't know. My grandma gave my mother the story by way of explaining a part, even if a small part, of my father's always-angry, always-tired life. Perhaps to make it tolerable for her? A story passed down from woman to woman to protect themselves and their children against straight male rage.

My grandma remarried, to a man named Bill Stevens, doubling one name while pushing aside another. My father took on his stepfather's name, then was sent to live with relatives.

One Saturday night in the early eighties, my drunken grandmother papered the floor, the furniture, the shelves, the tables, and the windowsills of her downtown apartment with family photos. She held down the photos with near-empty vodka bottles. She stuffed each bottle with a thick white candle. The firefighters told my parents that a tipped bottle shot wax out onto the photos and furniture. Burnt, sodden photos plastered the apartment, and my mom spent the next snowy Sunday morning sifting through the charred edges. Mom stacked the photos in cardboard boxes to save for my dad and my dad's half-brother. Grandma Stevens told me later in a sort of conspiratorial whisper that she liked, even craved, the reflections of the flames in the thick vodka.

In the summer of '89 I visited Los Angeles with my then-boyfriend. My father insisted that I go see my grandmother in the rest home where she lived. He himself hadn't seen her or talked to her for the past ten years of her life. I didn't want to go, but he insisted. She was my grandmother. I drove down to Ventura from Santa Barbara to take her out for lunch. Burned, brittle from too many years of too much drink, she mistook me for my father. At first she knew it was me; but as the lunch wore on, she called me "Mike" and talked in a daze about things I couldn't follow, people I didn't know, the games her family had played on her. She pleaded for the reasons God had taken away what she had. Grandma Stevens fumbled the air with her hands as she attempted to narrate events that had effects, though no immediate effects, on my life. I reminded her that I wasn't my dad. She asked me if I were married. I said that I had a lover. She decided she needed to rest. She had a doctor's appointment that afternoon. She gathered up her personal effects and stuffed them into her purse.

If there were a photo in front of you, it would be white-bordered (black-and-white but really grays), a photo of a handsome young man in a white cotton T-shirt standing against a shiny, then-new car. He wears cotton pants and has a thin waist and strong biceps. The shade of gray suggests that the pants are probably blue. The white, ragged border of the photo is stamped with a truncated date: '44. The young man looks back at the camera and out of the photo, but he doesn't smile broadly, only slightly. He stares cross-armed into the camera.

# Tune In, Get Off, Come Out:
## California Dreamin' and My Age of Aqueerius
### by Dolissa Medina

It was one of those HBO specials with Dick Cavett as host. As neon letters spelled out the word YESTERYEAR in the opening sequence, a montage of newsreel footage covered my TV. I sat watching, half noticing the 1969 graphic that had appeared on the screen. This was, after all, 1981, and my ten-year-old brain on summer vacation was not too keen on a history lesson. But when the music started, everything changed.

*"When the moon is in the seventh house / And Jupiter aligns with Mars / Then peace will guide the planets / And love will steer the stars / This is the dawning of the Age of Aquarius..."*

I knew this song!

**February 6, 1971.** *A wrinkled little baby opens her mouth. Proud dad takes a picture; creative mom sticks the snap in a photo album and writes underneath:* THE YAWNING OF AQUARIUS.

My early childhood memories have always included staring at this photo of myself and reading the caption. I soon learned the song associated with these words when my dad placed an album on his "hi-fi" stereo and let the groovy vibes rip.

Well, not exactly. It was "Aquarius/Let the Sunshine In," sure enough, but a rather pristine rendition by the Ray Coniff singers. My father, the furthest thing from a hippie, was a fan of "easy listening" and other types of elevator music. My childhood was subsequently

29

wrought with the trauma of prolonged exposure to *The Lawrence Welk Show*, and so I never understood the true antiestablishment context of this hippie anthem.

That is, until that day in 1981 when a familiar song played with new and fascinating images. I sat before that TV screen and watched, intrigued by the wild-haired people dancing barefoot in the park, the chorus of fists and protest signs, and the naked children in a far-off jungle, running for their lives—images unlike anything I had seen before. I left Dick Cavett that day with more than a history lesson. I had learned about a new way of life.

By the sixth grade I was not yet wearing flowers in my hair. Nor was I using words like "groovy" or donning peace signs. I was primarily known as the class tomboy: a kid who was, ironically, still into guns, toy soldiers, and playing war (so much for nonviolence). I shared this tomboy title with a girl named Harriet, my rather athletic buddy who dug skateboarding and Hacky Sack. Thinking back on that friendship, I realize she was my first girl crush—and probably a baby dyke too. But we were both still far off from realizing our crystal pink persuasion.

So in the meantime, I daydreamed about a decade long before my own. With my discovery of the Woodstock Nation, my conversion to more Gandhian ways in junior high inevitably followed. Camouflage got traded for tie-dye. I practiced flashing the peace sign in front of the mirror. And key phrases like "question authority," "far out," and "free love" became a part of my daily vocabulary.

Sadly, it didn't take long to realize that there were few "far out" things from the sixties still left. And for my generation, free love carried a price. For me and countless others of Reagan Nation, *AIDS* became a four-letter word almost at the same time as *fuck*.

**February 6, 1981.** *This is the bombing of the Age of Aquarius.* I don't remember too much about my tenth birthday except for the fact that I shared it with the new president of the United States. At that time I had no way of knowing that hundreds of gay men were sick and dying. Nor did I know who Ronald Reagan was or how he would fit into my sixties/eighties time warp.

Looking back on the eighties, I resent that those years, which were so formative to me sexually, included a rise in conservatism, embodied by Reagan, paralleled by the rise of a fatal new sexual disease. Erroneously perceived to target only my kind (queers and ethnic minorities), the disease was ignored by conservatives and religious fundamentalists, who preferred that God clear us off the face of His Earth in one sweep of a holy snot wipe.

This disdain for difference was nothing new. I remember watching the last scene in *Easy Rider,* in which rednecks blew away Peter Fonda and Dennis Hopper for being longhairs. The scene disturbed me greatly, as I was given yet another example of a mentality as American as apple pie: "If it's not like you, kill it."

Given that I was a queer feminist hippie chick living in a small town, my teenage years were not easy. In high school I developed a reputation as the "school radical," channeling most of my repressed sexual energy into sixties-style politics. *Better to be the class activist than the class dyke,* I thought. On the surface, my outdated verbiage and weird dress already marked me as different. But hell, this was the era of parachute pants, leg warmers, and glitter gloves on one hand. I was not about to conform—inside or out.

So as Michael Jackson sang "Beat It" on MTV, I beat off my mind to magazine pictures and old TV images of sexy social revolution. Footage of Woodstock in New York and riots in Chicago fascinated me, but what really blew me away were the be-ins in Golden Gate Park. It was here—in these images of San Francisco's Haight-Ashbury district—that I first discovered the geographic birthplace of my magical, mythical world. There was something about the visual appeal of this city—its lime-green-and-orange Victorians, its roller-coaster hills—that embodied the playfulness and freedom of an era.

The sixties were long gone, I knew, but San Francisco was still very much alive. Maybe one day I could escape there. Besides, wasn't that where all the gay people lived?

*This is the dawning of the Age of Aqueerius.* In my lust for total knowledge of the sixties, I also stumbled upon the history of another revolution, one not so well-publicized. Despite all the talk about riots and subcultures, when the raised fist of an insurgent had a limp wrist, no one paid much attention.

June 27, 1969. Greenwich Village. Poor Black and Latino drag queens—tired of years of police harassment and routine raids on their gay bars—fight back, sparking three days of riots that become for lesbians, gays, bisexuals, and transgendered folks, the Legend of Stonewall. It is the shot heard round the nation for the modern gay rights movement.

I'll never forget the day my best friend and I stumbled onto this morsel of hidden history on the shelves of our public library. We must have been fifteen by then. Reagan was in his second term in office, and we were each probably on our third same-sex crush. Interestingly enough, a sixties revival was also taking shape. Classmates who had previously made fun of me were now accessorizing with trendy rhinestone peace jewelry. As I watched an important personal symbol turn into a fashion statement, I thought, *Well, at least no one's going to steal the pink triangle.*

To a large degree, I think that's why Stonewall was such an important discovery for me. It gave me a sense of connection, a site where peace sign and pink triangle could merge into one. In the story of Stonewall, I encountered something I had never before experienced: the intersection of my gay and hippie identities.

I mean, this was happening in *1969*, man! Less than two months before the Woodstock festival in upstate New York, urban queers in the Big Apple were staging a happening of their own, taking a bite out of bacon and stiletto-kicking some serious ass. I was captivated by the notion of men in high heels fighting men in blue. One account told of demonstrators forming chorus-girl kick lines in response to police riot formation, and—quite literally—dancing at their revolution.

It was all so incredible and beautiful; for me, the Legend of Stonewall remains a modern-day fairy tale of psychedelic proportions. It seems, at times, otherworldly in the surreal images it inspires and yet so familiar and inevitable given the cultural context in which it occurred. A gay revolution simply could not have happened at a more appropriate moment in time. The language of liberation was on everyone's lips, and marginalized groups were drawing inspiration from one another.

Hippie and gay subcultures were no exception. I often think about the influence gay culture had on the language of the flower children. One can see how hippie expressions such as "What a drag" and "He's straight" (i.e., "establishment") were inspired by gay bar slang—itself influenced by black culture of the Jazz Age, which affected the beatniks, who preceded the hippies, etc.—a cosmic full circle.

As a young activist, I too drew inspiration from these many cultures and political movements. But I also realized the responsibility of appropriation. To wear peace signs was all fine and groovy, but what was I doing now to make a difference? In addition to other social justice issues, the historical presence of the gay rights movement—sparked by Stonewall—was a crucial factor in the development of my political consciousness. I believe that, had I been alive in the sixties, I would have been a part of the many mass movements for social justice. Yet I also wonder how my sexuality would have been perceived in this pre-gay rights decade. Would I have compromised—even sacrificed—a major aspect of myself to fit in with "The Cause"?

Indeed, many of these so-called progressive movements of the sixties harbored intense homophobia, racism, and/or sexism even as they professed to value equality. As I realized this over time, I lost many of my romantic notions about this decade. But the power of the sixties never left me. It fed my imagination, giving me passion and hope for human possibility. Such is the magic of our myths.

Stonewall, for me, became a favorite bedtime story. As with the sixties, it gave me something to dream about during my difficult adolescent years, when, inspired by my hippie ideology, I turned on and tuned in to the possibility of resisting any authority that labeled me as "other."

I also dropped out, not in the conventional sixties sense but definitely in a sexual way. It was a conscious choice, an unfortunate strategy of self-protection. In my teen years I witnessed my cousin (the other lavender sheep of the family) die of AIDS. This experience brought home the psychological terror first faced by my generation. In the deepest coil of my young queer psyche, to pursue the affirmation of our life was to invite death. The faggot skeletons dying in hospital wards were proof of this, my historical and cultural milieu. Never mind the fact that I was apparently in a low-risk category; my cousin embodied a community fighting for its human right to exist. We all shared the same tainted blood.

My cousin was also the one who had gotten away, leaving home and family for the same streets where my Stonewall heroines had struggled. Watching him die, I feared my own big-city failure. Would I ever make it to San Francisco? What if the sixties spirit I hoped for was no longer there? Could I ever dream of possibility again without an overwhelming sense of shame? Instead of escaping into drugs, the only mind-expanding thing I did those years was to write in my high school journal, in which I struggled with these and other questions. And so while my peers waged adolescent revolution between the thighs of their young lovers, I crawled into empty, open notebooks and licked paper vulvas with my pen.

I must have licked a damn lot of pages, because at age twenty I arrived in San Francisco with the virginal flowers in my pubic hair still intact. But I didn't care. My migration to San Francisco was primarily an act of self-love. I didn't come here looking for sex or even for a twenty-five-year time warp. I simply needed a place where there is freedom to exist and evolve. Such potential for human exploration remains inherent here, in my tiny little city by the bay.

I often joke that San Francisco was my first lover. We've lived together for four years now, and my heart still smiles when I see her curvaceous hills and cascading thick white fog of hair. San Francisco, so I've been told, is also considered an Aquarian city. Indeed, there's no place like home.

I have to admit, however, the Haight no longer holds the same fascination for me. Times have changed too much for me to act like it's still 1969, and I couldn't care less that Jerry Garcia's dead. Interestingly, the gay Castro district has also gone down the same road—the homos there are much more homogenous than I first thought. And so I currently live as a bi-girl "homegirl" de la Mission, a comfortable neighborhood for my Chicana identity.

One benefit of this residence has been the people I have met: older activists, artists, and cultural workers whose experiences give my own identities a real sense of historical context and continuity. There is no fragmentation of self in this *familia;* many of these friends are women, Chicana, queer—*and* ex-hippies! To put a human face on history is a beautiful experience. I feel lucky for these intergenerational friendships. We speak across political and personal paradigms, creating collective self-discovery. Such relationships, I'm convinced, will renew our community as we tear down the closet door to a new millennium. They also prove to me that Generation Q has a lot to learn from some aging queens and dykes. Then again, they could learn a lot from us too. Hippies, homos, or hipsters, we're all heading toward a new age.

The dawning of Aqueerius is here. Let's advance the evolutionary trip.

*Envoys From Planet FagDyke*

# Coming Out Under Fire
# (Thank God They Used Rubber Bullets)
# by Kelly McQuain

West Virginia: the most northern of the southern states and the most southern of the northern states—hillbilly country through and through. That's what my dad's always called it, and he's lived there all his life. Evenings, you might find him chewing the fat with his cronies in one of the fast food restaurants that have sprung up along old Route 33 like mushrooms on cow dung.

McDonald's offers comely high school girls behind the checkout counter, and Hardee's is open all night for truckers to tank up on cheap coffee. Scottie's, a local favorite, snags the morning crowd with its greasy-spoon breakfasts. Even the rented house I grew up in has been converted to a Kentucky Fried Chicken. These venues, with their stock of hardened coal miners, weather-worn farmers, oily mechanics, and splintered construction workers, are not where you'd expect battles for social tolerance to be waged and won. But it does happen here in the mountain state—and with no small thanks to my father.

In November 1988 I came out to my family in the worst way possible—drunk and by phone. I had just returned to college in Philadelphia after having survived a trip home for my maternal grandmother's funeral. My out-of-state boyfriend offered no solace—showing up on weekends with another man's hickeys on his neck. My depression deepened. Compared to me, Sylvia Plath was an "up" person. Deciding that the best course of action was to get everything difficult done in one week, I got a bottle of scotch, picked up the phone, and confessed all to Mom and Dad. Between sobs of despair I spit out the words "I'm gay!" like projectile vomit. I was waging war against a world that had so recently cost me my favorite grandparent, my first true love, my self-respect, and my confidence for as long as I could remember. Who better to lash out at than the two people responsible for bringing me into the battleground in the first place?

"Really?" asked my father.

"Yes, really," I snapped.

"I kind of expected as much," Mom said with a sigh. Then, "Have you been drinking?" Her father and brother were both alcoholics. She was used to boozy late-night harangues. Though I had recently turned twenty-one, she still gave me the hairy eyeball if I so much as looked at a six-pack.

"Yes, I've been drinking!" I shouted. "But that's not the goddamned point!"

A teary conversation ensued, during which my parents expressed the timeless parent-to-child sentiment "We still love you, but we don't understand you." Always a bet hedger, Mom added, "I still care, though I don't necessarily approve." What happened? I had expected raging tempers, fiery expletives, my name torn out of the will. True, we had always been close—but it was in a hand-to-hand combat sort of way. This was too easy. I kept waiting for them to slam down the phone in disgust. But they didn't. As I cried into the receiver, my anger slowly abated. In the end I agreed to lay off the sauce. We'd discuss the "gay issue" more at Christmas.

Maybe my parents were luring me into a trap. I kept a lookout over my shoulder for suspicious vans full of burly men, kidnappers sent to spirit me away to a deprogramming camp in the mountains.

But nothing happened. At the holidays, when I told my sisters, all I got were open mouths and raised eyebrows. My older brother simply responded with, "Tell me something I don't know." Wait a minute! Why weren't Bibles being slammed upside my head? My family was reacting the wrong way! True, my brother added, "Make a pass at me, and I'll slug you," but that was more a product of ignorance than homophobia. The gangly Geek, as they called him back in high school, didn't have anything to worry about. Perhaps if Johnny Depp joined the family, we could negotiate—but my real brother? Ugh!

I told the Geek on an uncommonly warm December night as we walked to the grocery store for beer. What should have been Christmas snow was a rainy drizzle. I thought of similar solitary walks before I came out to my family, when I would trace the steel train tracks that laced the town's industrial park, scouting for a locomotive to hurl myself under. But the coal trains had stopped running through town long ago. On the most despondent occasions, I would call the Appalachian Mental Health Center from a phone booth, hoping they'd talk me out of my suicidal urges. "Why do you want to kill yourself?" the operator always asked. I hemmed and hawed, unable to spit out the words but grateful for someone—anyone—to talk to.

Things got a little better when, at sixteen, I came out to Annette—a laid-back friend whom I had stolen from the Geek. Annette had recently returned to high school to finish a degree put on hold eight years before by the birth of her son. She had survived an abusive, short-lived marriage and was now a lesbian wanna-be. On long walks we often mused about the roots of her sexual attraction to women: Was she gay as the result of a poor marriage, or had a poor marriage prompted her to consider dormant inclinations? Was she gay at all if she hadn't yet acted on her feelings? My case was more clear-cut: In junior high my brief attraction to girls had been "the stage," and my crushes on coaches, peers, and underwear models in the Sears catalog was the true direction of my compass needle.

Confiding in Annette let off just enough steam to survive small-town West Virginia. She listened patiently to my inchoate longings and bought me beer and Boone's Farm wine that I'd quaff in abundance on overnight camping trips with my two best friends from childhood—trips that often ended in drunken streaking or mutual jerking off, which we'd pretend to block out in the guilty light of morning. Treading water, I waited for college, when departure would mean an end to isolation. I had no gay newspapers, magazines, or books to teach me patience or what to expect—only occasional TV movies in which gays either hustled, were killed, or died from disease. Still, I yearned for escape, wondering whether it would ever come. Days plodded one into the next, my burgeoning desires bludgeoned into self-loathing at a time when they should have been as light as air, suffused with discovery, innocence.

When I finally left on scholarship for college, I hoped that the hypocritical preachers and unsympathetic teachers who conveniently let homophobic slurs slide by would choke on my dust. I never dreamed that once I left Elkins, West Virginia, there could ever again be a place for me there.

But maybe you have to leave town in order to come home again.

In my absence, small-town life ticked on as usual, tongues wagging, people nagging each other over which way to build the new four-lane extension, whether to change the high school's name. Oh, there were picnics and birthdays too—but sadly it's the controversies and disappointments, the long-standing enmities that tend to collect in our minds as life strains through us. For instance, while I was away a grudge match broke out between my paternal grandfather and Sherri, my dad's first cousin. Granddad wouldn't let Sherri get her greedy hands on some inheritance money she thought she was entitled to. He claimed the money was for maintaining a nurse for Sherri's aging mother and aunt and that he was tired of Sherri's pot-smoking son's mooching off the two old ladies. My grandfather said he thought the boy needed to clean up his act. "You're one to talk," Sherri countered. "Your grandson's a faggot." Her second husband had supposedly seen me entering a notorious homo party at a local hotel, whooping it up with the gay owner (an Iran-Contra fund-raiser and reputed crony of Ollie North's. Clearly Sherri did not know my taste in men).

My grandfather and grandmother pshawed and shucked in disbelief. On my dad's next visit, my stepgrandmother told him, "Sherri was over here talking trash about your son. She's says he's, he's—" (I can picture her gray eyebrows scrunching toward her steel-wool hairdo) "a homosexual!" (Lips pursed as if she'd swallowed a lemon.)

Did Dad deny it? Did he cook up a more palatable explanation? No. "You'd better make sure what you're mad at Sherri for," he said, "because as far as Kelly being gay, it's true. Though I don't know nothing about no parties at the Motor Lodge."

Dad related this story one Christmas on the way home from picking me up at the train station in Pittsburgh. Before I came out, silence always sat between us like an invisible wall. Now we had plenty to talk about: him, news about back home; me, the latest gay rights rhetoric. I still felt the need to push the envelope, to test his limits and his love. I was amused that although Sherri's facts were totally off-base, her deduction had proved correct. My painstaking ruse had been for naught; some people, at least, could hone in on the truth like a shark on a bleeding fish. Still, I was sorry to have been outed to my grandparents on Sherri's terms and not my own. But I was impressed at my father's response to the situation.

"Maybe if I'd known about those 'wild parties,' I'd never have left town," I joked.

\* \* \*

Since then Dad hasn't flinched when gay issues arise in conversation. For example, shooting the bull with some old-timers over coffee in Hardee's one evening, Dad's ears pricked up at a stray comment made by our former neighbor Winston Kooper. His wife, chatting with church friends the next booth over, had been my after-school baby-sitter years ago. Dad listened patiently as Mr. Kooper went off about the horror of gays in the military and AIDS as God's revenge. Mr. Kooper pictured homosexuals as the promiscuous stereotypes drilled into his head by the *700 Club*. He speculated that gays must turn out "that way" of their own volition or because of how they were raised.

Dad cleared his throat. "I don't know that that's necessarily true," he said. "People who grow up to be gay you don't treat different or discipline any different when they're young. 'Cause when you get right down to it, Winston, you helped raise one. Kelly was over at your house after school for years. He turned out to be gay."

Dad told me this months later, over breakfast at Scottie's. Dad always came here for sausage gravy and biscuits, home fries, and greasy eggs—a heart attack on a plate. A bleached blond waitress poured us more coffee; her eyebrows looked like they'd been torn out by a seam ripper and then drawn back in. As she shuffled off, Dad described the stunned look on Mr. Kooper's face: "At that moment the issue of gays was kind of soft-pedaled a bit 'cause it made Winston think. As far as I know, Kelly, it's not like you were molested or raised any different than anyone else." He sipped his coffee. "Our talk gave Winston a little food for thought. I don't know if it changed his mind any. But it made him think."

As Dad signaled the waitress for our check, I asked him to characterize West Virginians' disposition toward gays. "Most people don't have an attitude one way or another. They don't think there's many gays round here. When the subject does come up, they tend toward the stereotypes and jokes. They just don't have the knowledge that gay people don't all talk funny or have a broken wrist."

"Mine healed real properly," I told him. I'm always the smart-ass.

Dad just kept going. "Most people in West Virginia don't think about gays one way or another until they read a headline about AIDS or see somethin' sensational on the nightly news. They're too involved in their own lives. They only get involved in thinking about gays or black people or Jewish people when something calls it to their attention."

*A white man's luxury,* I thought to myself. I fished for more. "But why, when people finally do think about gays, do they so often strike out at them?"

"Ignorance," Dad said simply. "Just stupid ignorance."

He made them sound pitiable. A little too forgivable, I thought. Still, I said, "I think it's good that you're battling ignorance."

"But it's not like I crusade," he chuckled, dismissing the significance of his actions. "Not like I start out each day trying to battle muleheadedness. I just hope when I do meet ignorance, I don't ignore it but face it head on." The waitress brought our check, and Dad fumbled for his wallet. "But we all backslide now and then," he continued, "with stupid jokes and stuff, which is dumb." He put a few bills on the table. "Even you, Kelly, are sometimes quick to judge 'narrow minds.' "

"Ah, but I call it righteous passion," I told him.

"So does the other side," said Dad. "So do they." He took a final sip of coffee. "Some people don't know they're ignorant." He reached for his coat. "I hope I know I'm ignorant. Maybe then I won't stay that way."

We got up to leave. The blond waitress smiled our way, and I snuck an extra buck onto Dad's fifty-cent tip.

**\* \* \***

Those who dismiss hillbillies as simple country rubes would miss the fine nuances of my father's character. But it exists, there beneath the flannel shirt and full belly, the trademark cowboy hat that he lifts indoors to reveal a DA cut he's worn all his life, the hair gone gray from the years. He doesn't lie. He's never cheated. He possesses the kind of stubborn honesty that makes it hard to get ahead, though his jack-of-all-trades attitude hasn't helped either. At various times he's been a sign painter, a storekeeper, a real estate salesman, a political candidate, a land developer, a talk-show host on public-access TV, and an auctioneer. Our hometown is comfortable with Dad no matter how many times he reinvents himself, no matter who he is. As a gay man, I wish people would treat me the same way. Although my family has proved accepting, I still quake when rednecks hurl hateful epithets from their jacked-up trucks. Their fingers are never far from the rifles in the gun racks behind their heads. Hate crimes can and do happen, even in sleepy little hamlets like Elkins, West Virginia. Yet Dad never seems nervous about defending me. I'm not sure if he's courageous or a bit naive, but I'm certain now that he loves me. My coming-out has proved more traumatic for me than for him. I'm impressed that he's the one talking openly about my sexuality with my grandparents while I remain tongue-tied.

Will such openness change anything? I do not know. Even my father admits our hometown is deadlocked in homogeneity, reluctant to transform. It's not so different in Philadelphia, where I live now. Just two weeks ago my friend Peter was bashed with a brick to the head by a mob of children. And during the writing of this essay, I was threatened on the street by a man who wanted to "bust my faggot ass." My father too easily forgets that being straight affords him luxuries that I can't take for granted; he is beyond the scope of much abuse. But my dad does not rest altogether comfortably on such luxury. In wars of quiet conversation, he blasts rounds of subtle artillery. He wages on, battling ignorance no matter what he says—and for that I am proud.

# How I Got My Boots
## by Jim Davis-Rosenthal

OK, it's a stereotype, but what's a girl to do but go shopping? Deciding that I needed to get more in touch with the Wyoming rancher within, I thought, *Boots! Cowboy boots! Patsy Cline!* I called Dad up and asked him about the traction of cowboy boots.

"Should I buy cowboy boots with all the snow we have here?"

"What you need, Son, is a brand called Durango. They also call them 'trucker boots,' because truckers can't have their foot slipping off the pedals, so they have rubber soles instead of leather."

I was ready. My first stop was Boulder's only country-western store (to my knowledge) in the mall. But they had only a small selection of boots and really snobby employees, so I was foiled until my next trip to Denver. Denver had two boot boutiques, one way out east and the other closer to downtown.

I decided to head out east first and then try the downtown store. I drove my little blue Japanese pickup—the ones GM described as "little faggot trucks" a couple years back, prompting a successful boycott in which the city of San Francisco pulled all of their purchase contracts with GM. I drove and drove until I was almost in Kansas. The city had disappeared, and what had been a major thoroughfare had been reduced to a two-lane country road. Just when I thought I'd gone too far, I spotted an old truck stop over on the left. Sure enough, that's where the store was, right next to a liquor store. I drove into the parking lot and saw: Ford truck, Ford truck, Ford truck, four-by-four, Ford truck, Blazer, Ford truck, four-by-four, Blazer.

I thought, *You've got to be butch! How would Jodie Foster do this?* As I walked to the store, I decided I should put on a Wyoming accent so I might get out of there alive.

There were lots of boots, many more than in Boulder. I picked up a few and looked at the prices. The first pair I liked were $1,100 Tony Lamas. I couldn't figure out where the sizes were, so I didn't know which ones to look at.

"Lookin' for boots?" A salesman had come up behind me.

"Yep." I remembered to maintain my Wyoming facade. "Say, how're these sized?"

"They ain't sized. You just pick out the style you like, and we got 'em back in the stockroom." Oops! My first major mistake. "Well, what color are you looking for?" he asked. The Tony Lamas had been red and snakeskin.

"Oh, I dunno. Maybe black or gray?"

"How 'bout brown?" he said.

"Sure. That'd be fine." I thought it was probably best not to sound too picky.

"Well, what price range are you lookin' for?"

"Oh, I guess under a hundred. Hey, you got a brand named Durango?" As with many things in life, you sound like you know what you're doing if you can name a brand.

"No. I don't carry Durangos, but I'll show you my lower-end boots down here." I was so insulted. Me, a fag, and he was showing me the "lower-end" merchandise. He showed me a pair that had a slick leather sole on them.

"Uh, I was kinda lookin' for something called 'trucker boots'— y'know, they's got a rubber sole."

"Well, do you want 'em for work or for country-swing?"

"Oh, a little bit of both, I guess."

"OK, I've got a brand called Acme that might do the job." He showed me some styles, and I picked out a few to try.

As we were looking at a few other pair, he turned and looked at me. "Say, you look awful familiar. Do you work at Anchor Paints?"

"No. Don't work there." I kept my answers very brief so as not to give away my fake accent.

"Well, where do you work?"

I lowered my voice a little. "Uh, at the university."

"Well, whatcha do there?"

"Um, I teach."

"I don't know you from there, 'cause I never took a class there. How 'bout a concert? Been to a concert lately?"

"No, no concerts."

"Well, I don't know. You sure do look familiar." We went back to trying on more boots. I tried on several pair, and none fit quite right, so we kept trying different widths and sizes. Boots, I learned, are very different from ruby slippers. Finally we picked out a few styles, and he said, "Well, why don't you come back in the storeroom, and we'll grab these sizes. Besides, I've got another style back there we don't have out front."

Now, this is probably the point at which some boys and girls want the story to go in a certain direction. Here we are in a storeroom: leather piled from floor to ceiling and a musty, sweaty smell. No one else around, and my heart was pounding. But not for the reason you might think.

This place had boots! They were boxed and piled about fifteen feet from floor to ceiling, and the aisles were very tight. He walked back fast, pulling boots off the shelf at a rapid pace. We were about halfway back in the storeroom when he got real quiet and said, "I know where I know you from. Amendment 2. You was on television!" I got real nervous.

"Yeah," he said. "That reporter was asking you all those stupid questions. I was so pissed off. I voted 'no' myself."

"Well, thank you." I said. I was really relieved because I had suspected that he knew me from the television coverage of my activism but probably couldn't place me. My Wyoming relatives had seen me in drag during the Gulf War on cable television as one of the Ladies In Support of the President (LISP)—in fact, that is how I came out to my extended family. So it wasn't unusual for people to recognize me.

We went back out to the front. As I was trying on more boots, a woman came into the store and headed for the back. She was also looking at the boots.

He called out to her, "Mary?"

She looked back and answered, "Dan?" It was his day for recognizing people.

Turns out, they had gone to high school together some sixteen years ago. They talked for a long time, and I heard bits and pieces of the conversation. After a while she went up to the front of the store, and I told him I had picked out a pair I liked.

He pulled me aside and said, "Now I got something to tell you." A big grin appeared on his face.

Another employee called from across the room, "Hey! What're you grinnin' about?"

"Nothing," he said, "nothing." He pulled me further aside and spoke real low and soft. "Now, you keep this quiet."

"Sure," I said.

"That woman that was just in here—Mary?" I nodded in recognition. He continued, "Well, in high school, Mary and I, we had the same boyfriend."

So that's how I got my boots.

# Brainy Smurf and the Council Bluffs Pride Parade
## by Ricco V. Siasoco

When my boyfriend, Scott, tells me that we've been invited to join his friends at the parade, I politely say that I'm not interested. I have yet to attend any kind of gay event. I'm uncertain whether I am afraid of confirming the stereotypical images gay pride events carry for me (an abundance of leather pants and shirtless vests or drag queens screaming, "You *go,* girl!") or if I'm simply not as secure in my identity as I claim to be. Scott, however, seems intent on our attending this year as a couple. His intentions aren't unreasonable; we've been dating for a year now, and this relationship is the first one of significant lasting power for either of us.

When I was a kid growing up in Iowa, I never missed the opportunity to strut my stuff at the annual Council Bluffs Pride Parade. A progressive, well-organized event that brought together elementary schools, community colleges, local businesses, and ordinary citizens like my folks, it was eagerly anticipated in the sleepy Midwestern town where I spent my first eighteen years.

This was not a gay pride parade. It was a parade that celebrated generic pride in our farms, our heritage, our families, our small-town goodness.

Trouble was, I didn't grow up on a farm. The closest experience I can recall was a field trip where, in an attempt to produce milk, I squeezed a cow's udder too tightly and she kicked mud on my cherished pair of parachute pants.

## BRAINY SMURF AND THE COUNCIL BLUFFS PRIDE PARADE

My family was not a typical white Iowan farmer family. My parents immigrated to the United States from the Philippines twenty-seven years ago. There were five other Filipino families in Council Bluffs then, and my parents were close friends with all of them. In fact, my mother was the founder of the Filipino-American Association of Iowa. Even before I had entered kindergarten, my cousins and I used to perform the *tinikling*, a barefoot dance between two long bamboo poles that were slammed against each other like bear traps. While our friends played Little League and took gymnastics lessons, we toured the state with the Fil-Am Association of Iowa's only Filipino dance troupe.

I was the only one of my six siblings born in the States. My childhood was a kind of Jack Lemmon-Tony Curtis combination of Filipino traditions and American holidays. We feasted on *lumpia* (egg rolls) and fried rice on the same plate with turkey and mashed potatoes.

My participation in the Council Bluffs Pride Parade was a way I felt linked to my community. Scott asks me, "Isn't the Boston Pride Parade a contemporary version of this concept?" When we discuss it further, my hesitation seems to be the only variable that holds us back.

**\* \* \***

I don't believe growing up in Iowa was necessarily different from the experience of my friends who grew up in Massachusetts or Hawaii. Our generation shared a powerful signifier: television. In separate worlds, thousands of miles apart, with differing families and neighborhoods and incomes, we wasted our afternoons in front of a box that flickered with an electronic pulse. We all relate the early events in our lives to television images—ask any person under twenty-five about their memory of the Challenger explosion. It will not only trigger a blue sky shattered by a chilling dandelion of smoke, but it will also bring back other youthful memories tied to that particular moment. I remember passing an ingenuous note to Kris Capel (pledging her eternal devotion for one kiss) in the hallway of our junior high school minutes before I viewed the space shuttle explosion in my homeroom class.

At home I watched the boob tube religiously, sympathizing with Bobby Brady in his trials as the youngest child in the most all-American family I could enviously imagine. I developed a crush on Ricky

51

Schroeder of *Silver Spoons* fame and fantasized that I led his charmed life as a rich blond orphan who slept in a bed shaped like a miniature race car; Ricky was constantly battling the dilemma of boys climbing through his bedroom window. Heck, I remember thinking, we even bore the same initials. I was convinced that Ricky Schroeder and Ricco Siasoco were twins who had unfortunately been separated at birth.

Like others in my television generation, I learned many of my social graces from television role models—though the tutors I selected may have been more offbeat than my peers. In fact, the earliest romantic notions I remember are connected to the Smurfs.

Yes, the Smurfs. Sure, they were blue and about one inch tall, but their "Smurferrific" appeal lay in their ability to exist with thirty men—but only one woman. Their village even nurtured Baby Smurf, who was, of course, male. And Hefty Smurf—let's just say his bare chest and tattoo of love were the apple of my seven-year-old eye.

My fascination with Smurf culture led me to found a club with my classmates at Gunn Elementary School. I single-handedly selected the members of my club, the best-looking boys in class. Mike Stone was Handy Smurf, whom I chose to be president because I wanted to be his stalwart right-hand man. I christened myself Brainy Smurf, vice president of our chic Smurf clique. Chad Pechacek and Shad Coppock and the rest rounded out our cozy clan. I quickly and conveniently ditched Smurfette.

We held our first meeting at Mike's house. Following an obligatory game of Donkey Kong on his Atari and after his mother had served us Rice Krispies treats and grape Kool-Aid (my mother always offered my friends *chicharon*—better known in the States as pork rinds—and vinegar), we trudged into his backyard to commence the first gathering of the Smurf Club, Council Bluffs legion.

In my mind I considered our fraternity the springboard for a network of Smurf clubs nationwide. However, after a few minutes of unengaging conversation about our nemesis, Gargamel, the other Smurfs were stirred to mutiny and reinvented themselves as Luke Skywalker, Darth Vader, and the elusive Storm Troopers.

As I reflect on it now, the meeting of the Smurf club was the first occasion in which I felt I was an outsider. The other boys wanted to be space warriors. I was alone in my ambition to portray my cartoon role model.

In those days all I wanted was to be part of a group. As I entered high school, this urge to belong became even more vital. I wanted to be "one of the guys," to pass as one of the clean-cut American kids. I wanted my worries to fall away from an ever-increasing, desirous fascination I had developed for other boys. Sex always floated in my mind, lingered during algebra class, and materialized in embarrassing daydreams not of the most popular girl but of the track star sitting in the row ahead of me.

I joined anything and everything: the Boy Scouts of America, our community theater group, a pen-pal club, a tae kwon do organization, the speech and debate team, my high school yearbook staff, the altar boys of St. Patrick's church. Now I am twenty-three years old, and it seems that everything I want is clearly the opposite; I've grown to savor the anonymity I maintain in a crowded room.

My friends (I cringe at the thought of speaking for a "generation") seem to share a perspective on sexuality that is not identical to that of generations past. We're not eager to wear our sexuality on our sleeves or pink triangles on our backpacks. I think most of us want to lead quiet lives, gay or straight, without the separatist identities of previous generations.

This is why I waffle when Scott proposes the gay pride parade. One minute I am stubborn as a mule in my unwillingness to attend. The next, I am inclined to follow his friends. In our twelve months together, Scott has developed his own method of handling my constant indecision. He ignores it.

*** 

Most of Scott's friends, standing beside us on the cracked Boston sidewalk, are gay. "Why don't you have any straight friends?" I ask, as if I am of superior worth because my friends are breeders. Instead of answering me, he dons a pair of sunglasses.

We're standing at the intersection of Stuart and Clarendon streets, with the monolithic John Hancock building behind us. The stereotypical images I harbor of gay men are present, but I'm surprised by the balanced number of subdued men who appear to be unconcerned with their image. A pack of guys in the crosswalk are casually dressed for the humidity of a Boston summer: knee-length shorts, T-shirts, baseball caps. And there are hordes of people my age: a young generation in its twenties, gay, and proud to be out on this sweltering June day.

Creeping down Clarendon Street, flatbed trailers move at the leisurely pace of my mother in her Saturday kitchen. The parade route is four rows deep with people. To one of Scott's friends, I point out a significant number of children sitting on the curb, waiting for the spectacle to begin.

The Council Bluffs Pride Parade, unlike this, was not a bonanza of massive floats or outrageous, elaborately costumed performances. It was comprised of hand-lettered signs, a battalion of pickup trucks, and purple balloons blown up by Miss Pashby's second-grade class. It would fall behind and last an hour too long. It was hand-dipped corn dogs and raunchy bean burritos. It was Council Bluffs, in all its corn-cob glory.

You knew what to expect; my mother was able to snap pictures of me marching down Main Street, to add later to her collection in boxes beside the washing machine. Dad got to drink Pabst Blue Ribbon and eat *chicharon* with his buddies in the parking lot of the bank where he worked. Me, I looked forward to the opportunity to walk in the parade with my peers. To show the people in my community that I belonged.

A handsome young Japanese man approaches us on the sidewalk. He's a Calvin Klein-ish waif for the nineties, with a tight haircut and a T-shirt bearing a blockish logo that reads Q&A. He walks directly to me and hands me a flyer, oblivious to the rest of our group. Scott erupts in laughter when he reads the words printed on the flyer's cover. Q&A, it reads, THE QUEER AND ASIAN ALLIANCE OF BOSTON. Suddenly it occurs to me—I will forever be a minority within a minority.

However, I am not unique. My generation (here I go tackling the cumbersome job of Mr. Generational Spokesman) is an unparalleled mishmash of minorities. We are Gay Asian Smurf Enthusiasts From Iowa, Black Midwestern Mormons, Jewish Artists with Disabilities, Bisexual Southern Democrats, Straight Cross-dressing Cabdrivers, Single Protestant Mothers in Chiropractic Schools. However, we are a group of young people who choose not to be identified by these tidy, impersonal categories. We look forward to relegating those labels to the past.

I fold the yellow flyer into thirds and toss it into a nearby trash can. "Wait," Scott says, "you're throwing away the first group where you truly belong!" With a goofy grin, he takes my free hand in his, and we laugh.

# The All-American Queer Pakistani Girl
## by Surina A. Khan

I don't know if my grandmother is dead or alive. I can't remember the last time I saw her—it must have been at least ten years ago, when I was in Pakistan for a visit. She was my only living grandparent, and her health was beginning to fail. Every once in a while, I think she's probably dead and no one bothered to tell me.

I'm completely out of touch with my Pakistani life. I can hardly speak Urdu, my first language; I certainly can't read or write it. I have no idea how many cousins I have. I know my father comes from a large family—eleven brothers and sisters—but I don't know all their names. I've never read the Koran, and I don't have faith in Islam.

As a kid, I remember being constantly reminded that I was different—by my accent, my brown skin color, my mother's traditional clothing, and the smell of the food we ate. And so I consciously Americanized myself. I spent my early childhood perfecting my American accent, my adolescence affirming my American identity to others, and my late teens rejecting my Pakistani heritage. Now, at the age of twenty-seven, I'm feeling the void I created for myself.

Sometimes I think of what my life would be like if my parents hadn't moved to Connecticut in 1973, when I was five. Most of my family has since moved back to Pakistan, and up until seven years ago, when I came out, I went back somewhat regularly. But I never liked going back. It made me feel stifled, constrained. People were always talking about getting married. First it was, "You're almost old enough to start thinking about finding a nice husband," then, "When are you getting married?" Now I imagine they'd say, with disappointment, "You'll be an old maid."

My family is more liberal than most of Pakistani society. By American standards that translates into conservative (my mother raised money for George Bush). But I was brought up in a family that valued education, independence, integrity, and love. I never had to worry about getting pressured into an arranged marriage, even though several of my first cousins were—sometimes to each other. Once I went to a wedding in which the bride and groom saw each other for the first time when someone passed them a mirror after their wedding ceremony and they both looked into it at once. That's when I started thinking my family was "modern."

Unfortunately they live in a fundamentalist culture that won't tolerate me. I can't even bring myself to visit Pakistan. The last time I went back was seven years ago, for my father's funeral, and sometimes I wonder if the next time will be for my mother's funeral. She asks me to come visit every time I talk to her. I used to tell her I was too busy, that I couldn't get away. But three years ago I finally answered her truthfully. I told her that I didn't like the idea of traveling to a country that lashed lesbians one hundred times in public. More important, I didn't feel comfortable visiting when she and I had not talked about anything important in my life since I had come out to her.

Pakistan has always been my parents' answer to everything. When they found out my sisters were smoking pot in the late 1970s, they shipped all of us back. "You need to get in touch with the Pakistani culture," my mother would say. When my oldest sister got hooked on transcendental meditation and started walking around the house in a trance, my father packed her up and put her on a plane back to the homeland. She's been there ever since. Being the youngest of six, I wised up quickly. I waited to drop my bomb until after I had moved out of the house and was financially independent. If I had come out while I was still living in my parents' home, you can bet I'd have been on the next flight to Islamabad.

When I came out to my mother, she suggested I go back to Pakistan for a few months. "Just get away from it all," she begged. "You need some time. Clear your head." But I knew better. And when I insisted that I was queer and was going to move to Washington, D.C., to live with my girlfriend, Robin (now my ex-girlfriend, much to my mother's delight), she tried another scare tactic: "You and your lover better watch out. There's a large Pakistani community in D.C., and they'll find out about you. They'll break your legs, mutilate your face." That pretty much did it for me. My mother had just validated all my fears associated with Pakistan. I cut all ties with the community, including my family. *Pakistan* became synonymous with *homophobia.*

My mother disowned me when I didn't heed her advice. But a year later, when Robin and I broke up, my mother came back into my life. It was partly motivated by wishful thinking on her part. I do give her credit, though, not only for nurturing the strength in me to live by my convictions with integrity and honesty but also for eventually trying to understand me. I'll never forget the day I took her to see a lawyer friend of mine. She was on the verge of settling a lawsuit started by my father before he died and was unhappy with her lawyer. I took her to see Maggie Cassella, a lawyer/comedian based in Hartford, Connecticut, where I was again living. "I presume this woman's a lesbian," my mother said in the car on the way to Maggie's office. "Yes, she is," I replied, thinking, *Oh, no, here it comes again.* But my mother took me by surprise. "Well, the men aren't helping me; I might as well go to the dykes." I didn't think she even knew the word *dyke.* Now, *that* was a moment.

Her changing attitude about my lesbian identity was instilling in me a desire to reclaim my Pakistani identity. The best way to do this, I decided, would be to seek out other Pakistani lesbians. I barely knew any Pakistanis aside from my family, and I sure as hell didn't know, or even know of, any Pakistani lesbians. I was just naive enough to think I was the only one.

It wasn't easy for me even to arrive at the concept of a Pakistani lesbian. Having rejected my culture from a young age, I identified only as a lesbian when I came out, and in my zeal to be all-American, I threw myself into the American queer liberation movement. I did not realize that there is an active South Asian gay and lesbian community in the United States—and that many of us are here precisely because we're able to be queer and out in the Western world.

South Asian culture is rampant with homophobia—so much so that most people in South Asia literally don't have words for homosexuality, which is viewed as a Western phenomenon despite the fact that images of gays and lesbians have been a part of the subcontinent's history for thousands of years. In the temples of Khajuraho and Konarak in India, there are images of same-gender couples—male and female—in intimate positions. One temple carving depicts two women caressing each other, while another shows four women engaged in sexual play. There are also references to homosexuality in the *Kāma-sūtra*, the ancient Indian text on the diversities of sex. Babar, the founder of the Mughal dynasty in India, is said to have been gay, as was Abu Nawas, a famous Islamic poet. The fact is that homosexuality is as native to South Asia as is heterosexuality. But since the culture pressures South Asian women to reject our sexual identity, many South Asian queers living in the United States reject South Asian culture in turn. As a result, we are often isolated from one another.

Despite the odds, I started my search for queer people from South Asia—and I found them, all across America, Canada, and England. Connecting with this network and talking with other queer South Asians has begun to fill the void I've been feeling. But just as it took me years to reject my Pakistani heritage, it will likely take me as long, if not longer, to reintegrate my culture into my life as it is now.

I'm not ready to go back to Pakistan. But I am ready to start examining the hostility I feel toward a part of myself I thought I had discarded long ago.

# Fitting
## by Charlotte Cooper

### Snappy Introduction

Things don't fit me. Zips won't fasten, buttons pop, jeans become wedged at my knees. I don't fit. I'm neither one thing nor the other. Seats are too narrow for me, turnstiles trap me. Emotional doors have been shut on me and political spaces cordoned off. When you see me on telly, I am a gross huffing pig about to collapse. I am a stealer of energy; I'll pilfer your work. I am greedy. I want what I shouldn't have. I am an assault on your aesthetics. I sit on a fence, and I hide behind privilege. Some people want me to be beautiful; some see me as a potential Queen Dyke; others want me to get married; you're telling me I should be thin. Don't hold your breath.

Let me explain. I am usually either bisexual, queer, or a bi-dyke. And I am fat, for always. Half a life of dieting has taught me that my body will never be an average size, that I am *supposed* to look this way. My pussy gets confused by that pesky gender thing; it's always both or neither, just not one at the expense of the other. So what! I have never been or wanted to be straight or normal in any of my lives.

I'm making it sound easy, but I know it isn't. My difficulties with these two chicken-and-egg identities erupted when people tried to squeeze me into a predetermined mould. This process began when I found out that my young fat body was a hot topic on quite a few agendas. I suppose it happened this way because my fatness has always been more visible than my sexuality. If only they had known!

My mother orchestrated my first diet when I was about seven. She worked as a nurse and was embroiled in a culture of health and sickness that taught her that fatness was a curse, an abomination, and the root of all disease. I think my body must have terrified her, a woman who fought her own fatness with diet sheets brought home from the clinic where she worked. Mum passed them on to me, smooth transition from mother to daughter. My inheritance was seamless. Excuse me, I'm shedding a tear for myself as a young woman wanting to slice off parts of her own repellent body and magic her belly away. I look so beautiful in old photographs. But now I have some other things to tell you.

A lucky thirteen years later, I began the process of rejecting the appalling fatphobia that was crushing me to death. Around the same time, I began to articulate my bisexuality.

### Fat and Queer in Mid Wales

Imagine you are here: It is 1987, 1988, 1989, and 1990, and I am eighteen, nineteen, twenty, twenty-one years old. I'm living in Aberystwyth, a small seaside town, where I am completing my first degree at the University of Wales. I went to college to escape the hellhole of my family life. Mum had recently died of breast cancer, and when I moved to Ab, I didn't know that my beautiful brother Paul would also be gone up to heaven in a car crash within the year. So there I was.

I was the fattest person I knew in Aberystwyth, but that was nothing special because I had always been the fattest person I knew. I continued to diet and obsess about my weight the way I always had. I bought and ate low-calorie products, I exercised, I smoked, I craved and binged on junk, I bought clothes that were too small for me in the hope that I would fit into them, I experienced a constant nagging guilt about the food I ate, I felt shame when I saw my reflection, and I fantasized often about myself as a thin woman. I felt that my inability to be thin was a measure of my personal failure in life.

Living alone enabled me to become more independent and autonomous than I had ever been before. I became politically active, and my politics had a most spectacular impact on my personal life. Other generations have agitated around the Miner's Strike, student loans, or the Criminal Justice Bill, but in my experience student activism focused exclusively on sexuality. Nationally, Section 28 of the

Local Government Bill was the big issue; this law prevented local authorities from "promoting" homosexuality—in effect it censored queer voices and lives. In Ab we campaigned to introduce a Lesbian and Gay Officer to the Student Union Executive; the campaign failed. Aberystwyth was a small, conservative, religious, and isolated town whose values were reflected in the student population. To desire your own sex was a very big deal.

I became part of a small group of people, mostly queer, who lived in each other's pockets. We shared the same politics, we laughed big and loud at the small-mindedness in this smallest of small towns, and as a result our faces were known and our sexualities constantly scrutinized. In other generations, queers have sometimes lived without hassle in homophobic communities because there was no language, no conceptualization of what *queer* meant. But for our group it was different: We were named. It was as though we were envoys from Planet FagDyke. The good people of Ab knew who we were and what we represented; they'd seen people like us on telly, and they had language for us, all right.

We lit fires beneath one another's beds and swung the spotlight on one another. Some people leaped out of the closet just in time, like a jack-in-the-box; others were forced out; and I can remember a few who made outrageous efforts to stay in. I came out when I said "I am bisexual." I didn't proclaim it in the middle of the street; I just assumed people knew, and if anybody asked me, I told them. But something felt weird, as if I were invisible.

In the midst of all the politics was a stifling rigidity. Political correctness made icons out of individuals and organizations without regard for questions of censorship and freedom of expression. Some people were ostracized for disagreeing with the party line, and heaps of scorn were dumped on others simply for asking questions. You were blamed for not knowing, you felt guilty for not knowing, and as a result there were lots of us sitting and analyzing in libraries instead of getting out on the streets. Separatism was popular, and personalities, ideas, sexualities, and appearances were categorized: "Us" and "Them." To me, now, this behavior seems typical of people under attack, which indeed was exactly what was happening to queer communities through punitive legislation and backlash. It was as if everybody were in shock, battening down the hatches and preparing for the storm.

I felt weirdly invisible because no one could read me as bisexual. Bisexuality did not fit here, it was not recognized as valid, and—sh!— it was not safe to ask too many questions. So when several lesbian icons told me that bisexuals were sucking the lifeblood from them, I believed and internalized it. They said that they would never sully their cunts by having relationships with bisexual women, and here I was wondering why they didn't want to be introduced to my boyfriend! Close lesbian friends refused to acknowledge my bisexuality, implying that one day I'd meet the right woman. I hoped so too because I thought that would make everything a lot easier. Meanwhile, I found myself in the ridiculous position of trying to pass as a dyke in lesbian-only spaces. The absurdity was lost on me; all I knew was that it was a lie—it felt wrong. There was nowhere else for me to go, but I felt so guilty, worrying that my presence was polluting the purity of all that lesbian energy, worrying that I was spying on them, seeing myself as an enemy infiltrator, and fulfilling their mythology about me.

Bizarrely, I think my appearance as a fat and punky woman protected me from my cohorts to some extent because I was built in the image of a figurehead for radical dykehood. The shit hit the fan that day I cut off my Mohican. I couldn't believe how disappointed people were—as if my hair had let them down! People close to me made no fuss about my fatness—they knew they shouldn't. Perhaps they knew it was "wrong" to make fun of fat people, and probably they were secretly glad they weren't fat themselves. However, most of my friends, although impeccably right-on in other areas, gave themselves away in the odd "harmless" comment: Outsiders and enemies were "fat bastards/arseholes/wankers/cunts." A gay man with whom I was close told me "You're not fat" to make me feel better (deep in denial, I was so grateful), and a lesbian friend called herself "fat" whenever she did something stupid, childish, or pathetic. So insensitive! My head began to pound, my body and my desires were dominating my life, and yet there was this big silence. I had no way of articulating the way I felt; I just knew that I didn't belong.

## Big Fat Changes

Up until Ab I had felt good about my sexuality. As a lusty child I had looked forward to the days when I would be able to express sexiness without getting smacked wrists from Mum. Learning to be proud of my fatness was much more difficult because then, as now, the people

I was close to, as well as strangers, experts—in fact, everyone in the world—could not stop yakking about it. My self-acceptance was tenuous at the best of times. I still wanted to be thin. I read a couple of books which were supposed to be about being fat and loving yourself but whose subtext really went something like, "self-acceptance is the first step to weight loss." More promising to me was news of a conference in London for fat women. I didn't go. It didn't occur to me that I could have gone; I made excuses such as "I can't afford it" and "It's too far." Inside I felt exhilarated that such an event could take place. Could that be me there? Could I call myself fat and feel proud? I held my breath, shut my eyes, wished, and waited.

I began a long-distance relationship with Keith. He pressured me to lose weight with promises of love as a reward. He told me that he would love me more if I looked like Alice in Wonderland—me with my dyed-red, dreadlocked Mohican! I went on a diet for him. (Good girl, Charlotte, good girl.) He ditched me two days before Christmas for a woman who was small and blond and really did look like Alice in Wonderland. You know when ex-alcoholics and junkies talk about waking up in the gutter in a pool of vomit and deciding to pick themselves up and get on with the show? That happened to me: I stopped dieting forever.

Well, sort of. It took ages to stop choosing diet drinks ("I prefer the taste"—yeah, right), to stop cringing when I saw photos of myself, to stop wishing my body away, to start feeling at home in my skin, and to begin being proud of my difference. Even now it's still a process for me. However, the shock created by Keith and his Alice-in-Wonderland fantasy effected one fundamental shift: I stopped blaming myself.

### Fuck You, Fuck You All, Fuck You Very Much
Growing up as a fat bi-dyke, I didn't fit anywhere, and fitting was paramount. At the time it seemed as if other people I knew were able to enjoy and develop their sexualities much more freely than I. I felt that my true self was unwelcome, that I should tiptoe around, that I shouldn't really trust anyone, that there was something wrong with me, and really, that I was offensive.

The utopian scene that chewed me up and spat me out was actually a dystopian nightmare. PC appeared to be so progressive and hopeful— "Let's include everyone." Very good, gold star for effort. But I was being stamped on, and I thought it was my fault, that it was up to me to change—not that the system was stinking rotten. I suppose that I should have been less trusting. The devil on my shoulder sneers "Sucker!" while the angel on the other side commiserates: "How were you to know?"

I have since realized that I spook lesbians, gays, and straights in a very profound way, and therefore my existence is important. Check out your queer history and remember how the S/Msters blew away the hypocrisy that ran like a thread through many lesbian and gay organizations in the mid eighties. Take note of how something so private as wanting to fist your lover or to be whipped into submission turned out to have relevance for even the most vanilla among us, touching on issues of consent, taboo, and inclusion (thank you, brave queer perverts; I am down on my knees and kissing your boots in gratitude). In a similar way, when I demand space in queer communities, my body brings into question stuff about queer aesthetics and desirability. And my sexuality means that you proud Kinsey six fags or perfect one-hundred-percent lesbians have to ask yourselves if you've ever had a twinge of het lust in your loins. This can be a tricky question to answer if your whole identity is based on homo sex. I'm sorry, do I make you uncomfortable?

## Five Years Gone

I've had a lot of problems in listening to myself and feeling strong in who I am; a lot of people wanted to impose their own agendas. In some ways I still feel shaky; for example, I can never take it for granted that anyone would be interested in me as a sex partner. I've never developed that confidence that would enable me to come on to people, and I dream of it. I wish I could have fucked around when I was younger. Now that I'm older and in a long-term relationship, I'm beginning to consider the possibility of nonmonogamy, which scares me but which also represents a new freedom.

But I have never felt stronger. Are you ready for this? I feel lucky to be fat and lucky to be bisexual. My difference is neutral and uncontrived. Others struggle to stand out from the crowd, but I was never part of the fucking crowd!

I am a trailblazer.

I don't fit.

I'm glad I don't fit.

*My Real Love Was Pop Culture*

# Rocky Horror Schoolgirl
## by Sarah Pemberton Strong

The first time I saw *The Rocky Horror Picture Show,* I was twelve years old and on a field trip with my eighth-grade class. Really. It was our teacher's idea to take us. This was an alternative school in Cambridge, Massachusetts, in 1980; we all had hippie parents, and Carter was still president. Besides, *Rocky Horror* was a relatively new happening at the time, and our parents didn't know what it was about. Neither did we.

Just before midnight on a Friday evening in October, I stood with a gaggle of twelve- and thirteen-year-olds in the long line of adults outside the Exeter Street Theater. We had dressed up for the occasion, and I was shivering in my costume, a black velvet cape whose purple silk lining had rotted away. We had painted our faces and brought props too; in school the day before, our teacher had passed out mimeographed lists of what we'd need. Like my classmates, I carried a shopping bag filled with the essentials: rice, newspapers, a squirt gun, toilet paper, and toast. Surrounded by adults as we waited for the theater to open its doors, we tugged at our costumes and poked each other, giggling at the novelty of being out so late.

At age twelve I was not totally naive. I'd spent a summer in Provincetown and had seen drag queens pushing baby carriages down the street. I had found *The Joy of Sex* under my parents' bed and read it. And the teacher who had organized this educational experience was a gay activist who on the second week of school had come out to the whole class. But sex and sexuality were still something for other people, something to be curious about from a distance. In other words, I was over *The Brady Bunch,* but I had never been kissed. Sex was not yet a participatory experience. It was not yet mine.

We went into the theater, and the show began. At first it was like a food fight; some stupid people got married, and we threw rice; then there was a rainstorm, and we all squirted our water guns. A bunch of people in sunglasses and tuxedos danced, and we stood up and danced too. Good clean fun.

And then Tim Curry walked on.

Six feet of smooth body poured into a black satin merry widow and fishnet stockings. Those huge eyes with makeup for days, and those buff shoulders. Lips begging to be bitten. That mane of hair. He was *hot. I* was hot—oh, my God! I bit my knuckles. I crossed my legs. I couldn't take my eyes off the screen, not even when someone in the balcony threw a cold frankfurter down my back. And during the scene in which Dr. Frank N Furter goes down on Janet and then on Brad, something inside me fell off the shelf of childhood and broke open. Tim Curry's head went down, Brad's legs went up, and my life was altered for good—and I knew it and was terrified.

Tim Curry? *Tim Curry?* When you're a twelve-year-old girl in 1980, you're supposed to have a crush on Shaun Cassidy or Parker Stevenson. But there I was in spasms over a transvestite mad scientist in spike heels who brandishes a whip and fucks boys, girls, and space aliens. What was happening to me? For the rest of the film I sat there in quiet panic. It was exactly the same feeling I had a few years later when I made out with a girl for the first time. It was the panic of realizing that there was no going back—a realization that came to me before I understood what I was moving toward—and that it was a good thing. That came later. Back then, however, all I felt was panic. I couldn't deal. I blocked it out.

Years later, little by little, I unblocked it. I moved to San Francisco, came out a few times (bi, dyke, bi), fucked girls, fucked boys, did it in fishnets and in handcuffs, with leather strap-ons and peeled bananas and blindfolds. I learned to love the smell of latex in the morning. And I was under the impression that I'd acquired all these tastes in San Francisco. I'd forgotten all about *Rocky Horror.*

Thirteen years later I'm in Boston again for the holidays. I'm sitting in my mom's living room with a friend I've known since seventh grade. It's late in the evening the day after Christmas, and we're bored. We don't want to go to a bar, and it's too late to see a movie. Then Brooke says she thinks there's a midnight showing of *The Rocky Horror Picture Show* in Harvard Square. How about that?

*Rocky Horror?* Haven't seen it since I saw it with her, haven't thought about it in years. "I'll get the rice," says Brooke. "You make the toast." And we're off. We ransack my younger brother's room for a squirt gun. We steal a roll of toilet paper from the bathroom, grab a couple of old newspapers, and head for the Square.

The theater is small but full. Most of the crowd looks suspiciously suburban, and there's not a costume in sight. Down in front there is one group of teenagers with hair dyed colors not found in nature, but this isn't in honor of the show; they always look that way.

The lights dim. The cast of the live revue saunters out, and the actor playing Frank N Furter steps forward and cracks his whip. I shiver. (Yeah, with a-a-antici… You know.) But then he makes an announcement.

"We want you all to enjoy yourselves and yell at the screen and dance in the aisles, but I remind you that throwing things in the theater is not permitted."

*Wha-a-at?*

He struts a little and continues. "Do not throw toast, rice, toilet paper, or anything else. It's too dangerous."

*Dangerous?* Brooke and I look at each other in disbelief. Unprotected sex is dangerous. Smoking crack is dangerous. Walking alone in my neighborhood at night is dangerous. But being hit with a piece of dry bread? This is *Rocky Horror;* you *have* to throw things. We look around the theater to see if anyone else is shocked and dismayed. No one is. Suddenly I feel old. *The Rocky Horror Picture Show,* like punk music and certain lesbian fashion wear, has entered the mainstream and lost its nasty edge. It's been made safe.

To make matters worse, once the movie starts we discover that the theater has ordered the ushers to stand in the aisles and yell at the screen unfunny retorts of their own invention, just to get things going. Fortunately, none of this succeeds in wrecking the movie. *Rocky Horror* is that good. It's still funny, it's still nasty, the music is still great, and the audience ignores the goons in the aisles and yells the real stuff. I sit there and soak it all in twice—once as the adult I am now, and once as that sweet and gangly twelve-year-old on the threshold of sexual awakening.

"Come in," says Riff Raff. "You're wet."

Yeah.

When it's all over I've decided three things. First, despite the theater's best attempts to wreck the experience, for my money Tim Curry is still far and away the hottest gender-fuck on celluloid. Second, it's too bad Susan Sarandon didn't have a scene in butch drag; I might have come out that much sooner. And last, thank God I now live in San Francisco, which is probably as close to Transsexual, Transylvania, as you can get without leaving the planet.

# The Village People, *Tiger Beat,* and Me
## by Michael Thomas Ford

On June 27, 1969, while a small crowd of fed-up bar patrons plucked beer bottles off a Greenwich Village sidewalk and began the revolution that would change my life forever, I was sleeping comfortably in a crib half a world away in my family's house in Monrovia, Liberia. Four days away from celebrating my ninth month of life, I had been in the world for less time than I had been inside my mother, who, when my scheduled entrance was delayed by more than three weeks, had finally demanded that I be removed by force without the benefit of a sweeping orchestral score or flattering lighting. Oblivious to the fact that back in my native land, my people were waging a war of independence, I rolled over, looked up at the bright African sky, and joyfully wet myself.

Living as we were in the relative isolation of a government compound, I doubt that the news of the Stonewall riots ever reached my family. Even if it had, it probably would not have brought much more than amused smiles to their faces. Accustomed to living in some of the world's more notorious trouble spots, they had seen more than one uprising in their lives and certainly far bloodier ones than that being waged by the angry queers back home. In fact, had my CIA-operative father witnessed firsthand the motley group of drag queens and poorly armed freedom fighters advancing against New York's finest, his first thought would likely have been that their use of high heels as weaponry showed great resourcefulness but that in the greater scheme of things, taking control of an oppressive military regime required more-practical footwear and far less mascara.

Thus, blissfully ignorant of the changing times back in America, I grew up happily in my jungle surroundings. *Gay* meant nothing to me as I toddled through the world looking for adventure, which came in the forms of alligators, large spiders, and once, rather spectacularly, a surprisingly determined cobra that decided one morning to take up residence in my sandbox. I was rescued from all of these things by my watchful sisters and my parents, who noted with deep regret my seemingly unerring ability to find the most deadly and quarrelsome creatures in the vicinity and attempt either to make friends with them or to put them in my mouth.

Miraculously, in the several years in which we lived in Liberia—and later in Zaire—I managed to survive not only several bites from various fauna but also a tumble into a nearby river and a severe head injury that brought me closer to death than anyone would have liked and left me both slightly dented on one side and rather forgetful of things. But survive I did, and at the age of seven, with my father's assignment over and my parents breathing a sigh of relief at having managed not to misplace a single of their three children during almost eighteen years of constant travel, I boarded a plane and half a day later landed back in America for good.

Picking a child out of a life in which popular culture consisted solely of occasional showings of *Mighty Mouse* in African dialects and evenings spent listening to recordings of *Victory at Sea* and dropping him squarely into the middle of the seventies is surely one of the more wryly humorous social experiments my parents ever undertook. I arrived in America just in time to catch the blossoming of the golden age of Farrah Fawcett, and I was spellbound. After years of thinking that life consisted of little more than playing with building blocks and that Peter, Paul, and Mary were the musical Trinity above which none other triumphed, suddenly I was surrounded by movies, music, and television I had never known existed. The moment I sat down in the family room of our new home and turned on the first real television set we'd ever owned, I watched the screen bloom into a full-color picture of Kristy McNichol and was bathed in a celestial light more powerful than any baptism my born-again Christian mother could have asked for.

Although at the time I had no idea that what I was doing was developing a queer aesthetic, skewed as it might have been, I launched myself wholeheartedly into a celebration of all that was gay in my little world. My older sisters, both a decade ahead of me, had missed out on many things by dint of spending their teen years in Africa and so were not much help to me. Their sole concession to the camp life of 1975 was to develop enthusiastic fascinations for both latch hook and macramé, which they undertook with abandon until the house fair near rustled with the sounds of yarn being yanked through colored grids and twine being forced into all manner of lovely shapes. For a time I even found myself drawn into this mysteriously wondrous world, sitting on my bed and listening repeatedly to a recording of Walt Disney's *The Aristocats* while feverishly filling in the face of a brown and yellow dog pillow with lengths of yarn and an ingenious metal hook.

But my real love was pop culture, and I became its slavish acolyte. By age eight I had memorized every episode of *Charlie's Angels,* begging my parents to let me stay up past my bedtime on Tuesday nights to watch Kelly, Jill, and Sabrina puzzle out an endless stream of mediocre mysteries. While I feigned interest in the stories, the thin plots were immaterial to me. What I lived for was the hair, the clothes, and the cars. I confusedly fell in love with Jaclyn Smith, mistaking my lust for her red hot pants and unfailing ability to flip her hair seductively over her shoulders while nabbing a would-be kidnapper for early heterosexual leanings. I felt a strange kinship for Kate Jackson's dykey Sabrina and probably should have realized more than I did when my favorite episode was the one in which the girls are captured by white slavers and held in an all-women's prison by stern matrons with severe hair.

My devotion manifested itself in the form of the world's largest collection of *Charlie's Angels* trading cards. I spent hours riding my bike (a Huffy racer, of course) to the nearby 7-Eleven and buying up as many packs of cards as I could, along with a handful of Pixy Stix so as not to appear too single-minded. Racing home, I would sit and tear the wrappers off feverishly, discarding the wooden slab of gum in my anxious need to see if I had managed to choose cards I hadn't already collected. New ones—especially those featuring Kelly—would be put in places of honor, to be viewed reverently until they were replaced by fresher offerings a few days later. The others were tucked neatly into shoe boxes and stored under the bed, where I would think of them and be happy.

Because we had been away for so long, I saw in television reruns what many of my contemporaries had already seen a few years before me. Deprived for so long, I now spent hours in front of the television, eating TV dinners of Salisbury steak with Tater Tots and chocolate pudding and flipping through episodes of *Adam 12, Emergency,* and even *Flipper.* Occasionally I would give in to my mother's pleas for something educational and turn for a few minutes to *The Electric Company* and *Zoom.* But as soon as she was gone, I would rush for the knob and feast once more upon thirty minutes of pure joy watching the father on *Flipper* drive his boat around Florida's waters in nothing but the smallest shorts.

Just as I was unaware that my attraction to Sabrina, Kelly, and Jill had anything to do with an innate attraction to camp, I was equally oblivious to the fact that the reason I found *Adam 12, Star Trek,* and *Emergency* so captivating was the men. Strong, dark, and deliciously hairy, they were like nothing I'd ever seen before. My previous heroes had always been cartoon action figures with plastic skin, molded hair, and not even a hint of sex about them. While I could imagine riding below the waves with Aquaman on gigantic orange sea horses or soaring with Hawkman above the clouds, I got a much bigger thrill from watching the men of *Adam 12* running around in their policeman's uniforms and from seeing Captain Kirk's solid body so clearly defined by his skintight suit and leather boots. They were living, breathing men, not at all like my cartoon heroes, and I quickly fell in love with all of them. I imagined them rescuing me from evildoers and all sorts of natural disasters, their deep voices soothing in my ear as I fell asleep safe in their arms.

My bible during these wonder years was the inimitable *Tiger Beat* magazine. Though it was ostensibly aimed at teenage girls, I am convinced that *Tiger Beat* was the creation of some brilliant Charles Nelson Reilly fairy godmother who wanted to offer salvation to all the struggling prepubescent queens of America. Sold in every grocery store in the country, it featured pages and pages of pictures and gossip about my favorite stars, almost all of whom were male. The cover was invariably a montage of shots of Leif Garrett, Shaun Cassidy, and the Bay City Rollers wearing tight pants and open shirts. It was enough to cause a coronary event in any red-blooded American queer. While the men of *Tiger Beat* weren't generally the supermasculine men of my television dramas—they more often sported the thin, pale, almost genderless look popular in those days—looking at their pictures touched a part of me that was beginning to blossom after hours of watching *Love, American Style* and wondering what all the fuss was about this romance business.

While my mother loaded up her cart with Hostess Ho Hos, Hawaiian Punch, Rice-A-Roni, and other delicacies of the 1970s, I sat on the floor near the magazine rack poring over issues of *Tiger Beat.* Sometimes I would dip into its older sister, *16,* but it wasn't the same. *16* was too, well, sophisticated. It tried to discuss serious issues such as acting ability and singing prowess. I wanted to know about clothes, about who kissed better than who, and about with whom I could win a date if I answered all of the trivia questions correctly. I remember distinctly one contest in which readers were asked to write down a word that rhymed with *Leif* in order to win a night on the town with the willowy, redheaded Mr. Garrett, the shots of whom in tight white shorts seductively unzipped at the top made me dizzy. I anxiously scribbled SAFE onto the form, convinced that the judges would be overwhelmed by both my knowledge of Scandinavian pronunciation and my choice of such a nurturing example with which to rhyme Leif's name. I mailed it off and waited for the phone to ring. When it didn't, I consoled myself with Dolly Madison Raspberry Zingers and switched my allegiance to Shaun Cassidy.

Shaun, in fact, was becoming the leading man in my life. Once I'd seen him on-screen with Parker Stevenson in *The Hardy Boys Mysteries,* I was hooked. While the darker, more masculine Parker was closer to my romantic type, such as it was, something about Shaun spoke to me. I went to Dart Drug and plunked down two dollars for a poster of him wearing a shiny silver jacket open to the groin. I placed it above my bed, and every night I would go to sleep under the watchful eye of the man who sang "Da Doo Ron Ron" and "That's Rock 'n' Roll" just to me. I even went so far as to send him letters and a picture of myself and my dogs, having culled his address from a list of celebrity addresses I had dutifully ordered from the back pages of *Dynamite!* magazine. When they too went unanswered, I understood why my sisters looked so miserable after hours of sitting by the phone waiting for errant boyfriends to call.

As the years boogied on beneath the splintered light of the glitter ball, I grew into my queer self more and more. With my friend Stephanie I discovered roller disco, and we spent every Friday night from 1976 to 1978 rolling around the floor to the strains of Gloria Gaynor, the Bee Gees, Amii Stewart, and our favorite, Rod Stewart, whose "Do Ya Think I'm Sexy" thrilled us no end and sent us screaming madly around the rink, our sweaty hands clasped tightly together as we created magic beneath the wheels of our skates. During the summers we would sit in Stephanie's pink Holly Hobbie bedroom and listen to the sound tracks to *Grease* and *Saturday Night Fever,* both of which we were forbidden to actually go see. To make up for missing what we were sure were the most exciting sexual adventures ever committed to film, we would take turns reading the raciest passages from equally forbidden books such as *Endless Love* and Judy Blume's *Forever,* easily finding the pages by searching for the dog-ears placed there by countless other readers before us.

Life for me was sweet—an endless stream of music, movies, and skateboarding. I fell in love with Harrison Ford in *Star Wars,* the first non-Disney movie I was ever allowed to see. I developed a crush on the oldest brother on *Eight Is Enough.* My mother introduced me to *West Side Story,* and for weeks afterward I was haunted by dreams of Latino men with dark hair and crisp white shirts. I begged my parents for a shiny green satin jacket and purple velour shirts, which I wore everywhere. Watching *The Hollywood Squares,* I stared wide-eyed at Peter Allen and Wayland Flowers and Madame, wondering why they seemed so much more interesting and alive than the more mundane guests such as Valerie Harper, Pam Dawber, and Lauren Tewes, whose Julie on *The Love Boat* was never a match for Gopher's peculiar charm.

Then, in 1978, during the summer before my tenth birthday, something miraculous happened, something that would mark my official entry into the queer world with such fabulous fanfare that it would be unmistakable. In July of that long, glorious summer when my life hung delicately between childhood and adolescence, the Village People released their album *Macho Man.* While it may not have rocked the charts, it certainly blew open more than a few closet doors in my life, even if I was unaware of it at the time. I still remember begging my older sister to drive me to the mall to get it. I had heard the song on the radio, and knew I had to have it.

After surrendering several weeks' worth of allowance, I took the record home, ripped off the cellophane covering, and put it on my cheap little record player. As the sounds of men's voices filled the walls of my patriotically decorated red, white, and blue wallpapered bedroom, I found heaven. I sat on my bed and listened to "Macho Man" over and over, the whole time staring at the album cover. More than the music, I was drawn to the images of the men on the sleeve. In their costumes they were like something out of a dream to me, rugged angels sent to bring me a message of salvation and a vision of the promised land.

I was especially enchanted by the construction worker, David Hodo. His mustache, his work boots, and the rolled-up sleeves of his blue work shirt captivated me. I wondered what secrets he kept behind his dark aviator sunglasses. I stared at his invitingly tight jeans, and wicked thoughts stirred in my head. Alas, I would later find out that of all the members he was the only one who professed to be straight. It would become a recurring and disappointing theme in my life.

I had no idea which village it was that the Village People came from, and had never even heard of *the* Village whence they took their name. I only knew that I wanted to go where men looked like my construction worker. I pictured a town where the streets were swarming with men in jeans and work boots, their shirts opened to reveal broad chests covered in hair. I imagined them all at the YMCA, doing things that weren't quite clear in my mind but that I was sure involved lots of brotherly love and singing. The songs spoke to me of a place where people could be free and happy, and that sounded good to me, even if I had no idea what an American Indian in full headdress had to do with it.

My mother, perhaps sensing something I didn't, suddenly forbid the playing of Village People records in the house. Swept up as she was in a frenzy of Baptist fervor, many things suddenly ceased to be appropriate for my consumption, including rock and roll, PG-rated movies, and anything that had pictures of unicorns on it, which she firmly believed were symbols of the devil and drug use. I don't think she actually connected my devotion to David Hodo and his friends as an obvious expression of my queer self. After all, she hadn't blinked at the Shaun Cassidy posters or the green satin jacket. But whatever her reasons, she made the Village People and all they stood for firmly off-limits.

But like Bonhoffer in his German prison, I managed to maintain my devotion despite her watchful eye. I heard the Village People on the radio and saw their pictures in *Tiger Beat*, from whose contests I longed to win nights on the town with them. And, of course, there was the group's eagerly awaited film debut in *Can't Stop the Music*, which rivaled only *KISS Meets the Phantom of the Park*. It all stayed firmly rooted in my mind, even when several years later disco was dead and the Village People became nothing more than a glittery memory in the bargain bins at Musicland.

Ten years after that magical summer of 1978, at the age of twenty, I would come to live for several years right in the heart of Greenwich Village, in a small studio apartment on Carmine Street. It was my first exposure to gay life and was almost as unsettling to me as being dropped headlong into the culture of my late childhood had been. I expected the Village to be filled with men who, if they didn't exactly dress like David Hodo, nonetheless claimed their sexuality proudly and wore it well. After all, if Gordon Merrick was right (and I fervently hoped he was), there were men making love everywhere around me with wild abandon. With a little luck, I could be one of them.

Instead what I found was a city ravaged by the AIDS crisis. While I was not ignorant about AIDS, I was in no way fully aware of what it had done to my community. Sheltered by three years at a small religious college where "liberal" had nothing to do with either the arts or the curriculum, I had managed to remain far from the real world and its touch. Despite being only half an hour from the city, I had somehow held tightly to a vision of New York as a teeming sexual playground for queer people. It was a vision created partly by my own desires but also partly by what I'd heard about for so long in songs and in stories. Now that I was actually there, seeing the playground littered with the remains of a party that had ended before I'd even arrived, I was faced with reality. The party was over.

I did find the men. And some of them did look like the Village People's construction worker. In fact, on my very first visit to a gay bar, the historic Monster on Sheridan Square, I was picked up by a man who could have stepped out of a Marlboro ad. Complete with work boots, white T-shirt, and mustache, he fixed me with his dark eyes and asked if he could buy me a beer. For one brief, heart-stopping moment, it was as if the man from my childhood fantasies had come to life. But after the beer came the discussion about the two friends he'd buried that same week, and the sadness in his voice told me that beneath the macho-man fantasy lay a darker world, one that had little to do with music and dancing and much more to do with death and loss.

Later that evening, walking home past the Stonewall Inn and the site of the event that changed my life without my even knowing it, I felt angry. I felt as though all of the struggle that the riots represented ought to have resulted in joyous lives for queer women and men. Instead I was walking through a village where the people, instead of dancing in the streets to the strains of "I Will Survive" and "We Are Family," were withering and dying while the echoes of old disco songs called to them like sirens promising great treasures but yielding up only death. The jubilant sounds of Donna Summer's "Last Dance" had faded ominously into the somber moaning of Morrissey, and it just wasn't the same.

I have never really felt cheated by AIDS, at least not for long. I do not look back at the sexual freedoms of the 1970s and wish that they were mine. I am a firm believer that things are seldom as good as we remember, and I suspect that applies to what many young queer men see in their minds when they insist on lamenting the loss of what they somehow perceive as a birthright of endless sex with beautiful partners who never age, let alone die.

What I do feel I have lost—and what a whole generation of men and women has lost—is some of the innocence that ran rampant in those days of bad hair, worse clothes, and way too much blue eye shadow. Watching Greg Brady transform himself from high school geek to rock star Johnny Bravo, I thought that maybe life was going to be filled with all kinds of possibilities, even for those of us who never really fit in. After all, wasn't the whole point of *Saturday Night Fever* that everyone can be a star, if only for a moment? And wasn't the point of "YMCA" that every young man at least had the option, whether he chose to take it or not, of being one of the boys? Now it seems some of those promised possibilities have been taken back.

There is currently a new wave of 1970s nostalgia that seems to be attracting a generation a decade or so younger than me. The clothes, the music, and the ideals that hung in front of me like a shining star as a child are now being dragged out of storage to be hung in front of another group of young people like a beacon calling them backward into a past that was never theirs. Just as many of my peers longed to belong to the Woodstock generation, putting on tie-dye and dropping out to the sounds of the Beatles even though they were really a decade too late for it, these young women and men don bell-bottoms and clutch *Josie and the Pussycats* lunch boxes tightly in their eager little hands despite the fact that many don't remember life before Ronald Reagan and *Beverly Hills 90210*.

These people who now embrace the relics of my childhood are doing it, I believe, because the future is much more terrifying to them than the past. Looking ahead to the potential of death in every kiss and a country ruled by men who hate who and what they are, it is easier to retreat back to a time when Stevie Nicks gave us her "Dreams" and anything wrong in life could be forgotten by putting an Olivia Newton-John eight-track into the player and driving to the mall with the windows down. It's much more comforting to surround ourselves with what reeks of the fun and the carefree—even if it was at its heart fairly hollow—than it is to admit that what we are left with is the remains of a party that got out of anyone's control.

Queer young people are certainly not alone in wondering why the dance had to end before they had a chance to shine. But especially for queer men there seems to be a fierce determination to hang on for as long as possible to the illusion. For men of my generation, the promises of the 1970s never quite came true, not through any fault of our older brothers but because the beat just can't go on forever unchanged. Many of us speak in wounded tones of having lost our youth, of having been cheated out of a life that others said would be ours when we were old enough to claim it. When Vicki Sue Robinson—now surely nearing fifty if not already there—goes from gay bar to gay bar singing "Turn the Beat Around," the audience, many of them barely old enough to remember when the song first filled discos and roller rinks, waves their hands and sings with her, believing she can make it all right again.

Recreating the past has, I suppose, some sense of comfort in it, especially when the future seems lifeless in comparison. But it seems peculiar to rewrite what actually happened. No matter how many disco balls we hang up or how cleverly we recreate the kitsch of 1978, it is still a false image. When the Pet Shop Boys sing the Village People's "Go West" today, it may be amusing, but it has little of the anthemic lure that the original had. Instead it is a chilly reminder that what we thought was the clear voice of freedom calling us to our promised land has turned instead into some synthesized, passionless echo of the original. Like Dorothy discovering that the voice of the great and powerful Oz was nothing more than the well-meaning cries of an impotent old man behind a curtain, we have discovered that there never really was anything in the black bag for us after all. Even Kelly, Jill, and Sabrina can't rescue us from this one.

It is easy to be angry over what we never got to do. It is easy to talk about how good a past was that most of us know only secondhand. What is harder is making a new future out of what we've learned from it and admitting that maybe a lot of it was done with dry ice and mirrors. As tempting as it is to reach back and try to grab a last handful of whatever is left of our childhoods and what we thought might be our futures, we need to construct something new and even something very different from what we expected with what we have left. As queer people we have to look forward, not back. The answers aren't waiting in the past to be discovered like Leonard Nimoy digging up the lost ark on *In Search of....* Just as we deserved more than scratchy 45s of "Stayin' Alive" as history books and Gordon Merrick novels as how-to manuals, the next generation deserves more than futile attempts at resurrecting a past that has gone the way of K-tel records and Ginsu knives.

Still, on the days when yet another friend has been diagnosed as positive or when I hear of another teenager who has killed herself because life is still too hard for some of us, I wish I had my collection of *Charlie's Angels* trading cards and *Tiger Beat* magazines. If I did, I would spread them all out on the floor, put "Macho Man" on the stereo, and feel it all come rushing back, if only for three minutes and twenty-five seconds.

## My Life in Darkened Movie Theaters
## by K. Burdette

When I was a child, I imagined the ritual of dating going something like this: Boy arrives at girl's house. Boy waits downstairs, making awkward conversation with girl's parents as he waits for girl to get ready. Girl glides downstairs, hurriedly says good-bye to parents. Parents warn boy not to keep their daughter out too late. Boy and girl go to the movies, where they might hold hands, neck, or, depending on the girl's mores, do more.

The first time anyone ever asked me out, we went to the movies. I noticed a couple making out in the back row and pointed them out to my friend, hoping to give him ideas. Likewise, my one and only semblance of a heterosexual romance took place before a cinematic background. We fell in love shortly after *Underworld U.S.A.* Breathlessly held hands during *Life Is Sweet*. (I found Jane Horrocks captivating.) Didn't speak for months after *The Double Life of Veronique*. Reconciled to *Zentropa* and *Blowup*. Spent the night together after *Shock Corridor*. And didn't see each other again after *Children of Paradise*. I remember lying on my back half-naked and hearing him ask if I wanted him to go get a jar of peanut butter after we'd seen that Mike Leigh film. In my mind and in my experience, both the cinema and cinemagoing are bound up with the culture of heterosexuality. The cinema was not just a place to fall in love—with your companion or with a screen star—but a primer on how love might be enacted.

Ironically, it was in a movie theater, watching the trailer for an upcoming feature, that I realized that heterosexuality, as an identity and as a lifestyle, was impossible for me. The trailer was for a girl-centered coming-of-age film, and the particular image that led to my revelation was that of the young, beautiful heroine looking up glowingly at the man she loved as he fucked her in the missionary position. For the first time, I was struck by the disparity between the image on-screen and my own life. This was an experience I'd never had and, in all probability, never would. I cried—not because of any aversion I had to a queer identity or lifestyle but because I would never be able to share in the collective cliché of being a young woman getting fucked in the missionary position by a man she loved. From that point on a whole slew of cultural signs, rites, and values suddenly became meaningless to me.

My epiphany was the more surprising—and the more devastating—because I had always been aware of my marginality in relation to other sorts of "normalcy." As a mixed-race bastard adoptee and as a willfully unfeminine girl, I'd never experienced the pleasures of recognizing my likeness or even having the existence of persons like myself acknowledged by popular cultural texts.

Lacking that experience, I had never been conscious of missing it. But heterosexual privilege was one privilege I *had* experienced. Although I'd never had a boyfriend, I never considered that I wouldn't have one eventually, and it didn't occur to me that my attractions to girls were anything other than platonic. Heterosexuality had been my hope for some sort of normalcy in at least one area of my life. The realization that I would live life as a *queer* mixed-race bastard adoptee was shattering. The representations that had previously failed to address me as a half-Korean tomboy of dubious parentage—television shows, pop songs, advertisements for everything from deodorant to chewing gum to automobiles—now utterly excluded me, a self-identified queer. And they did so with my full knowledge, tearing from me my last connection to the cultural commons.

In the end, then, it was as a queer person that I truly grasped the sources of my alienation. Until that moment in the movie theater, I never understood the underpinnings of the vague but substantial sense of not belonging I'd felt all my life. And with that understanding came intense rage—because the images in which I'm supposed to find meaning say nothing to me; because in the eyes of mass culture, I am a nonentity; and because I can do nothing about it.

# Evolution Starts With a TV
# Heroine and a Plaid Dish Towel
## by Tom Musbach

Something happened when I started watching television reruns of *Batman* when I was a young boy—something peculiar and not peculiar. I found a hero whom I longed to imitate, and this longing, while relatively short-lived in its original form, continued to extend an influence over other phases of my development. These phases, similar to eras of evolutionary progression, I call my Batgirl Periods.

In 1970 I was a happy four-year-old, loved by my parents and progressing on a "normal" path of boyhood development in suburban Cleveland, Ohio. Most every day was spent playing in the yard with my younger brother and sisters—until *Batman* aired.

All playtime activities stopped once the show's animated opening began. We fixed our attention on the cartoon renderings of Batman and Robin leaping into the Batmobile and speeding into the horizon under a bat symbol projected onto the night sky. The familiar theme song raised our expectations for daring rescues and death-defying escapes from garish villains. We were ready for adventure.

As the cartoon continued I hoped for the occasional sight of Batman and Robin being followed by a masked female costar, Batgirl, on a motorcycle. She made the show great.

The first few scenes revealed the unmasked civilian Batgirl as an ordinary librarian, smart but plain, with a bad pixie haircut. When she got wind that trouble was brewing in Gotham City, however, she transformed herself into an agile, no-nonsense beauty. As Batgirl she was glamorous, especially on the motorcycle, with her shoulder-length wig and cape blowing behind her. She mesmerized me like no other fictional character, and I absorbed every move she made. When she walked into a roomful of villains, she radiated confidence. A few graceful kicks to the chops with her high-heeled boots—a nice contrast to the guys' punches—always gave her the upper hand.

My feeling was not attraction (I do remember, however, enjoying the sight of Batman and Robin in tights). I couldn't explain it, but I wanted to be like her. Perhaps it was her difference: She was not the ordinary male superhero. Superheroes were the rage, after all, for kids in my neighborhood. But Batman and Robin—as well as Superman, Aquaman, and Spider-Man—were not icons I emulated as I fantasized about my future. My imagination seized upon Batgirl, and thus began the Early Batgirl Period.

Once the show was over, my brother and sisters and I reenacted the episode, and I inevitably chose to play Batgirl. I didn't always get my way, since there were only two boys; when I did, we sacrificed Robin.

I approached the role very seriously; I was an infant drag queen who wanted to "pass" as a convincing Batgirl. I went into the kitchen, grabbed a dish towel, and put it on my head. After fitting a cap over the towel, I suddenly had long hair. I borrowed my baby sister's blanket from her crib and tied one end of it around my neck, making a cape. My glamorous transformation was complete once I stood on my tiptoes, pretending to wear heels.

I don't remember what else we did as part of the *Batman* reenactment. All I cared about was running swiftly to create the sensation of wind blowing my long plaid hair and raggedy cape. Sometimes I sacrificed the tiptoes in order to intensify the flowing effect. I pretended to be pretty, agile, and confident, my young soul feasting on the imagery. Deep inside I wondered whether I could someday fulfill this fantasy with more-realistic accessories.

One day my father came home from work as we were playing. Every night when he arrived, we stopped our activities and ran to greet him, screaming, "Dad's home! Yay!" We hugged whatever part of him we could grab and told him about our day. He in turn affirmed how good we were. This day, however, was different.

My father's usually benign expression became stern once he saw me running toward him. We started telling him about our activities, and I announced that I was Batgirl. He immediately ripped the dish towel off my head, saying, "Don't let me see you do this again. Boys are not supposed to pretend they are girls."

I sensed my face getting red. I felt humiliated. Though I didn't know why, I had done something wrong that day. I immediately suppressed my Batgirl fantasy in obedience to my father. I assumed that my father's message applied only to dressing up like a girl. His words hadn't conditioned me to "genderize" most playtime activities, so some of my interests continued toward "girl" activities.

In the first grade I noticed during recess that some kids had invented several challenging and fun games around the simple act of jumping a rope that was twirled by two other children. I was attracted, so I joined this group and found that I performed well and had a good time. I didn't think it odd that I was the only boy in the group.

Most of the other boys had a different impression. They hurled words such as "sissy" and "girlie," the insults becoming brands that sealed my reputation over time. A year or two later, "faggot" and "gay" entered the lexicon of insults. I figured from the context—no thanks to Webster's—that the kids weren't calling me a cigarette or even a happy cigarette. I had no idea what those words meant; I just knew they weren't terms of endearment. I contradicted my tormentors every time I could—"I am not a faggot." I couldn't be, because it was obviously a horrible thing that made everyone hate me. I was just being me.

I learned the meaning of the word *gay* before leaving elementary school, and I rejected it more vigorously. The word applied to a sexual practice, I thought, and I had barely reached puberty. Being gay had nothing to do with who I was.

Meanwhile, I graduated from jump rope to gymnastics. I had befriended two gymnasts in my neighborhood, and the three of us did tumbling runs across our yards for hours. The two girls helped me learn front and back walkovers, among other tricks, and I soon performed the moves flawlessly. I was becoming acrobatic and graceful—that was all that mattered to me. Other boys slid into bases; I did roundoffs and handsprings. This was my Middle Batgirl Period.

I learned a few years later that walkovers were not men's moves, nor was the balance beam an apparatus for men—this knowledge came long after I had spent months perfecting a cartwheel routine on a beam that my sisters and I had convinced my father to build. I may have been one of the most talented boys in girls' gymnastics in the whole state of Ohio.

This was not the achievement I wanted. When strangers actually took me for a girl or had a hard time determining my sex, my self-esteem did a nosedive. A teacher once told my mother at a parent-teacher conference that I was a fine student but that he had had difficulty telling whether I was a boy or girl when I first joined his class. When I answered the phone, adults on the other end often assumed that I was my mother. These and other experiences humiliated me. I had never intended to become a girl; I just wanted to do what I enjoyed.

By the time I reached my teens, I had renounced all girlish ways in order to survive. Enduring the constant stream of insults from classmates took most of my energy, and I spent the rest achieving superior grades in my schoolwork. I often felt attracted to other boys in school, but I refused to even consider the possibility that I might be gay. I had no intention of validating their malice toward me.

Though I trained myself to act more typically male, my inner desires did not change. They were manifest in my devotion to *The Mary Tyler Moore Show* and figure-skating programs. Although I did not want to be a woman, I could not stop identifying with confident, independent, and graceful women.

My perspective on gay identity changed in college when I discovered a campus organization for gay and lesbian students. I hadn't the courage to attend any of the meetings, but I did make sure to walk by the student center as attendees were gathering. Once I had identified a few members, I observed them around campus throughout the year. How did they cope in classrooms full of straight students? How did they react to their visibility in the dining halls? My observation period lasted years, but it provided good data: My gay peers were able to function as integrated parts of society while being honest about their identity. Many of their attributes, furthermore, spanned the gender spectrum, and they were comfortable with themselves.

At age twenty-seven, nearly five years after graduating from college, I finally came out. It was no surprise to some of my friends, who joked, "It's about time, girl! We were wondering when you would get a clue." It obviously took a long time for me to realize that "gay" was not a horrible brand—it's a real part of my whole identity. That realization changed my life and enabled me to express myself more fully. I finally let go of my masculinity issues: There was nothing wrong with me.

Which brings me to the Late Batgirl Period. Last Halloween I joined a group of friends who were putting together a costumed troupe with a choreographed routine to entertain the crowd that gathers each year in San Francisco's Castro district. Our identity was very specific: a drill team from the West Lubbock, Texas, Community College for Women. The dozen of us wore specially made purple vests and miniskirts, long white gloves with fringe, and little white cowboy hats atop big hair.

It was my first time doing drag, and my preparations were meticulous. I put curlers in my brunet shoulder-length wig and gathered a host of cosmetics. I summoned my old knowledge of theater makeup and deduced beauty tips from the endless ads I had absorbed in *Vanity Fair* over the years. I slowly and methodically painted my face while the other guys joked about my intensity. I wanted to have fun, just like they did, but I was serious about doing it right.

After I finished, a woman who had helped us get ready for the crowds told me I looked beautiful. "Seriously, if I were a lesbian," she said, "I would go for you." I knew my fantasy was off to a good start.

Soon all twelve of us were marching in formation down Castro Street, stopping traffic. It was the Saturday night before Halloween, and many folks were costumed. As we marched we waved to everybody and shouted greetings in falsetto voices with Southern accents. Every hundred yards or so, we performed our dance for pedestrians who had stopped to watch.

It was thrilling. I had no concern about being recognized; I was a totally different person. I strutted, sashayed, and threw my all into my drag persona, Pristine, an amalgam of Batgirl, Nadia Comaneci, and Mary Richards.

Nobody ripped off my wig or questioned my masculinity. I was able to live out my fantasy of transformation: Like Batgirl, I had experienced going from plain to pretty. What felt best, however, was finally following my imagination without fearing what others thought. I indulged a part of me that relishes creative expressions of beauty, movement, and humor, and my drag participation intensified my appreciation of those graces. I let my inner queen have her day, and it was great fun.

The day after the adventure, however, I was content to return to my life as a plain man with short hair—just like the heroine returning to her stack of library books.

But as the wind blew through my wig that Halloween, I remembered the boy who was too scared to imitate a character who had captured his imagination. Now, as a man, I was free to pretend. The seed sown by *Batman* reruns finally flowered, and I expressed a part of myself that had been dormant for twenty-five years. The portrait that had begun with a four-year-old obsessed by a TV heroine was finally complete in a purple-and-white ensemble topped with springy curls and Iced Raisin eye shadow. Alas, the costume bore no resemblance to Batgirl's. That achievement will surely herald the Postmodern Batgirl Period.

*A Difficult Floating Garden*

# Problems

## by A. Rey Pamatmat

I am young.
I am gay.
I am in love.
This is what life is all about.
All I want right now is to feel something real. All I want to think about is holding Jeremy's hand as I am walking down the street. All I want is to cuddle up next to him on the couch while Letterman babbles in the middle-of-the-night background. I want to sit up on the roof of my building and point out the World Trade Center and the Empire State Building and the apartment windows across the street, telling him the numerous stories I have seen unfold there. I want thighs rubbed under tables in small cafés, stolen kisses while no one is looking, and slow, luxurious sex on sunny summer weekends until twelve-thirty in the afternoon.

I hold the receiver up to my right ear and hear the trancelike hum of the dial tone. My finger fumbles for the buttons in a giddy sort of excitement and begins punching out the seven-digit Touch-Tone lifeline across Manhattan. The computer-generated phone rings buzz with background fuzz until I hear the pickup click promptly after the second ring.

*Hmmmmmmm...*
*Beep-bip-bop-bip-boop-beep-boop*
*Rrring...(cruck)*

*Rrring... (crckl)*
*chu-click*

"Hello?" Disappointment hits me with the sound of Jeremy's roommate's voice, hollow and unsure.

"Hello, Jeremy there?" I ask with a brashness that spits out my broken expectations. They roll off of him.

"Yeah, just a minute."

I spend a few seconds wondering about the propriety of my romantic delusions in this time when fact is more important than fiction and history more important than memory. It would be nice to forget that I live in a world in which individuals are no longer human beings with desires. It would be nice to forget that individuals are now things cobbled together from different politics and philosophies, that they exist only as political statements, representations of interest, demographic, and marketing groups. But I can never forget. In this age of de facto political activism, I am never allowed to forget that I am a native-born, Pacific Islander-American, religiously freethinking, Piscean, essentialist, postmodernist, poststructuralist, post-Stonewall, alternatively lifestyled, uncloseted, self-identified gay, part-time vegetarian male.

All right.

"Hello?"

I can deal with that.

"Hello? Anyone there?"

The soothing sound of Jeremy's voice lifts me from my reverie, implanting visions of his beauty in my head. I see his inquisitive face, its features melting effortlessly together from proud forehead to sloping nose to full, strong cheeks to serious lips to meek, blunt chin. The image of his eyes with their heady blue irises enfolds me even though I know that behind that dream-inducing exterior is a person who can gently focus and solidify my erratic and unharnessed energies. Even now the sound of his voice pulls me from my far-reaching, undirected heights of chaotic thought and sets me down within the simple act of conversation.

"Hi, it's Rey."

He speaks again, but now a familiar warmth has filled his voice. "Hey, what's up?"

"Not much. Just felt like calling. How was work today?"

# PROBLEMS

Jeremy is a journalist in a temporary research position at an international newsmagazine. I constantly marvel at his ability to report and the way this talent puts him in a position to affect the consciousness of a nation. He constantly marvels at my ability to take simple words and phrases and manipulate them into poems and stories that affect the unconscious of the reader. It is this sort of reciprocal awe that fuels our relationship and drives us to fully complement and complete each other. His facts with my fictions, his actions with my emotions, his realities with my visions, the ways in which our existences buttress each other endlessly excites and amazes me.

"It was fine, but man, am I tired," he says. "I feel like I could just fall into my bed and melt." I begin to wonder whether he will be able to come over tonight, but I save the verbalization of the question for later. "What about you?" he asks. "Did you work today?"

In an entirely absurd way, it upsets me that he does not have my work schedule memorized or at least documented.

"No," I answer, preparing to conceal my silliness with an explanation. "I packed. I'm nearly finished putting away all of my things, and I'm going to start moving some stuff over to my new place tomorrow."

"Good," he says as a laugh fraught with innuendo begins to creep underneath his voice. "I can't wait."

Through some stroke of ill luck, the beginning of my relationship with Jeremy coincided with the beginning of strained relations with my roommate, Tim. The two are not connected, at least not in my mind, for Tim had decided that I must move out a week before I began seeing Jeremy. Tim, however, insists on using anything possible to fuel his anger toward me. Jeremy's invasion of Tim's all-too-spare space has been a common theme this past month. It would be just as easy, Tim says, and it would better satisfy all parties if we would just fuck at Jeremy's place.

"Will he be there tonight?"

But that solution has its own slew of problems.

"Who?" Jeremy asks.

"Your roommate. I was thinking that maybe I could go over there tonight."

"No," says Jeremy after some uncomfortable consideration. "I think he's going to be here."

Jeremy is still in the closet.

To everyone.

Even to me sometimes.

He takes a moment to overcome the small wisps of fear-filled flame that I can feel raging over the phone. Then he suggests excitedly, "How about I go over there, and we go up on the roof?"

"Well…"

"C'mon. We'll be really careful and quiet until we get up there. Tim won't even notice I've been over."

"I don't know," I protest halfheartedly. "Tim and I are finally getting along now that I'm starting to move. I don't want to up the tension again."

"I know."

"But let me think about it."

I often wonder what it is exactly that I feel for Jeremy. I often wonder about the nature of love altogether. Does that sort of idyllic romantic bliss of which people have spoken throughout the ages exist? And if so, is that bliss love? In my mind it seems that three weeks is entirely too soon for me to feel love for him or for anyone, and yet we have both admitted that we have never experienced such depth of feeling with anyone else in our lives. With its various roadblocks and obstacles—everything from closets to roommates—it is hardly that idyllic romantic bliss at every minute.

And yet gay loves seem to be the only ones that could achieve such ecstatic heights. There are no set processes, no road maps, no clichéd examples of typical disappointments, and hardly any self-help books to aid in forging the way. Instead two young, strong people must push ahead together and follow their own path. Together they must decide for themselves what their relationship will be and the boundaries within which it will function. They decide for themselves how they will deal with closets or with race, with sexual expressiveness or with age, with appearance, with public affection, with careers, with family, with children, with commitment, with laws, with religion, with politics, with homophobia, and with hate crimes.

And, of course, with other things.

"Did you make the appointment?"

Such situations have their own slew of problems.

"Yes," I answer.

"When is it?"

"Well, since it had to be on a Monday so we could go together, they couldn't get us in for two weeks."

"Oh, yeah," Jeremy replies. "How do we get our appointments back-to-back?"

"When you call the hot line, just tell the counselor your number and say someone reserved a space for you at the Upper East Side clinic," I explain.

"Upper East Side…didn't they have any closer clinics?"

"Yeah, but I've never been up there before. I thought it could be a mini-adventure."

"Up where?"

"One Hundred and Fifteenth Street."

He begins to chuckle at my criterion for choosing Department of Health centers. I cannot help joining him for a bit, giving the tense topic of conversation a much-needed release.

"All right," he continues. "You used our birthdays as the numbers, right?"

"Yep."

There is a pause as he tries to piece it together for himself. Then, defeated, Jeremy asks, "When is it, then?"

"June nineteenth at one p.m."

"OK…oh, wait, damn."

"What?" I ask, masking my dismay and knowing that I am failing. "What's the matter?"

"I forgot, the Friday before that is when I leave for New Hampshire. I don't get back until Monday evening."

"Shit."

I feel a sudden weight pull at me as disappointment grips me around the middle. I am confused by this sudden anxiety; everything was fine when we planned to go together. When Jeremy originally suggested we stop in as a pair, it gave the situation a silly sort of date-like irony. The prospect of going to the health department alone, however, seemed to give my impending appointment a more real and certainly more intimidating edge. There was no longer any sense of fun about it.

"We'll just call and make it for the week after."

"No," I groan, thinking how sweet it is of him to offer. "I'll leave mine the way it is. Just go ahead and make yours for the next week. I keep thinking that if I postpone my first antibody test once, I'll just keep on doing it."

"No, you won't," Jeremy says. "I won't let you."

"It's all right. I should go for myself anyway."

"You sure you'll be all right?"

"Yes, Mother."

There is a pause that fills my ear with background phone fuzz as Jeremy considers what I have said. It occurs to me that he may want me to accompany him because he is the frightened one, but I immediately dismiss this as untrue. If either one of us will turn up positive, it will without a doubt be me.

"OK...I'll call tomorrow and make my appointment."

"OK."

More phone fuzz.

"Hey...come on over," I offer. "I'm sure Tim will never know."

"Good," comes his voice across the miles. It is once again filled with its encouraging warmth. "I'll be over in a bit."

"I'll wait downstairs on the steps so you don't have to buzz."

"Y'know," Jeremy adds, "I kind of think of the roof as our place."

"So do I."

I hear a warm acknowledgment and then, "All right, talk to you in a bit."

"Bye."

Such situations have their own slew of problems.

I return the phone to its cradle and immediately wish that I could settle into someone's arms the same way. I remind myself that Jeremy is already on his way and set about straightening my room as my mind, no longer under his sway, begins its typical wanton wandering.

Can any sort of bliss exist with such a shadow looming over it? I am nineteen years old, and one of my most significant and lasting relationships has already been with a man who is HIV-positive. Another of my boyfriends possibly seroconverted during the period we were together. I do not remember a time when HIV was not a part of dating. AIDS awareness came hand in hand with pubic hair and long before my first actual feelings of love.

All I want right now is to feel something real.

All I have right now is to think about chances to get tested together. All I have are the memories of holding people in the dark as they worried whether this fever signaled seroconversion. I have late nights thinking about someone's rash or someone's cold or someone's weight loss. I have evidence of mortality for them, for myself, for everyone I love, and for everyone with whom I have sex.

I am young.

I am gay.

I am in love.

This is what life is all about.

# A Difficult Floating Garden
## by Pete McDade

He says I'll leave him for a woman. He says it with a smile, and we both laugh at this, one of our many running gags (which are, after all, the blood of any relationship), but we both know he isn't completely kidding. I can't promise I won't, and I don't think he could believe me if I did, no matter how much he wanted to. Let's be fair, though: Could he promise me he wouldn't leave me for another man?

We're far from reaching the point where people make those kinds of promises, and we both know it. One of my problems is that I'm still not convinced that point exists, and I don't see how I can be sure until I show up one day with a dreamy glow around my eyes and a suitcase packed for the future. I'm hoping that that skepticism makes me more like the people who refused to believe the world could be round— benign fools, easy to cast in an understanding light even though they were proved so dramatically wrong—than like people who refuse to believe there's an afterlife, humanists who, I suspect, may be the ones proved right when all is said and done. (Talk about your frustrating victories: Being proved right means not having any chance to gloat across the clouds at anyone.)

He played the piano for me last night. There's a sort of big rec room on the bottom floor of his dormitory—you know, TV, Ping-Pong tables, angst-stained couches—and stuck in the corner is this old upright, surprisingly more in tune than not. I sat on the counter of the nearby microwave-popcorn nerve center, at first only watching his fingers as he began playing, to see how naturally they moved toward the keys. As big a fan of logic and common sense as anyone, I also believe that some things, like the ability to look natural while playing a musical instrument, just cannot be taught. I was impressed immediately, though, with the way his hands glided over the keys and noticed for the first time that his fingers were a little longer and thinner than they had to be. Because he was fated to play the piano? Or did a desire while he was young, still growing—maybe even before he knew that desire was there—somehow shape his fingers like that? I moved my eyes up from his hands and looked at his face. His eyes were closed so he could somehow see the music better. He played Bach—he says everyone starts with Bach—and finally inspired me to close my own. He didn't play long, plenty of stray notes and a few awkward stops and starts, but those five minutes or so provided one of those powerful glimpses that we all want with the people we're starting to know: a way to see if our time is being spent wisely. I was convinced. Resoundingly convinced. Almost too convinced. I know now that if he gets really good, gets much better than good, at the piano before we stop seeing each other, I won't want to stop.

Once again my mind drifts to that mythical land of Making Vows You Mean to Keep: I suspect that one of the paths that leads there must involve simple endurance and staying power, and I wonder if I shouldn't at least try that approach once and see what happens. Don't misunderstand me. In my heart I am certain not only that such a land exists but that there are many ways to get there and that I will someday stumble upon one of them, but the difference between that kind of facile certainty and a true conviction is that one is something you cultivate because it makes it easier to keep going—and, like caffeine, it needs to be replenished often to work—and the other is something you never lose no matter how bad things may seem.

He says he doesn't think he's ever been in love and isn't sure he's capable of it. I think he's not only love-ready but starving for the chance to show someone. I haven't said that to him yet because someone once said something similar to me, so I know it's a thing more difficult to hear about yourself than it should be.

We were talking, this other friend and I, when suddenly he looked me directly in the eyes, put his hand on my shoulder, and said, "You poor guy. Just waiting for someone to love." Not someone to love me but someone to love. It was true (maybe still is) and was said with only the best intentions (almost like a compliment, I think), and yet it was so true and so well-intended that it hurt. I distinctly remember wincing from the pain. Almost embarrassed to be caught standing there, my arms filling to the point of strain and overflow with all this built-up love I needed to deliver upon someone.

So even though I want to tell him that he is capable of love, that I see love someday flooding his entire being, and that it will be a miracle—like suddenly watching a movie in a wide-screen theater instead of on a wristwatch TV or like a caveman having the concept of space travel (or even space, for that matter) explained to him—I say nothing. I don't want him to feel embarrassed, knowing that I've seen (or at least think I have) him standing there, holding all that stuff in his arms.

I'm sitting here trying to come to grips with this after having spent my first twenty-four-hour period with him. Sleep and all, which means the real down-and-dirty truths—like toothbrushing habits (he squeezes the toothpaste from the middle, like me, but is more concerned with the cleanliness of the tube opening) and late-night body noises and odors (which is worse, anyway? Given the choice, I don't know which I'd sooner be rid of)—were finally exposed. We both stood up to the glare fairly well, I think.

Without our even talking about it, without my even being fully conscious of it, I find myself more and more forgiving of little habits that annoyed me and breaking myself of tics I developed in my long period of solitude that I sense annoy him. Not only is the sex still too good, but even more alarming to the budding world-weary cynic that flourished in that period of solitude is the occasional sense of absolute...fondness I have when I look across the room at him. Love can be fought fairly easily because it has developed such a bad reputation over the years and has been revealed as a charlatan so many times. True and genuine fondness is a difficult floating garden.

I slept well last night too, next to him. In the morning our bodies naturally pulled to a spoon shape that is most desirable, most symbolic of finding some other half of the broken key. This has happened to me very few times before, and, as is true with all forms of comfort and senses of intangibly feeling natural, it is something I'm convinced is impossible to be taught.

So what is it that makes any sort of true commitment still seem an impossible step? Anything we plan further into the future than the next couple of days is done only in the sketchiest terms imaginable and with the traditional running-gag disclaimer, "If we still know each other." Is this inability to call whatever it is we're doing something more serious than "whatever it is we're doing" an affliction of my infamously lazy generation? Or is it more specifically a problem of homosexuals: Without the carrot of marriage to keep us going, is it too risky to get too attached? There will never be a piece of paper, after all, that makes any union between two men or two women legal anywhere; certainly not in my lifetime and not in yours either, unless you have yet to enter the first grade, and even then I doubt it. And I'm the Optimistic One in my circle of friends.

Or is the inability to commit a problem automatically attached to the word *bisexual?* Is the word itself not an impossibility, an imaginary friend I've made up to keep myself from ever having to finalize...well, anything? I'm convinced it isn't, but history's full of people who have convinced themselves of the ludicrous.

Again I pray: let me be a flat-worlder.

He asks sometimes, very casually and cautiously, what I think will happen, and I say proudly—maybe too proudly—that I have no fucking idea. I figure that admitting this turns it from a fault to some sort of asset. It's one I hope to find myself without one day, since it is so desperately an asset of the Completely Independent, the Completely Alone.

I don't want to be completely anything.

# My Life as a Baby Dyke, or, Ode to a Pretty Schoolgirl
## by Bree Coven

I knew I was queer by the time I reached fourth grade and fell in love with the new girl in school. Her name was Christine. As soon as Miss Taylor assigned her the desk next to mine and she admired my Smurf eraser and asked to borrow a pencil, I knew we were destined to be best friends.

Christine was beautiful and smart, wore purple every day, and had the same family problems and embarrassing Pink Panther bicycle (the one with the panther's face for a seat) as I did. We played together almost every day after school. My favorite game was "Desert Island," loosely based on *The Blue Lagoon*, except both of us were Brooke Shields. The game involved pretending we were shipwrecked, losing all our clothes in the water, and clinging for dear life to the raft that was, in reality, Christine's four-poster bed with the Holly Hobbie sheets. Sometimes our oceanic adventures would lead us to romance, and once we'd made sure the door was locked, we'd kiss until it was time for dinner.

In my prepubescent passion I wrote her syrupy love poems professing my undying love and gave her my favorite beaded bracelet to wear. She in turn ceremoniously presented me with her treasured unicorn sticker collection and a lock of her strawberry-blond hair. It was 1981, a few years before I heard anything about AIDS, so we thought nothing of it when we pricked our index fingers with a sewing needle and pushed them tightly together, solemnly swearing to remain "blood sisters" evermore.

One day after spending the night at Christine's house, I skipped home to my mother and announced, "Mommy, I want to marry Christine when I grow up. By the way, what's a lesbian?" I had never heard the word before, but when I bragged to the kids on the playground about my plans to marry Christine, I was informed that girls can't marry girls and that anyone who wants to is a lesbian. My mother was quiet for a minute. Then she said, "A lesbian is just someone who hasn't met the right man yet." I went, "Oh." So I didn't come out that year, at age nine, but I did keep on kissing Christine. And no, I never met that fictitious "right man." I met the right woman, several times, years later, but that's another story.

I never forgot Christine. Our friendship drifted ages ago when my family moved away and she entered junior high, got into the "popular crowd," and started signing her letters to me, "Love ya—dearly, not queerly." I have no idea where she is today—probably nested somewhere in New England suburbia with a husband and 2.5 kids. But I have fond memories of that first childhood crush. It's the first of many pages in the dusty scrapbook of my life as a baby dyke.

# Till Death Do Us Part
## by Catherine Saalfield

I usually feel like a fugitive. But I can never figure out what I'm escaping from. I guess for all my cozy and open family nurturing, I was still overexposed to the Way of Life that includes male-female bonding at all costs, usually in the form of marriage. But at the same time, I've been told and shown that whatever I want to do is OK. Coming out as a big happy dyke was easy enough since I wasn't ever pathologized or taken to shrinks and shock therapy. I've successfully learned to unpack negative media images, and I have access to lesbian-made representations. Yet as I've found "my people," I find us not fitting in to one homogenous queer pool, not following the same patterns or paths, stepping out of even the elusive and intangible common boundaries we've been drawn to. Furthermore, Coming Out in the Age of AIDS is a particular refugee story unto itself. No one—queer or straight—prepared me for this. They didn't know how to, and they didn't know they had to. We are all going through this one together.

After many noble attempts I'm still unable to pinpoint the very first time I felt twinges for a girl, so I've actually lost interest in the origin story. Instead I experienced coming out as a change in temperature, where the possibilities of a before only emerge afterward. And there really isn't a final afterward because we aren't around for evaluation at that point, are we? We're left to a process of locating ourselves in relation to those who came before us and those who surround us today. The dawning of my kisses with women, then sunny and rainy queer pride marches, ecstatic affairs, and perpetual reinventions have led me to chilly evenings in hospital rooms, beeping instruments, bloody needles taped into people's wrists. I'm running from this tragedy as much as from anything else. Yet, the romance—loving those who are "the beautiful, the tender, the kind…the intelligent, the witty, the brave"—still courses through me, gets me up and out, keeps me out and about.

When my best pal Ray Navarro used to speak about Coming Out in the Age of AIDS, he spoke of a lost erotic feast that his forebrothers enjoyed; of a threat to his life, his lover's life, and his friends' lives; of a tightly woven but anxious community born of miserable global conditions. Ray was a Chicano faggot in his early twenties. I'm a white twenty-six-year-old dyke. From there the frayed threads of a strange time, of a double displacement tied to the queerness of HIV, must be pulled apart, realigned, realized. What was the impact of AIDS on Ray and me as this unlikely pair, and what did my being a lesbian have to do with any of it? How, generally, has the crisis reshaped the way a whole generation of dykes and fags love and fuck and think and die? How, specifically, did Ray's illness, our activism, our intellectual banter, and our sex talks shape my lesbian life? I can ask because I know I'm not alone in my transgression, this evolution or revolution, or simply in this historical moment: New York City, the early 1990s.

Ray Navarro and I met over activism one night. For us, ACT UP (the AIDS Coalition to Unleash Power) was a thick, desperate, flamboyant, euphoric embryo of dyke and fag culture that became whatever we made of it and exceeded everything we wanted it to be. There were no strings attached, only discovery. There were no presumptions: Getting grabbed in my gender-fuck crotch by horny boys made me laugh. There were no rules except Robert's. As we relished our unwitting but insistent Way of Life, we couldn't have been more alive. There was no background music; that starts now.

Ray died on November 9, 1990, right after he turned twenty-six, back when Soul II Soul's "Keep on Movin' " made perfect sense. In the few years of our virtual inseparability, we experienced an unusual relationship at once charged and obliged by a lack of role models. We had a subtle and discreet but apparently hard-to-disguise sexual attraction to each other. Our energetic intrigue and drive motivated hours of collaborative rigmarole: talking endlessly, teasing, competing, taunting, and then shooting and editing our world on videotape. We huddled in front of the computer, at work on another joint article, pressing our knees together under the desk. We provided soda, sweatshirts, coffee, and aspirin for each other. Anything to keep him comfortable, anything to keep her focused. We made each other's phone calls and we made each other's lunch.

Although we differed rarely, we could never agree about the weather. Ray hated the cold. He loved the summer. (The one drawback was having to acknowledge my barely clad breasts more often.) I, on the other hand, love the fall most—it makes me hungry. I'm reminded of this wonderful photograph—his first autumn in New York, fresh from balmy Southern California. Wrapped in a big blue scarf, he's sleepy and freezing on a SoHo corner. His face is a crisp red from the wind. He's smiling despite the frost on the ground around him. In fact, he's smiling at the irony of any pleasure in subzero temperatures.

At an ACT UP talent show in 1989, Ray and his posse all got up in drag to shimmy to Bowie's "Boys Keep Swinging" (which we referred to as "Boys Just Wanna Be Girls"), which roared over the bad bar stereo system. He wouldn't tell me beforehand what he was going to wear that night. I walked into the glitz, scoping for RGs (real girls) just in time for a sultry voice in my ear, "Hello, dahling." I spun around to gaze upon the tackiest of barflies.

"Ray," I addressed him, "you are the life of my party." He was oh-so-fine in his seventies-mod queen role. His body swelled and swayed on cue, and his cheeks narrowed in all the right places. But that's the only time I can remember not finding him devastatingly seductive—when he assumed the generic trappings of a girl. I told him so. "You're having an identification problem," he insisted. "I'll never be the straight girl groupie your getup requires," I countered. "But as long as you put your jeans back on tomorrow, I'll still love you."

Despite our seemingly opposed objects of fascination and desire, what continues to amaze me—mostly because I haven't found the same degree of intimacy with many other men—is how we did connect about sex and sexuality. It was spurred by a mutually deviant curiosity and, I suppose, that obscure erotic charge between us. I wouldn't have known that the domain remained open for cross-gender duck talk if I hadn't spent four years in ACT UP, one of the hottest pickup spots in the city for outdoorsy, politically active, and (safer) sex-positive boys. I learned that thinking about sex a lot was OK, and I learned to share the pleasure openly with my boy friends.

We all want an intense connection that is genuinely erotic, not conservative, paranoid, or preoccupied with concerns about infection. We all want to get off. Unapologetically, although with considerable explanation, I have ventured in and out of playful conversation and communal fantasy with the guys. After two ACT UP buddies ducked out of the barroom chat for some fresh air in the back room, I was told that it was a real testament to the depth and trust in their relationship that they could embark on this adventure together. They could look the other way. "Besides, it's pretty dark in there." On the contrary, the jury is still out on how we might ultimately define or recognize "promiscuity" in girl circles. Concurrent lesbian lifelines involve living with ex-lovers, sharing ex-lovers, fucking ex-lovers, networking with ex-lovers for new ones, recreating space and significance. At least these patterns deviate from my image of straights divided by social class, sex, and community, locked up in those infernal, privatized dwellings, casting a whimsical, jealous eye toward the bonding happening around and, pointedly, regardless, of them.

More smoothly with Ray than with many lesbians (at least earlier on), I could relive my playtime, draw it out, have it during any cup of coffee. We arrived at this place simultaneously: He set me up with my first city-based girlfriend, and I called him the next morning when I woke up saddle-sore and shy. Once when we were sitting across from each other, ingesting caffeine and talking about intimacy and sex, I inadvertently raised his consciousness about dyke proclivities. This great-looking girl walked by, and all he saw was my face as I glanced over his shoulder at her butt and the way her hair stood out on the base of her neck. I was satisfied when she twisted around to check out the heated stare. Eye contact. I turned back to Ray without registering my digression and caught his demanding grin. "What?" I begged. He shrugged, saying, "I've just never seen a woman cruise another woman before." He didn't stop talking about it for days.

We partied together every Tuesday night at Rock and Roll Fag Bar, which had all these naked boys and fashionably undressed girls drinking, flirting, dancing, strategizing, and making out. That's where I learned about his playtime theories: His boyfriend in Los Angeles and his boyfriends in the back rooms. "I want that kind of freedom," I whined. He wanted me to have it. With him, though? It came up. It fell away. We nurtured our attraction in public spaces and during "business hours." He perched on the stool behind me at the computer because I typed faster. I worked the keys while he worked the hormones. He sat beside last night's dildos (now freshly scrubbed) and suggested, "Go ahead and strap mine on." I appreciated his intellectual acrobatics, his ability to displace the significance of his dick and imagine it as removable for my benefit. He was intensely sensual. We took pleasure in the necessary anxiety over our sexual difference. We created new conditions of sexual excitement.

When I fantasized about fucking Ray—which I was wont to do in the privacy of my own mind—it was all about power and not at all about revenge. It was about both of us locked in that raw and ticklish space, playing with dos and don'ts. It was about giving him pleasure, although I didn't ever imagine getting him off without coming myself. I don't trust men enough to attempt such traditional patterns. This was about me having the upper hand, topping a boy who did boys as a girl who did girls. The version of "bisexuality" in the film *A Different Story* is not what I mean.

Nonetheless, when Ray's stunning former girlfriend came to town to visit, I saw his credits on the Kinsey scale slip to middling. He didn't remove his eyes from her face while she was around. He fought more with his lover at that time and spoke modestly of the woman after she left. But I wasn't jealous. Other times he slept over naked with another friend, a straight girl. OK, then I was slightly jealous. But something less explicable, less conventional, more perverted, and unusual happened between us. When he stayed over with me, we never fully undressed. We got in bed casually and did that thing where you turn your back immediately but carry on the conversation so they know you're not mad, then push into each other and spoon before the issue of whether or not to have sex can come up. When the alarm clock rang, we ducked out of it again. "Things are erotic in the morning," he once said. "That's the only way I can describe it."

Instead of penises and nipples, the law of the father (in general, theoretical terms) came up in our bed. And in our writing, which for us was sex: ecstatic and passionate. We were neo-protos, lots of (psychoanalytic) theory mixed with historical materialism and street activism. We decided one afternoon that theory without politics was unconsciousness. That guilt without sex was death. That a body without organs was orgasm. And that seminars without sex were sleep. Marxism to us was a methodology for asking questions, a theoretical framework, a problematic but also revolutionary political practice. We didn't valorize any form of "point the finger" Marxism. And if an empiricist believed that meaning is out in the world and an idealist believed that meaning is in someone's head, we figured a Marxist not only goes about producing meaning in relation to social structures but also gets off on it.

One of our heady little rampages would start something like this: "Ideology tells only half the story. You have to move away from where theoretical doubt might lead you." The immediate retort went: "Don't be anti-intellectual. If you don't engage ideas on a (variably) theoretical level, you ultimately short-circuit and disallow practice." The other one would say (and the speakers are fairly interchangeable), "I think we agree. I think thinking is practice. What could we do without it?" And then the lowest cut would rear its ugly head: "You're being neodialectical." Comebacks at this point were difficult to muster: "Who's got the attitude problem? Not me, you...you subtheoretical bag of uncombed hair. Neo, my butt. That's not critical intervention. That's television."

Of course, we performed the heavy theory jag for our sex lives too. By way of collective investigation, we transformed myths instead of settling for role reversals. While Ray and I were friends, I was involved in an obsessive butch-butch love thang. Ray reveled in its apparent contradictions since neutralization of lesbianism so often takes the wrongful form of positing male and female roles, of naturalizing butch-femme stereotypes without a clue about power and kinky sex. Ray liked to muse over stories about how my lover and I turned the blissfully ignorant straight world inside out, like when we kissed on the corner and dumb boys in dumb cars yelled out the windows, "Faggots!" (And I thought it was supposed to be butch dykes on the street who get recognized for what they really are.)

We talked about butch-femme, about how for the gurlz the key is not only—or even necessarily ever—identifying with how or that the top gets aroused. In a variety of forms, fashions and leather bits, aggressive desire for the object plays out as seduction. Ray rarely grokked the particularly butch girl control bit without some lubrication. Not surprisingly, the butch-butch quality of my relationship totally threw him for a loop. "Why not drop the labels if you aren't going to adhere to them?" he'd ask. I had to review the lesbian fundamentals beyond a unified, generic Queer Way of Life, finally stammering, "You want us to lose our identities so easily...and just be girls together? Forget it!" Somehow he understood this interpretation. Sex talk (and sexual attraction) between devoted gay boys and girls is really "irregular" in the most titillating and productive sense of the word.

People didn't think Ray and I were normal even when we were holding hands. But unlike some close dyke-fag relationships, ours wasn't threatened by gender, and, boom, our Way of Life was, for all intents and purposes, thoroughly natural. The enigma of the feminine hit us in distinct ways, and we transformed its literalness into a thrill of deciphering. Dicks and dildos weren't in any competition in our world since the spin-off of the slip-on resonates for both dykes and fags. We divorced the question of sexuality from the question of gender and spoke of our lovers without relying on assumptions about male and female. We played with identity and played with genitalia. But still...we didn't *do* it.

Having been socialized by such a reprehensibly homophobic society, one so scared of any and all difference, our little extended family resisted the impulses to settle for easy gender inversions or thoughtless internalizations. But when I say that gender never threatened Ray and me, I mean that we worked hard to liberate ourselves from it. It was the *sex* part of *sexuality* that scared the shit out of us. And HIV.

Ray once said, "I'm not so scared of the future. I'm scared of the present. The future only offers shadows. The present offers concrete, real things to be afraid of." Wriggling out from under the paranoia, I've posted a card on my wall, a quote by Gertrude Stein: "Considering how dangerous everything is, nothing is really very frightening."

Perhaps the emerging sexual vanguards will undo those parallel taboos about "unnatural sex" and "unnatural death." Perhaps Ray and my unnatural approach to our unnatural lives provided us with precisely the extended family we needed. As Audre Lorde wrote in her collection of essays, *Sister Outsider,* "In touch with the erotic, I become less willing to accept powerlessness." We organized our sex lives in terms of friends, community, activism, and living situations. We said to hell with an incest taboo that criminalizes us for sleeping with people who have slept with each other. It is ourselves, our lovers, and our movement we have to answer to.

In 1989, at the Fifth International AIDS Conference in Montreal, Ray's lover got sick. And then Ray got sick, and my thoughts of long hours with him in the hospital go on and on and on. We were so present there with him then, in his full presence, that the processing and the vivid evocation of those moments has all but undone them. Lying with him on his hospital bed, even when it was at his apartment, has lost all sensory value. Yet I know that having sex together was beyond question at that point. His body hurt, and he was so much smaller than I. My girlfriend at the time assures me that Ray and I would have slept together before he became ill if only I had been smaller. Perhaps this reflects an insurmountable allegiance to the classic geometry of husband and wife. Perhaps the necessary but promising mental gymnastics we played with in our platonic relationship were too challenging to transfer to the physical realm. In any case, when we lay there together, his *huevos* peeked out of his patterned boxers, and my long arms had no place to rest for fear of bruising his side or shoulder or butt.

When Ray was sick we still made cracks about all the dildos—the long ones, the butt plugs, double-headers—that I would find in his bureau as I fished around to get him some matching socks because he couldn't see and couldn't really be getting up. His mom, of course, searched daily through the same sex toys for socks, boxers, cassette tapes, rubbing alcohol—whatever ended up there in our perpetual effort to have everything he needed close at hand and put away at the same time. "She's going through your stuff, handling your extra cocks," I teased. "Does she ever ask?" He'd laugh, saying, "The more the merrier, the bigger the better." And then he'd cough.

Through those long hours differences between Ray and me— among dykes and fags—emerged so vividly. Our specific experiences belied our matching haircuts, similar hiking-boot style, and parallel syntax. Ultimately what Ray and I have in common from our distinct places in the HIV community formation is that we will both die. In Mexico they say, "We know when and where we were born, but we never know when and where we will die." When I remember that people die from all kinds of things other than HIV-related illnesses, I feel as vulnerable as the next. When I remember that, I feel closer to Ray. We aren't so different. We aren't so far apart. At least then we have death in common. At least now we have his.

# Remembrances of Things Past
## by Nels P. Highberg

I fell in love with a man. His name was Blane. This is where I always begin and I always stop. I have been trying to tell this story for three years. I've told bits and pieces to various people I knew before and after this all happened. I've written papers for school to compare my experience to larger social realities. I've written poems and pages in my journal. I've gotten my students to read literature that stresses the importance of breaking silence and telling the truth about all of our lives. I've spent more time and pages talking around the event that shapes every day of my life than I care to think about.

I fell in love with a man. His name was Blane. I was twenty-two. He told me he had AIDS a few weeks after we met. I certainly knew the facts, and while I was somewhat shocked, I was not that concerned. He told me that his doctor said things were going as well as possible; and when we had sex it was as safe as it could be. A quick call to a friend of mine who remained negative throughout his six-year relationship with a positive partner assured me that safe sex worked and that I really had nothing to worry about. Over the next seven months, we fell in love, had a commitment ceremony, and moved in together. Then he died.

For most people those are the important events. One of my later boyfriends asked how I could start a relationship with someone when there was no future. A friend from school asked what we talked about those last nights together. Someone else wondered how we could have sex in the first place. Those are important questions that I do think about, but they are not the points that shape my memory of that time.

There's a basic exercise in writing courses where you begin with the phrase *I remember* and keep going, discovering what's in your head and what you have to say about it. Often, remembering is pretty easy.

*I remember* my six-year-old niece coming into my bedroom a few weeks after Blane died. I had moved home for the rest of the summer. Sara was glad that she could see me whenever she visited Nanny and Poppa. I was sitting in a rocking chair watching TV while Sara stretched out across the bed. We talked about the horse she was learning to ride while I flipped through the channels and watched some movie for a couple of minutes. Then Sara said, "Nels, where's your friend, Blane?"

I wasn't quite sure what to say. Of my family, my mother was the only one who knew the entire story. Everyone else thought that he died of cancer because that's what his family had put in his obituary.

Blane met Sara when we visited my family for Easter. Sara remained cautious around strangers, just as she should. In our effort to make his entrance into my family easier, we spent some time wandering through local department stores to find some teddy bear or something to give her, not to buy her off but to give them a point of connection. We found a brown bunny in a pink flowered outfit, and he gave it to her the morning after we arrived. After that, whenever I called she wanted to talk to him too.

After she asked about him, I kept watching TV and said, "Well, he got really sick and died."

She asked, "Did he go to the hospital?"

I turned to her. "Yeah, but the doctors couldn't do anything. They tried, but he was too sick."

"So he's in heaven, like Duke?" Sara lived a few miles outside of the town where I grew up. Cows, cats, and other animals roamed all over the acres surrounding her house. Duke was a large mongrel that was bitten by a rattlesnake the year before. Death was not a foreign concept to her.

"Yeah, I guess so."

She wanted to know, "Do you miss him?"

"Yeah."

The thing that struck me about this conversation when I thought about it later was the fact that Sara was one of the few people to even mention Blane and ask about him. There were a couple of female friends, straight and lesbian, who called to see how I was doing. But none of the gay men I knew in Houston seemed to have anything to say to me. I understood why the friend I mentioned earlier who was in a relationship with a positive man never called; he knew there would be a time when he would be in my place, and I know it scared him. But I wanted some of the gay men I knew when I lived in the dorms or from my classes to say something. I wanted to feel less isolated from the community of which Blane and I were a part. I wanted a man like me to ask me what I was feeling. I did not know how to get the support I needed.

*I remember* going to Washington, D.C., for the National Women's Studies Association Conference a year after Blane died. It was June, and I was preparing to move to Ohio in September to begin work on an M.A. in women's studies. At the conference I met some people who would join me in graduate school and who have since become good friends. I started hearing about the ideas and theories that would shape my thinking for the next two years. The conference made me realize how ready I was for the future I had been thinking about for months.

Before I left for D.C., a good friend told me about the bars and places I should go to in my free time. The night after the conference began, I went to one of the bars on P Street. I have always loved the music in such places, though the meat-market atmosphere does tend to get on my nerves and keep me out. Still, there is something about going to a bar in a new city that seems familiar, even if the familiar means finding those elements that piss you off at home. I settled into a corner and watched the video screens for a while. Before the night was over, I had met a man from Boston named Dennis, and we walked around Dupont Circle for a while. He was at another conference a couple of blocks from mine. The next night we sat in one of those combination bookstore/coffee shops, where I drank a chocolate malted and he ate a slice of one of their special chocolate pies. We had gotten to the point in our life stories where I told him all about Blane and where I had been a year earlier.

Whenever I told this story to men, I always felt a knot in my stomach. The first man I met after Blane died found a reason to leave soon after I told him and never called me again. I thought every man would react the same way and told the story with that caution always in mind. A few moments after I told Dennis, he excused himself to go to the bathroom. I thought he left for good. The more time that passed, the tighter my stomach grew. I knew that this would be like it had been before. If I told men the truth, I would be marked as dangerous no matter what any test had to say. If I kept that part of my past secret, I would be denying one of the most significant relationships of my life. I looked at the empty chair across from me and wondered what to do. Then he returned. When I later went to the bathroom myself, I realized that it was up a flight of stairs and was so small that a line stood constant just inside the door. I guess I was being just a little paranoid.

*I remember* spending most of my Christmas vacation after my first quarter of graduate school with Richard, one of my best friends in Houston. The word *boyfriend* did not really describe him, but there was a physical side to our relationship that made us more than friends. When I lived in Houston, we dated other people even though we spent most of our time with each other. While driving me to the airport at the end of this trip, he asked, "Would you ever try a relationship with an HIV-positive man again?"

I paused. I had thought of the question myself before and since. Part of me focuses on the belief that you cannot control whom you love, and if I loved someone, I would want to be with him. But that other part of me thinks of what it was like to see Blane go from working every day to spending the entire day in bed to needing help getting in and out of the bathtub. Part of me thinks of the weeks after Blane died, when I thought I would be dead soon because my eyes could never focus on anything and it seemed like I could never completely sleep or fully wake up. Part of me wonders if I would want someone to want a relationship with me if I were the one who was HIV-positive.

In response to Richard's question, I just answered, "I don't really know." He said, "I don't think I could do it."

I was not able to see Richard at all during my next Christmas break. After deciding to change jobs, he moved back to his family, who lived close to Dallas. We spoke less often. I knew he spent his time trying to figure out what to do next with his life, and I knew he was not finding the answers easily. Toward the end of January, he called and said he was in the hospital.

"Wait a minute," I said, "what's going on? What's wrong?"

"AIDS."

I spent the rest of that weekend not knowing what to think. I left my wallet in my jeans when I threw them in the washer. I pissed off my students when I could not finish grading their papers. I wondered if this was going to happen every time I fell in love with a man. I felt selfish because I kept thinking, *How could I go through this again?* I felt trapped because I did not know what to do to help Richard. I felt stupid because even though I had been through this before, I did not know what to do now.

I resent that I never had the chance to grow up before I had to act like an adult. When Blane died one of my coworkers pointed out that most people do not lose their spouse until they are two or three times older than I am. Everything that has happened to me shapes my daily life, down to the books I teach and the way in which I treat those around me. Still, I don't know what to think about all of this. Each memory adds to the pile of events to consider as I try to figure this all out. At the same time, I do not know if "figuring this all out" is what I should be doing. But I do not know what else to do, and no one else seems to know either.

*Face-to-Face With Fears*
*and Strange Knowledges*

# How I Got Over Virus Envy
# and Learned to Love AIDS Clones
# by Robbie Scott Phillips

I have feelings too, you know. I found out I was HIV-negative. I felt let down more than anything else. *All* my friends are positive, and I fucked just as many guys as they did. I'm no wallflower, and I'm certainly not ugly! *Really.* I deserve recognition and attention too. It's no fun being the only one having fun at the ball while everyone else is popping AZT. Bummer. I feel so alone. Left behind. *Healthy.* I want a beeper too. And those cute little boxes that tell you which pills to take when? To die for. No pun intended, sweetie darling. The new chic look is thin, thin, thin. And I'm not talking Kate Moss here. I'm talking knocking on heaven's door. I can get the accessories, but no matter how hard I try, I can't get the look.

Here's the bottom line. Everyone else is getting all the pampering and attention. They're all in gorgeous hospital rooms *literally* getting their asses wiped by all the cute homos in town. Every HIV-negative queen in the city is an AIDS buddy or what-the-fuck-ever. None of them have any time for a healthy faggot like me. You gotta be dying to catch their eye. They've got so many liberal guilt issues to work out, they wouldn't dare go out with some poor HIV-negative like me. I mean, I went to an ACT UP meeting thinking at least some hot guys would be there, all sweaty and worked up about their cause, but please! I do better cruising hospitals. All I saw were six dykes and two old homos who missed getting infected.

My friends who are sick? What a drag. No one does poppers any-more. Sex in the public parks? Forget it. Like a scene out of *Night of the Living Dead*. If they *can* pry themselves away from their gorgeous nurses and warm hospital beds long enough to go out, I end up pay-ing. They've spent all their disposable income on medicine and med-ical bills, you see. *No one* takes me out anymore. No one has the cash. I even went to protest the high cost of experimental drugs on this one. I'm serious, not fucking around. They don't mind, though. If you have the luxury of knowing you're gonna die, think of all the credit cards you can max out. You're not gonna pay the bill. Every homo I know flies to France or wherever when they get diagnosed. When's the last time *I* went to Europe? I *pay* my bills.

Then there's this love bit. Everyone who's positive has miraculous-ly found the true monogamous love of his life. I can't find anyone to trick with, much less be my life partner. Positives are sick, but at least they're loved. People wait on them hand and foot too. When I had my anal wart removed, no one came to visit, but hook up some Mary to a respirator, and she has friends coming from across the country. Once they die too, forget it. Memorial services up the ass. Every queen in town weeping. I could get hit by a truck tomorrow, and my face isn't gonna be smiling out at you from the pages of *The Advocate*.

Just the words too—they're *positive*. Hooray! Sunshine! I'm nega-tive—zero, nothing.

I know. I'm bitter, and it's not right to be angry at these sick peo-ple. But I feel so left out. I've lost my community—the people who fuck without rubbers, do drugs, and dance all night. I'm not part of that postdiagnosis health craze. Sure, I can take vitamins, but *I* don't have enough pills for one of those little boxes, and I don't socialize at AA meetings. I tried the AIDS-Anon meetings, but everyone there's pathetic. I fit in nowhere. Ever since the doctor told me I was nega-tive. Nothing. Zero. I have feelings, and they're hurt. I still get tested every six months and keep my fingers crossed. All the AIDS Clones are so hyper about safe sex, though, so I'll probably always be a little old negative. I feel so ashamed. I feel so alone.

Next test's in two weeks. There's always hope, darling.

# Hear O Israel
## by Wayne Hoffman

I always turn the volume down when I'm watching old porn videos. Overall, I prefer them to the newer stuff—no flimsy plots, no bad dialogue, no bleached hair, no shaved chests. And the men never pretend to be straight; they are actually happy to be having sex with other men. But the music is unbearable. I'd rather watch in silence.

So I'm sitting on my couch, watching an old Colt movie. A friend once told me I was born two decades too late, but here I am, a 24-year-old mustached baby clone, jerking off to Bruno and a young Al Parker.

The clips are windows into another age, one I hear about but never lived in. Two men are working over a third, one fucking his ass, one fucking his face. They have hairy chests, mustaches and beards, work boots, leather vests. They ooze masculinity. I pump my cock.

Two men kneel over the third as we approach the climax. I scoot toward the television to catch the come shot in full view, careful not to blink and miss a second. One man shoots right into the third man's face. He opens his mouth and lifts his head to catch the stream on his tongue, gulping it down quickly so he can open his mouth and catch the next spurt. His mouth is hungry, his eyes glaze over.

I groan out loud. Eating come is my very favorite part of sex with men, and I resent the restrictions that keep me from doing it more often. I've tried it anyway—that's how I know I like it—and every once in a while, I let myself eat a load, even though I know it's against the rules. I always hit myself later, but the excitement and pleasure are worth the guilt.

I rewind the tape, watching the scene over and over until I am ready to explode.

*Stop*, I tell myself. I'm a young, attractive, horny guy. I don't need to be sitting here jerking off alone in my apartment on a Friday afternoon. I reach for the phone.

Now, I don't know anyone in the city yet, so I try out one of the phone sex lines—"twenty cents a minute, fifty cents for the first." I dial the Daddy Line, older men being my current obsession.

Two minutes of "Hello? Hello?" into empty space (seventy cents, I tell myself) as I watch the cum shot frame by frame, one hand on my cock, one hand on the remote. Finally, a response.

He tells me his name is Paul. "Mark," I say. He describes himself: tall and slim (strike one), clean shaven (strike two). But he is forty-two (one point), with a hairy chest (two points), and wants to get his dick sucked (three points). He also has a car and can pick me up in fifteen minutes (the clincher). I zip up my jeans, put on my boots, and get ready.

He's meeting me on the corner by the sub shop. I see a gray Chevy wagon turn the corner and pull over to the curb. Just one second to check him out, and I hope it's good news.

He looks like a forty-two-year-old Jewish man. Not unattractive, but not terribly sexy. My ex-lover used to joke that Jewish men don't age well. And I tend to agree. Here is Paul, drooping eyelids, heavy lips, and a visible self-effacement that no gentile could ever fake. A window on my own future? I approach the car.

Paul gets out. "You'll have to get in on my side," he says. "I got side-swiped last week, and the door on the passenger side doesn't open." He looks me over, seems pleased with his fate, smiles meekly.

"Or I could just get in the backseat," I suggest.

He opens the back door, and I climb in. I sit behind him, studying his thinning hair, as he asks me questions about my work, my life. I answer the questions as they come.

A familiar feeling washes over me in the backseat. I am being driven to Hebrew school, sitting in the back of a station wagon much like this one, Mr. Warsaw trying to make conversation with all the kids in the car pool. On Sundays my parents would take their turn, but

Tuesdays and Thursdays I sat behind the other kids' fathers, men who seemed inconceivably old at the time.

We drive to Paul's office, not too far from my apartment. The office is empty at this hour on a Friday evening. It's starting to get dark outside, and Paul does not turn on any lights. We stop our conversation and turn to each other.

"My real name is Eric," he tells me. Does it matter?

"And I'm Wayne," I confess. At least we both used fake names. For some reason this makes me feel less awkward.

He takes me in his arms, leaning down to kiss me. He kisses me as if he has no lips: His mouth is open, his tongue traces my lips, but his own lips remain dry, separate, uninvolved. Kissing for me is passionate and devouring, but this is somewhat detached. I reach up and unbutton two buttons of his oxford shirt, running my hand over his chest to his nipple. I squeeze gently. Eric moans and holds me tighter.

"You like it when Daddy holds you in his arms, don't you, boy?" he asks, eyes closed.

I hate role playing, but it does feel good. "Yes, Daddy," I whisper, sucking on his tongue. He untucks my T-shirt and reaches up to my nipple. I whimper a bit, melt into his arms.

His shirt is now completely unbuttoned, and I pull back a step, bending slightly to take his nipple in my mouth, rolling it softly between my teeth. He gasps, rubs the back of my neck. I trace the shaft of his cock, warm through the scratchy fabric of his work slacks. I keep it slow but steady, gradually increasing pressure on his cock. I like to make my daddy feel good.

We stop for a moment to take our clothes off, suddenly shy in the dim light. My boots go under the chair, my jeans and T-shirt folded neatly over the back. His slacks and oxford are tossed on the desk. He has become more attractive, more familiar. I run my hand lightly through his salt-and-pepper chest hair. As he encircles me in his arms, I rest my face against his chest, flicking my tongue over his nipples, cupping his balls in my hand as our cocks rub against our stomachs.

I am ready. Turning the chair around, I sit on the edge and pull him toward me. I take his cock in my mouth slowly and softly, licking the underside of his shaft. He moans and slides his dick in all the way. His head pokes at my throat, his balls brush my chin, and I inhale deeply, smelling his crotch up close.

"You like to suck Daddy's cock, don't you, boy?" he asks.

I look up into his eyes, his cock still in my mouth, and nod. Rather than say anything, I show my daddy just how much I like to suck his cock. I pull him in farther, sucking hard. I swirl my tongue over his head, rub my lips over the base of his shaft.

"I want to fuck your face, boy," he says. "Open your mouth."

Anything for my daddy. I open my mouth.

He holds my head in his hands and starts thrusting his cock between my lips. His cock is very thick, stretching my lips and scraping slightly against my teeth. He picks up speed, and his strokes get deeper. But he never tries to choke me, never gets violent. Doesn't want to hurt his boy, just reward him. I want to stay here forever.

He's getting close, I can tell. I reach up and pinch his nipple hard. He grunts. I go to work, sucking his cock in fast circles, flicking my tongue just under his head. I twist his nipple and pull on his balls.

"Oh, yeah, boy. Daddy's gonna give you his load. Daddy's gonna come!" he shouts.

He gives me a warning, a split second to decide. I decide to see it through to the end. To break the rules.

I pull back so just the head of his cock rests in my lips, so I can feel the come shoot against the back of my throat, land on my tongue. He shouts out loud, and his knees go weak. He steadies himself on my shoulders, shooting load after load into my mouth. I hold it in my mouth, filling up with his come, while I squeeze his balls, milking every last bit out of him. This is what I need.

He is empty. He tries to pull back, but I don't let him. I hold his cock, still semihard, in my mouth, licking very softly. With my mouth full and the taste of his come still fresh on my tongue, I jerk my cock furiously. It doesn't take long now.

"Oh, baby!" he shouts as I explode all over his office chair. I shoot into the air, still nursing his dick, careful not to hurt him in the midst of my excitement.

Only when I have finished do I let him remove himself from my mouth. We stand separate for the first time in minutes, Eric and Wayne, no longer Daddy and boy. A bit awkward and shy again. He excuses himself to get me a towel.

We make small talk during the cleanup: his office, his work, the city. I begin to get dressed, shirt first, then jeans. He is buttoning his shirt when he notices the time.

"Shit, it's already almost eight o'clock," he says. "I need to make a phone call. Do you want me to give you a lift home?"

"Sure."

"This'll just take a minute," he says. "Promise." I sit back down in the chair and look around the office. Diplomas, maps, papers. Nothing exceptional. I lick my lips.

He makes the call, sitting across the desk from me. I am uncomfortable sitting in on his conversation, but I have nowhere else to go. I look around and pretend not to listen.

"Denise?" he says. "It's me. How are you? Is Mother there? OK, thanks."

He covers the speaker and looks up at me to explain.

"My mother just had a stroke a couple of weeks ago. She's not doing too well. I don't think she's going to make it."

He seems matter-of-fact about it. I ask, "Is she at home or in a hospital?"

"Oh, she's at home, but with full-time care. It's sad, really. She was so on-the-ball, very sharp. And all of a sudden she's fading."

He shakes his head. I shake mine too.

"But I guess it's just part of life," he continues. "There's good and there's bad." I nod in agreement, but I can't help being surprised at how cavalier this sounds.

She's on the line. He turns away from me again.

"Hello, Mother. How are you?" He speaks loudly and slowly, like a teacher to a child. He repeats himself. "I said, how are you?... It's Eric, Mother, in New York." He looks at me and shrugs.

"Did you have a nice supper?... That's good. What did Denise make you?... For supper, Mother... No, I'm in New York, Mother... Yes, I'm coming to Florida on Thursday. Today is Friday. That's just a few days— Yes, we'll have a party when I get there. I'll be there soon. We'll have a party."

He is half listening to her, getting slightly frustrated at her lack of comprehension.

"Do you want to say the Shema with me? Come on, say it with me for Shabbat. With me, slowly. *Shema...Yisrael...Adonai...Eloheynu... Adonai...Echad.* Good."

I hear my Hebrew school teacher reading slowly with us and adding translations so we'd know what we were saying: "*Shema Yisrael Adonai Eloheynu Adonai Echad.* Hear O Israel, the Lord is our God, the Lord is One."

"Good. Do you want to say the *brucha* with me? Over the candles for Shabbat? OK, say it with me. *Baruch...Ata...* No, no, you say it for me." He pauses, listening to see if she remembers the prayer over the candles that she has probably recited every Friday for half a century, when she can't even remember what she had for dinner. She gets the words out slowly, with a few corrections and proddings from Eric.

"OK, Mother, is there anything else you wanted to tell me? No? OK, remember, I'll be there in a few days, on Thursday. Tell Denise to remind you. And I'll see you soon. Here's some hugs and kisses for you." He makes loud kisses into the receiver. Goofy, I think, but he's not too embarrassed.

He pauses for a moment after hanging up the phone, to compose himself. "Well, we'd better get going," he says. We file down to his car in silence. No playful touching in the elevator, no tender kiss goodbye.

I climb into the backseat again. As we take off across town, I try to start a conversation by asking about his recent accident, his dented station wagon. But the rumble of the engine is loud, and I have to strain to hear his answers. I lean forward to hear him better and try to catch his face in the rearview mirror. But the ride is too bumpy, and the night is too dark already. I can't make out his eyes and can't quite understand what he's saying.

He is pulling up close to the sub shop where he picked me up. "Where should I drop you?" he asks.

We are stopped at a red light a block from my apartment. "Right here is fine. Then you can turn and go back uptown."

He nods, and I unlock the back door.

"You have my number, right?" he asks.

I recite it back from memory, though I have not written it down.

"Good. I'd love to see you again, maybe go to dinner or a movie or something. Get to know you a bit better," he says, turning to face me.

"Sure, I'll call you," I say, knowing that I won't. I slam the door and turn away. The DON'T WALK sign is blinking, but I dart across the street, beating the light. Reaching the sidewalk, I take off for home, suddenly wanting to brush my teeth.

# The Scene and the Un-Scene: One Night
## Inside and Outside the Gay Leather Community
### by Emily Cotlier

I attended the twenty-fifth annual Centaurs Motorcycle Club Leather Weekend by myself. Standing alone in a crowd of a thousand at the Leather Cocktail Party on Saturday night, I felt as if I'd made a mistake. All around me tall, impressive leathermen—in full leather or half-naked, pierced and tattooed and girded with chains— were flirting, drinking, eating, cruising, and having a grand time. I was one of ten women in the crowd; of those ten women, I was the youngest at twenty-three. And I was not a happy camper. I'd come to this leather event in D.C. to distribute flyers for my hometown leather event; this was, admittedly, a thin excuse to see a particular butch top who was also at this event. But she had been too reined in by the responsibilities of her current leather title—and her primary lover— to spend more than an hour with me. I was physically sick with yearning for her. Or maybe I'd had too many of the fancy hors d'oeuvres.

It took me a few minutes to squirm through the crowd to the bathroom. "Excuse me! Pardon me! Girl cooties! Estrogen coming through!" My voice could barely be heard above the din. It was a relief to slink into the ladies' room. I stared into the mirror and sighed. I looked good: makeup in place; long, dark blond hair curling on the shoulders of my black crop top; my hourglass waist bare above a tiny black pleated miniskirt. I hadn't bothered to wear the sash or medal that said I had been Ms. Philadelphia Leather 1993; the sash was as big as a sandwich board on me, hiding my entire torso, and the medal made me feel as if I'd won a prize at some animal show. *Maybe if I looked more like a standard leatherdyke,* I thought, *in a pin vest and jeans with short hair, I'd be better at mingling with these strangers.*

After I'd wandered around for half an hour, bored, chatting uneasily with the few women at the fringes of the throng, my friend Nadia arrived. Like me, she was petite, very feminist, and twenty-three. Unlike me, she was new to the S/M scene, a novice submissive, charmingly timorous, and soft-spoken. It amused me to think that this meltingly gentle and quiet person was a riot grrrl. She hadn't done much S/M play or marched with leather contingents at queer pride parades or gone to any big S/M gatherings. She was excited at the prospect of attending her second women's S/M play party later that evening. I clung to her like a limpet, relieved to have some female pheromones to inhale after the musk of the leather-wrapped men.

Nadia was thrilled by the crowd for all of five minutes. Once she'd gotten an eyeful of body modifications and custom leatherwork, she realized the same thing I did: To the gay men tonight, we might as well have been invisible. We hung around with the top I was jonesin' over for a little while, but people kept congratulating the top for her title, and we felt like spare tires. After we threw some paper airplanes and got busted by a Centaur for littering the stage area, I suggested to Nadia that we go see what was happening in the other half of the club. The Centaurs' event was taking up only half of the largest gay dance club in D.C.; normal Saturday night stuff was happening on the other side. Maybe we could dance.

We squeezed our way through the one door allowing us to reach the other side, where a vanilla crowd was beginning to gather. Oddly enough, the music was worse. My outfit, so light and girlish at the leather party, was dark and severe compared to the gumball-colored rave boys and the sleek club chicks in silver spangles and daisy chiffon. I didn't know any of these people either, but somehow I didn't feel as bad about it as I did in the throng of leatherfolk.

By the time we went back to the leather party, the "Parade of Colors" had begun; in this event all the visiting S/M and motorcycle clubs showed their heraldic patches onstage and announced their names. We squirmed to the front and got an excellent view on one side of the stage, in between International Ms. Leather and

International Mr. Leather. I introduced Nadia to both of them, and she was thrilled. "Wow! Royalty!" she said. I giggled and hushed her as the evening's ceremony began.

First, some Centaurs Club officers came out. They were all over forty. Then, before the colors began, an honor guard stepped to the stage, bearing several national flags. The club officers led the crowd in the American, Canadian, English, and German national anthems. They even said the Pledge of Allegiance. Nadia was shocked. "I can't believe they're doing this! This is so weird and conservative!" I clasped her in a fierce hug, delighted that someone else felt the same way I did.

After the mumbly anthems, the first of seventy-five clubs started heading up to the stage. It was an impressive sight, if a little monotonous. We agreed that we'd split as soon as Nadia was sick of the spectacle. Just as returned with our coats and bags, the emcee boomed, "And now, all titleholders please line up to be presented!"

"Shit!" I'd thought I'd make it through the evening without having this inflicted on me, but no. Since the 1994 Philly titleholders weren't there, I felt obliged to go up. Besides, it would do the boys good to see that someone in a skirt belonged at their event. I ran up to the cluster of other leather titleholders. A man stepped back for me: "Ladies first," he said. The titleholder who went up before me was a well-respected female top. She was also nearly blind and walked haltingly, slowed by some mysterious pain, aided by her guide dog and her boy. Her fortitude was impressive. I felt very strange following her up onstage, young and lithe enough to take the steps two at a time, pouncing before the microphone and saying my name and title. I went to the side of the stage uneasy, almost guilty about the contrast between us in health and age.

Once we were dismissed Nadia and I fled without saying good-bye to anyone. In the parking lot, we jumped up and down and screamed "Girl! Girl! Girl! Girl! Girl! *Aaaaaaaaaa!*" Then we ran, laughing, to her dilapidated van. Running away from that ceremony made me feel as if I were playing hooky. The women's play party that we wanted to go to was being held at a professional dominatrix's dungeon in Maryland. Nadia had directions to the party, but she had no idea how to get to the highway they specified from the Navy yard area. We decided to just go north and ask for directions, and we sped off into the night.

As we drove, we talked. Nadia listened to me rant about the subtle and not-so-subtle sexism and ageism of the leather community. I told her about the "old school" leather system and the lesbian S/M sex wars of the mid eighties, about how the titleholder system had acquired its peculiar role in leather culture. I described my own struggle to be taken seriously as a young woman when my title flung me into the midst of the leather community. Nadia was very patient as I rambled. She was not, I noticed, a particularly good driver.

"The whole gay and lesbian leather scene is such a bizarre subculture!" I ranted. "And the most frustrating thing is that people don't think. They just do this profound, intense sexual stuff without doing a lot of self-examination or thinking about what power and sexuality mean, especially the guys. It's sexist, but it's so true! Listen, if you get bored, just let me—"

*Krannng!* The van lurched and swayed. "Shit!"

"I think we ran over a lane divider." We pulled over, and Nadia hopped out to check.

"I have a flat tire." she said, forlorn.

Nadia's spare tire was flat too. We had pulled over onto a grassy highway shoulder in a suburban area; several gas stations and the Master's Choice Motel were within sight. Nadia lent me an overcoat to drape over my outfit as we trekked over to these outposts of civilization. It was soothing to walk over the dewy grass. The evening was pleasantly cool.

"I'm having an epiphany, Nadia."

"Yeah?"

"I'm sick and tired of all this ritualistic title stuff. It's so ephemeral. I want to do something real with my energy, with my life. I want to write more. Cook more. Put more toward my career. I wouldn't mind getting laid more either. I need to play; it makes me feel physically ill not to play. It's weird. On one level I've gained a lot from the leather community, but on another level I haven't gained much at all—my life, especially my sex life, is more complicated and difficult. I've met so many more men than women, but it's the women who've made more of an impression on me…" I trailed off as we drew near the motel.

The next hour was as dull and nerve-racking as trying to get a AAA truck always is. My friend with whom I was staying, Nikki, and her friend Loreen found their way to our obscure location to retrieve me.

Nadia wanted to wait with her van. I bade her an affectionate good-bye; she looked lost in the motel lobby. Nikki, Loreen, and I decided not to go to the women's play party; it was one o'clock in the morning, and it would be two by the time we got there. Instead, we decided to go to an all-night diner.

I'd known Nikki since high school; she was brash, assertive, and a fast talker. Her startling green eyes were highlighted by her hennaed blunt cut. Loreen, a stunning young punk with a black buzz cut, pink lipstick, and tattooed eyebrows, was obviously able to keep up with her, conversationwise. They were both bisexual, more involved with men than with women and not terribly up about what was going on in the queer community. With a lot of high-energy chatting, we made our way to the diner.

Inside it was blindingly bright, full of high school and college students throwing french fries at each other. As we waited for a table, Nikki began to tease me good-naturedly about the scene I was supposed to have had that afternoon with the butch top. I told her about what hadn't gone down, and we dissected the whole incident. There was no need to be discreet with Nikki, thank heavens. We were done with the topic by the time we got a booth and ordered.

I turned to Nikki. "Remember when we used to come down here and visit Rachel, back when Rachel and I were lovers in high school? And we used to go to the IHOP after *The Rocky Horror Picture Show,* and we'd all order toast because we couldn't afford anything else?"

"Oh, my God, yes," Nikki replied. "At least we can get real food now."

"I felt like a total dweeb hanging out with all those punks, especially whenever I tried to wear black lipstick."

"Well, who wants to get black lipstick on their toast? Besides, you're better off than most of them now. You've got a degree and a real job, and you're still weird, doing all your S/M stuff."

"I guess. I still feel out of it at those leather things. I've been doing all this titleholder stuff for two years, for such a long time—and everyone is *still* older than I am. You're into S/M too, Nikki," I said, turning to Loreen. "In fact, Nikki was the first person I tried to top—who else do we know who's our age and into S/M?"

"Well, Rachel, Nadia, Sue, Elliott, and Sarah were for a while...Danny keeps avoiding it...Amy and Nina...Corwin...I know this guy Kevin..."

"I know some other people too, but they're all fucked up on drugs and stuff," Loreen said.

"Like, the S/M I was doing with Jesse wasn't fucked up?" Nikki and I both winced. Her relationship with nasty-boy Jesse had been an uncool, abusive, nonconsensual scene.

"Yeah," Nikki continued, "when I go to science-fiction conventions, I see some people doing unsafe things, flogging in the wrong places and doing bondage wrong and stuff, partly because they don't even want to admit they're doing it. Or maybe they're just doing it because it's in, part of the modern-primitive thing."

"Remember the time Rachel went to a con and she said she just drank people's blood all weekend?" I asked. "She was, what, thirteen at the time, in her vampire phase?"

"E-e-ew!" squealed Loreen.

"Oh, my God. That is so unsafe!" said Nikki.

Our food arrived. Conversation veered off into Nikki and Loreen's latest psychodrama. As they chortled over what kind of hot sauce to pour over some hapless guy's theoretically barbecued testicles, I sipped my milkshake. Looking at Nikki and Loreen nattering happily, I felt far older than they are. S/M had brought me face-to-face with fears and strange knowledges, with myself and my desires. Neither Nikki nor Nadia seemed to know what I was talking about, though they sympathized. Maybe S/M was important to them, but they seemed perfectly happy to live without it. Had they ever yearned to have the tension and pride beaten out of them, to taste the grassy bitterness of piss, to feel their blood sing against the thin bars of empty needles, to kneel and have the world contract to a dildo or a pair of boots? Did it make them feel sickeningly, excruciatingly resonant to do without? My few S/M friends who did understand were seven to twenty years older than I was.

I knew that the female titleholders I'd seen earlier at the leather party had been young turks when they were my age. Most of them were tops and had been befriended and mentored by gay men and the small coterie of skilled dyke tops. I guessed that they had gotten started, found their mentors, when they were my age or younger. Would any leatherman or cliquey top treat me like that? I was a femme bottom, not a top of any sort and not a butch—worthless currency to them, it seemed. I didn't feel like I belonged to this leather community, to any family or tribe. But was there anywhere else to go? Who was I supposed to connect with? What about Nadia and Nikki, other people my age in my fix?

Chilled from the milkshake, I pulled my leather jacket back on. The jacket was a perfect example of the whole dilemma. I'd bought it about a year ago at a fund-raising auction at a men's leather event. I'd been Ms. Philadelphia Leather of the year and, as often happened, the only woman at the event. The tiny biker jacket had been custom-made for a man who'd died of AIDS before he had a chance to wear it. Because it was so small, I was the only person there who could fit into it, and I snagged it for a hundred dollars. It was a year before I realized what the jacket could mean. I'd seen the label from the maker inside, though I hadn't recognized the name. Now I know that David Menkes was one of the most famous custom leatherworkers in the country. It was almost outrageous that I owned a jacket made by him. Also, leathermen and -women who acquire secondhand leathers and whips tend to take pride in the history of the former owners. It made me uneasy to think of the history and ritual that had been disrupted, the loveless way the jacket and the knowledge about it came to me.

It was three a.m. when we stumbled out of the diner to head home, our brains fuzzed by the carbohydrates and the late hour. I was very quiet in the car. Nikki and Loreen were still yakking when we got to Nikki's apartment, and it was clear they intended to talk for a while. Well, at least their mania meant that I'd been able to rattle on about what was under my skin and not feel like I was monopolizing the conversation. *What a weird night,* I thought. I'd been bounced between these extremes—the old-school gay men's leather community and my young peers—failing to reach the space I most wanted to be in, the space where queer S/M women were hanging out and playing together. I cleaned off my makeup and shucked my clothes to go to bed. Though I had hardly slept the night before, I couldn't settle down. Nikki finally crashed about an hour later. My body was seething with restless energy, haunted with longing and fear. I was still awake at dawn.

# Vanilla Means Having Sex With a White Person
## by Denise Tuggle

I am a working-class bicultural Black lesbian Buddhist martial artist incest survivor with a college education, and I think that's pretty neat. I've had to struggle all my life just to think I deserve to exist, because too many people think that being inclusive means saying, "I like all the parts of you that are just like me! You can sit at my table as long as you don't try to bring your whole self." My whole being makes these people uncomfortable, and I get blamed for that. Suddenly I am labeled a traitor not only by those who couldn't care less about me but also by people who are supposedly on my side.

I've been told to censor various parts of myself by friends, family, people of Color, and lesbians. The white side of my family showed their love by making me an "honorary white." My very Black middle-class girlfriend thinks, of course, that I should want to become middle-class, just like her. Proud Africentric Black heterosexuals will tell me in a heartbeat that Black gays are proof of the degeneration of the Black community. I care about "my" groups, all of them. But I belong to so many of them that I can see each one from the outside.

I've learned that each group has its own little head trips that it holds unquestioned. Refusing self-examination makes all of us weak, ignorant, and mean. I won't stand quiet and unquestioning about issues that divide us—and when I say "us," I'm talking about everyone in all of my groups. There are enough people in the world who want to erase the lives of people of Color, lesbians, *and* the working class. We don't need to make it easy for them. And yet I want to do more than survive. I want to transform, create, and grow. I had to preface in this way so you'll know where I'm coming from when I say that I want to look at perceptions and behaviors around S/M in the lesbian community.

The responses within the lesbian community to S/M (both as a topic of conversation and as a sexual practice) have been anything but neutral. Frankly, I am bored with this debate because it isn't going anywhere. I feel like lesbians aren't being candid about what informs our perspectives and biases on the subject. So I'll start by saying that I don't do S/M, and I do have criticisms. At the same time, I don't view lesbians who practice S/M as "the enemy" or as traitors.

When lesbians get skin to skin, all our shit surfaces. And once the shit's out there, it is like some sort of philosophical war zone. You know the camps. It's the S/M dykes versus the non-S/M dykes. Each camp self-righteously marches up and down, declaring "My way is The Way, and there is something wrong with anyone who is different!" Each sits in its foxhole taking shots at the other and yelling "Hooray for my side!" But actually, S/M and non-S/M lesbians are playing the same game. There is tacit agreement on the rules. We agree to loathe each other while feeling superior in our own position. Each side pushes the other to conform. And who each of us is doesn't seem to matter.

Although I am not into S/M, I am into passion, intimacy, sex, and power. I am dedicated to living my life true to this self-knowledge rather than in accordance with some pro or con dogma. Right there that gets me labeled as a traitor by some anti-S/M lesbians.

Yes! I love sex and passion and intimacy! I don't use these terms interchangeably, but rather, I consider them separate ingredients. There are people with whom I am intimate but not passionate or sexual—my brother or my mother, for example. There are people with whom I am passionate but not intimate or sexual, such as my kung fu buddies and the teenagers I work with.

It's the ingredients one chooses to use and the ways in which they are mixed that flavors an experience. Sex is like flour to me: It's an ingredient with not much flavor by itself, but when you add a whole lot of passion and honesty, a generous helping of intimacy, and a pinch of fantasy, you have my recipe for nirvana!

Where I run into trouble with both S/M dykes and non-S/M dykes is with two other ingredients: sensuality and power. I am both sensual and into my own power. Many people, including lesbians, seem unclear about these two things. For me, sensuality includes sex, passion, intimacy, and probably power as well. But many people find anything in the sensual category problematic—maybe because everyone craves intimacy, passion, sex, and power, and this need scares people.

I do know that my enjoyment of sex, power, passion, and intimacy both tantalizes and frightens many womyn. I was once told by an S/M lesbian that I would make a fantastic S/M dyke because of my commitment to power and passion. I know she genuinely meant it as a compliment, the same way some white people mean to compliment me when they say they think of me as one of them. However, I don't want to be submerged in someone else's category! I want to be celebrated for all that I am.

In their writings, presentations, and even in personal conversations, S/M dykes have not communicated a very clear idea of what constitutes S/M. Non-S/M womyn, however, are most definite on the subject. It is easy for us. Sadomasochism is finding sexual pleasure in inflicting pain or in having pain inflicted upon oneself. I don't see how this applies to me. I don't need to inflict pain or to be in pain to be powerful or passionate. Yeah, I like to kick and punch people for fun. I do it all the time in kung fu, but I don't get a sexual thrill from it. In fact, I don't ever intentionally inflict pain. When I execute a good punch or kick, I feel a fantastic rush! I revel in my power, my speed, and my self-control. But any fool can inflict pain. Any amateur can break a bone. It is far more impressive and much more difficult to exercise power without inflicting pain. In kung fu I strive to be able to punch and kick with full intensity yet maintain the control to make light contact. It is possible! We don't have to think like our oppressors.

Some S/M dykes have tried to identify S/M with specific sexual techniques. But S/M is not inherently the practice of any particular sexual technique. It is the application of pain with the technique that makes it S/M. For example, bondage is not innately an S/M practice. Good Vibrations, the West Coast lesbian toy store, sells rawhide restraints lined with lamb's wool. They work—they are fun, and they don't hurt. Fisting, role playing, even discipline need not be S/M, because none of them has to involve pain. (My current lover fancies herself the dominant one even though I can and do pin her whenever I feel like it. And if I make her say "please" before I let her up from being pinned, it is not to humiliate her. It is to gently remind her that if I lie on my back, it is because I choose it.)

I think S/M lesbians have appropriated these essentially non-S/M practices because their perceived illicit quality is exciting. The flip side of this is that non-S/M womyn end up labeling themselves S/M even though nothing they do involves pain. They just don't want to be viewed as sexually boring. I think the term *vanilla sex* was created by S/M lesbians as a reactionary cheap shot and that the term has stuck because we who do not involve pain in our sex have no name for ourselves. Maybe it is time we think one up! Personally, I do not accept the term *vanilla* as a put-down for people who do not use pain in bed. As far as I am concerned, *vanilla sex* means sex with a white person.

You know what, though? I can think of more than one boring, uptight PC dyke who put me to sleep in bed before we were done. I wonder about womyn like this. It's as if they are afraid that if they really get down, then they may like something "bad." Maybe this tenseness and rigidity is a reaction to some past sexual abuse—in which case uptight PC dykes may very well have something in common with many S/M lesbians.

Every single S/M dyke that I know has survived incest, rape, or both. Now, I know a lot of womyn are incest and/or rape survivors, but not every single one! As an incest survivor myself, I know that incest and molestation create profound chaos. I once went out with a womon who could orgasm only in one position. It just happened to be the position in which her father would rape her when she was a child. Incest haunts you. Things that seemingly have nothing to do with incest can unexpectedly evoke an incest response. For example, kung fu is a major part of my life. To this day I cannot be friends with my kung fu instructor. She is one of the most ethical, insightful, and generous people I know, but none of this matters. She is someone who has authority over me, and I have not been able to get over the fear that if I blur the boundary between us even slightly, then she will somehow make me cease to exist. It is an incest response, I know. It pains me and confuses my instructor. I don't yet know what will change it, but I do know that ignoring it only creates more chaos in my life.

I have been told by several S/M dykes that S/M empowers incest survivors by eroticizing the past damage of the incest or other sexual abuse. They say a womon takes control over her pain by choosing when, how, and by whom it will be inflicted. But I am not convinced that S/M is simply pleasurable empowerment, and I am concerned about womyn damaging themselves and their partners. As an incest survivor, I know that some wounds are much more difficult to heal than others. Some just don't heal. You can't decide to "take it back" after the damage is done.

I also know this as a Black womon. I see Black people damaging one another every day because of generation after generation of racial abuse. Black womyn tell each other, "You would be so pretty if you straightened your hair." Light Black womyn are considered more desirable than their darker sisters. Black womyn wear blue and green contact lenses—anything to change us into acceptable whiteness. We have been through so many hundreds of years of hating ourselves that it has become socially acceptable within our own community. We wear our anger and resentment with pride and as an armor—yet this does not change the essential truth that we hate ourselves. Such con-volutions only camouflage the problem, making it harder to rectify. So don't talk to me about empowering incest survivors via S/M. Eroticizing pain does not transform it. It only glosses it over. The wounds remain.

Race is a factor in S/M. I have met only one Black S/M dyke in my whole life, and I have been in and around the gay community since I was ten. I have heard rumors of Black S/M lesbians from white S/M lesbians. I have even been used as an example of one. I have met a few Asian S/M dykes, but S/M culture appears to me to be primarily white. Whether it really is, I don't know. But I think the ways in which race and power dynamics inform S/M culture need to be looked at and acknowledged.

I'm also concerned about the need for a battered-lesbian move-ment. Am I supposed to believe that it is a mere coincidence that the rise of this movement is occurring while S/M is in vogue in our com-munity? At the same time, many non-S/M womyn have abdicated any responsibility for lesbian battering by laying complete blame for the problem on the S/M dykes. Yet as long as S/M-lesbian paradigms do not acknowledge and include the existence of battered lesbians, the S/M dykes make themselves an easy target.

I think most lesbian paradigms have the same fatal flaw: They are always leaving someone out of their utopia. The ironic thing is that as a community we are much more inclusive than anyone else. Any lasting solution has got to include us all. We don't have to like everyone in order to include their existence in our worldview. As lesbians we must include all lesbians: S/M lesbians, battered lesbians, lesbians of Color, white lesbians, you name it. Not only that, any viable paradigm must include men of all races, bisexuals, transsexuals, drag queens, and white people. Just wishing some people would cease to exist doesn't work. I'm sure that at some point or another, each of us has experienced someone very actively wanting us to "just go away." It didn't work with us, and we shouldn't be doing that shit to anyone else.

For the most part I have disengaged from S/M lesbians. In my experience the martial-arts community and the S/M community do not overlap. We simply deal with issues of power and control differently. But as with men, as I feel less invaded by S/M lesbians, I've become more tolerant and philosophical about their existence. Ultimately what is right sexually is a wholly individual experience, beyond outside value judgments, and it is each person's right and responsibility to be honest with herself. Since I don't accept S/M and at the same time have no wish to annihilate its practitioners, I generally choose disengagement. Paradoxically, my version of inclusivity means saying, "There are some parts of you that I distinctly don't like. When we sit at the same table, we will have to negotiate."

# Stone
## by Nadya Arnaoot

For years I was haunted by the term *frigid*. I wasn't doing what I was supposed to do—that is, allowing myself to be fucked by men. And there was something really wrong with me for that. Inhibited, repressed. Prudish. Frigid.

I looked at girls with a terrible combination of smugness and self-loathing. I was above them and beneath them at the same time. I remember sitting behind one of my closest friends in high school, shortly after she told me she had let her boyfriend fuck her for the first time. And I kept thinking, disgusted, that she had a new hole poked in her body. I don't like to admit to that thought now, but that was what was going through my mind at the time: She had let him make a hole in her body. I was never going to let anyone do that to me—my body belonged to me and was whole in itself.

I watched as, one by one, my friends crossed that line, moving from fierce autonomy to the sticky business of boyfriends and fucking to using the word "we" all the time and endlessly agonizing over what some guy really meant when he said.... Sex and the loss of independence were intertwined; boys were emotionally and physically vampiric leeches. But everyone, it seemed, was crossing over to their side. That was what becoming a woman meant.

So I wouldn't be a woman. I would be something else, something above the physical and sexual, something detached and not quite human. But while I could call this difference superiority, the world called it something else entirely. The word for it was *frigid*. That was what they called a girl like me, a woman who refused sex.

Remembering the way I thought then, knowing that these old patterns still affect me today, I am both embarrassed and saddened. But this is the background to my troubled relationship with the word *stone*. You see, before I knew the word *stone*, I knew the word *frigid*.

With my first lover I learned that I love finger fucking. Putting my fingers inside another woman, feeling the warm, soft, moist place coming open for me, is a delicious and humbling thing. Physically the richness of sensations is astonishing: I feel as though I am living in my fingers. My hands, so frequently clumsy, fit perfectly inside another woman's body.

At the same time, I am astonished by other women's capacity to take pleasure in something that for me is painful and frightening—I cannot abide vaginal penetration. I clench up and freeze and hurt. Finger fucking another woman, I feel sensual pleasure, awe, and a trace of resentment that I cannot have the same pleasure. And is there, buried deep, a bit of contempt mixing with shame? After all, if we are different, then one of us must be superior. And I cannot decide which of us that is.

This ambivalence is not limited to vaginal penetration. For the few years that I have managed to be sexual, I have struggled between my desire to be touched and the difficulty of surrendering to another person's hands.

When I read the word *stone* in books such as *Stone Butch Blues*, I was both grateful and appalled. Here was a word other than *frigid* for a woman who does not permit herself to be touched. The word itself has a romantic sound—tough and strong and perhaps a little bit tragic. It sounds like my old kid ideas of self-containment, a word I would have picked back then to describe my refusal to allow penetration, violation, the interruption of my body's autonomy by another person's hand or penis. When I first ran into the word *stone*, I heard my own bravado, my own insistence that my way of being was valid. Not a lack but a strong presence. Stone.

At the same time, I was troubled by the word's inflexibility. Stone women never permitted themselves to be touched; they took pride in their untouchability. I desperately wanted to be touched, struggled against my own tendency to disassociate, to clench up under caresses as though under torture.

I also struggled against others' tendency to label me. I have had women, upon discovering that it is not easy for me to be touched, decide that it is not worth bothering at all. I shouldn't blame someone for being frightened when I become frightened, for not wanting to help me work through the barriers I so desperately want to work through, particularly since I have only recently been able to articulate my desire along with my fear. I shouldn't blame them for not reading my mind, for deciding to stop rather than risking rape by continuing, but I do. Part of me deeply resents the times that women have accepted pleasure at my hands and not reciprocated. Even when I have told them that they didn't have to.

I have never heard anyone but me say the word "stone" out loud. Some of my friends will refer to tops and bottoms when covering some of the same territory. I find the word *top* useful in describing particular moods or scenes—"I topped so and so" or "I'm feeling top tonight"—but it does not bring up the same richness and difficulty that *stone* does. I do find the words *bottom* and *submissive* useful in describing what it is like for me to permit myself to be touched. For gentle touches as well as for pain, I do need to submit, to make the very conscious effort of turning my body over to someone else. Sometimes it's easier for me to be touched in an S/M context than in less-defined make-out situations, where it isn't clear who is in control. It feels much safer to give away control if I know that someone else will take it.

I have been able to go further with my current lover in allowing myself to be touched than I have before. I think this is partly because this is the first time I've had a lover who is willing to do S/M with me, to scare me and hurt me and keep touching me after it gets difficult. We have a safe word, and I find it useful in two ways: I know that everything will stop—instantly—if I ask for it to, and I know that unless I ask for him to stop, he will continue. He doesn't read my nervousness as an automatic signal to stop, as my non-S/M lovers did.

And I find that as I learn to be touched, as I give my body to my lover who gives me pleasure, it is bittersweet. I am getting something delicious, physical, and sensual. Vulnerable. And I am giving up something as well, the power in not being touched, the pride of stone. This is something I have been wanting for years, and it is also something I used to swear I would never permit.

Giving up on stone.

*My Swollen Little Libido*

# The Creation of the Sluts
## by Cianna P. Stewart

J uly 10, 1992. We were finally assembled. Introductions, including our regular jobs: "writer/stripper," "prostitute," "photographer," "student/phone-sex worker," "construction worker," "stripper," "floor waxer/performer," "bookkeeper/lap dancer," "professional dominatrix," and me: "theater director. I'm here because Lani called me."

*Hi, Cianna. I'm calling all the sex divas I know. I want to send you a flyer for a new project I'm doing at Lyon-Martin Women's Health Services in San Francisco.*

*You call me a sex diva, and you know I'll have to say yes.*

An unusual team for a new HIV-prevention project designed to target women who have sex with women.

*Lani, I still think that was your most brilliant move, hiring a bunch of strippers and prostitutes and orgy-goers.*

*I just wanted some sex-positive women, that's all.*

That first day, I had no idea what kind of power we had, what we would achieve. I simply felt a little out of place and nervous. But definitely excited. I didn't think this was a groundbreaking idea, because it was so logical to me—and to everyone else there.

*The Peer Safer Sex Slut Team (PSSST) is one third of a project funded by the American Foundation for AIDS Research. The goal of this project is "to abolish the widely accepted myth that lesbians and bisexual women are not at risk for HIV, and to reduce their participation in behaviors that put them at risk from transmission of the virus." We will be targeting women who are more likely to have casual sex and are at a high risk for HIV transmission. We will be doing one-on-one interviews in bars, dance clubs, and sex clubs to find out what women know about HIV and safer sex and to what degree they're practicing it. We will also be educating through the interviews as well as through safer-sex demonstrations. What those demos look like and how you do your one-on-ones are up to this team.*

None of us was a conventionally trained HIV-prevention educator. And few of us had ever seen anything targeting us as women who have sex with women. We went through all the training you'd expect: sexually transmitted diseases, HIV symptoms in women, basic info on safer sex, getting pregnant and HIV, substance use and abuse and their connection with HIV, testing and treatment, the rules for us as employees of Lyon-Martin. Then we started to talk about what was out there and what we wanted to do. Getting private funding was critical because we wouldn't have been able to do our work with federal moneys. We could never have been as effective if we couldn't talk explicitly about sex. And our reputation would have been very different if we hadn't been able to take off our clothes.

*What are our own experiences with safer sex? What do we like? What don't we like? Are any of us practicing safer sex?*

These are the questions we started with, asking them of ourselves. I have since found that these questions are not often asked of educators. This has never made sense to me. And—even more amazing—educators don't often admit it if they don't like something or if they themselves are not practicing "one hundred percent safe sex, one hundred percent of the time." Or if they ever get bummed out or pissed off.

*What reasons have you heard from your friends about why they don't use safer sex?*

"I hate dental dams"; "I've never been taught how"; "I don't have to, lesbians don't get it"; "I hate the taste"; "All the information is conflicting. It's too scary. So I don't do anything anymore"; "I can't talk about sex"; "It takes too long"; "It's not real sex."

We decided that the best way to counteract all of this was to actually demonstrate safer-sex practices. Two women on the team had been doing basic safer-sex stage shows at a women's sex club already starting to take off in San Francisco. They were our first teachers. We learned (mostly through trial and embarrassing error) what didn't

THE CREATION OF THE SLUTS

work and developed whatever got the most response from the women in our audiences. We did "venue specific" demos, in what I have come to call "slut style." Every show consisted of a fact,

*The Centers for Disease Control and Prevention is the federal agency that tracks diseases. Did you know that their official definition of a lesbian is "a woman who has not slept with a man since 1977"? And you expect them to give us accurate information about how women are getting HIV?*

a tip,

*If you miss that slick, wet feeling of putting your hand inside her (or his) pussy, put some lube on the inside of the glove before you put it on. Then put some more on the outside before you slide it in. The glove feels like it just disappears.*

and a demo. We discussed and enacted all the different ways that women have sex with one another. We talked about play with any gender, with whatever body parts, with and without toys. We went from vanilla to S/M, from scripted fantasy to improv. We admitted our own fetishes and created new ones. We did "field research" and told people about our discoveries on how to use something differently, how to make something sexier, how to more than make do with what you have.

*Before you buy anything, take that tester bottle of lube and put a bit on your hand and rub it around so you can feel it. Then stick your fingers in your mouth—because taste is equally important.*

We talked about personal slut favorite brands of condoms, lube, toys, plastic wrap. We all gave up on dental dams (none of us liked them), and explored every alternative.

*When did I start keeping plastic wrap all over my house? I think it was after the time I was lashed to a pole with the stuff, then one woman got down on her knees in front of me and just stuck her head in my crotch and demonstrated with her tongue just how thin that plastic is. Before that, all my struggling just showed me how strong it was.*

We did silly, funny things. We did sexy, hot things. We stripped for one another and the audience. We covered each other in ice cream and chocolate syrup and licked it off. We turned gloves into flat sheets of latex ready for sucking on. We put condoms on with our mouths while our hands were tied behind our backs. We showed them all the best places to spank.

*The biggest mystery to me is still the fact that we were so innovative, that we were the only ones doing this. We started doing demos for boy groups who had heard of us, and they just went crazy over it. There have been so many boys doing demos for so long that I figured all this had been done, just not for us.*

We performed at street fairs and conferences, where we simulated everything or demonstrated sexy things to do while dressed. We went down on latex dildos strapped onto willing volunteers, stripped down to just-legal clothing, or stayed completely covered and still left nothing to the imagination. We talked about everything we like to do, licked up G-strings wrapped with plastic, lubed up the gloved hands of the nervous and played with their fingers until they had no trouble imagining how they could use this elsewhere.

And we answered their questions and admitted our own fears and anxieties. We spoke of our actual experiences and when it got hard for us. We found ourselves challenged by the histories of the women we talked to. We helped guide women through their fears about testing, relationships, safer sex. We talked with people in bars and clubs, found out what they knew and wanted to learn, and wrote new scenes in response. And no show, workshop, or demo was deemed successful if it didn't turn people on.

*I didn't realize that for some people it was hard to forget the word safer. Whereas to be a slut, you never forgot the word sex.*

# Waiver
## by Doug Mattis

My life changed when I was fourteen and I saw my gym teacher naked. I had come into the gym locker room to change into my phys-ed uniform. I distinctly remember hearing the shower running, and as I began to change, I thought someone from the class before mine was going to be late for his next class. As I pulled on my shorts, he walked out of the shower stalls.

Mr. Spano was (and remains, in my memory) the most beautiful thing I'd ever seen. He strode the length of the locker room toward his office completely naked. I watched, paralyzed by his thirty-year-old musculature. He saw me staring, dumbfounded, and held my gaze with his beautiful Italian face. Then he walked into his office, stood at an angle so that only I could see, and slowly toweled off. Soon I remembered the boys around me and broke his white-hot stare. I bolted.

Dealing internally with the revelation that I was attracted to men would have been so much easier if Mr. Spano hadn't been on to me. Each individual gym class was a nightmare, and although I never saw him naked again, there was plenty of interaction. He would constantly call on me to come stand with him in demonstration before the class, and he'd hold my shoulder while looking at me intensely under the guise of "advice from the coach." It would have been harassment, except that I probably just imagined the intent—I was completely in love with him. So much so, I could hardly be around him at all. I stammered responses idiotically and lost concentration during my classes afterward, fantasizing liberally and praying for the school day to end so I could run home and relieve myself.

I did, therefore, what any fourteen-year-old would want to do in this instance: I got a waiver for high school gym. But it wasn't easy. I had made the national figure skating team that year and was able to convince the principal of the high school that my involvement in skating (over twenty hours per week) would suffice for exercise and coordination activity—not to mention that I, in all likelihood, had a career in skating. I was a potential Olympic competitor. Why would I want to risk getting hurt and missing Nationals over a field-hockey injury?

All of this was easily understood by the principal.

"Unfortunately, Doug," he said, "any waiver would have to be signed by Mr. Spano, the director of phys-ed." He then promptly picked up the office phone and told Spano I'd be "right down to see him about a waiver." I thought I would shit.

The first thing Spano did was close the door to his office. I sat in the chair and let my frazzled mind wander enough to think that, in his tank top and football lace-up shorts, he never looked hotter. He sat across the desk from me and smiled cockily, asking why I thought I was so special that I deserved a waiver. Desperately collecting enough saliva, I told him what I had told the principal.

Spano went on a short tirade, claiming that there were many national athletes in the school and that I had no right to expect special treatment. I was actually flattered that he would go to such verbal efforts to persuade me to stay in the class. But then I remembered what it would be like to see him every day. Gulp!

"Mr. Spano," I said quietly, belying my fourteen years of age, "if you don't sign the waiver, I'll go to the superintendent of schools."

Mr. Spano rose above me like Mars, beginning to thunder. "Are you threatening me, boy?"

"I'm just telling you what I'm going to do." I was aghast at my own control, and considered it divine intervention.

Spano considered me for a long moment, and then sat down, smiling gorgeously at me. "Go for it, Doug."

Needless to say, I was out of gym in two days. All I had to do was think of subjecting my swollen little libido to Spano every day to give me courage. After the waiver was signed by the superintendent, Mr.

Spano couldn't even look at me in the halls. But he still looked at me in my dreams.

Figure skating had given me my first opportunity to avoid my sexual future—only later did I discover how many gay men skated!—and I put all my energy into my training. By the time I was a senior in high school, I had won Nationals, was on ABC Sports a couple of times, and was something of small-time sports celebrity in Philly. I had made the international team and was traveling for skating upwards of twenty-five weeks out of the year. It was exciting, but my high school class was voting me "Most Likely to Be Absent."

The night before my last final for math, I had come back from a trip to California, and the flight had gotten in late. I overslept and arrived fifteen minutes late for the final. At that point it is completely up to the proctor of the exam whether to admit a student to take it; and if I couldn't take my math final, I wouldn't graduate. Readying my plea, I knocked but paused as I saw Mr. Spano come to the door.

We stood looking at each other for a long moment through the glass in the door, and he smiled before slowly opening it. All of the students in the exam room paused to see our exchange, seemingly aware of its sexual history and electric tone.

"Mattis," he said slowly.

More silence.

"You've got me, Mr. Spano. It's up to you what happens. I'm sorry I'm late… What are you going to do?" Again, I was devastated by how calm I sounded in the presence of everything I then desired in a man.

There was a long moment, and suddenly I got a peek at the real Spano. His face softened, and to this day I have no idea what the implications of this were. He smiled and opened the door wider. "Come on in."

# The Mattress Papers
## by Tom Maroney

I had to go visit a friend, someone I have not visited or thought about in years, someone much smaller and less powerful than I am, someone hopeless and in trouble. I had to travel back, so far back, and the trip weighed heavily on my mind; it affected my body too. I slouched; drawing breath became painful. My eyes darted here and there, following dust motes and invisible energies. I did whatever I could to delay my journey, making long lists of things I had to accomplish before heading out. I would need this and this and had to make sure these needs were met while I was gone. Life would move forward while I went digging around in catacombs on my rescue mission.

Preparations for war! I was going in, like it or not, and my hate was pure, preserved through anesthetization, like a caul in a jar. I took it out and wore it, the juices dripping down my face. I turned to the task of weapon selection, rooting through the array of knives before me. In war, aesthetics are as important as utility. Should I bring a hunting knife, steely, made for gutting large animals? I pictured the Father this way, intestines spread out on the forest floor. Or a scalpel, a healer's tool, for going deep into creatures to discover their pain and draw it out? I am no veterinarian, no altruist! Surgery requires time and precision. But then, being a vegetarian, I'm not much of a hunter either. Bring them all, I said: chef's knife, scissors, paring knife, X-Acto blade, carrot peeler, everything that fits in the bag.

The air in the armory, dusty from years of disuse, made my sinuses run. This is where you appeared on the scene, remember? After the decision had been made, the tears ordered and packed in with the other supplies, ripe for shedding; after my heart had been twisted by the pain of memory like the arm of the cannery worker who caught his sleeve in the machine; there you were, eyeglasses in hand, popcorn, soda, a pillow for your rump. Racked with sneezes and coughs, I looked up to see you standing there gawking with your sympathetic eyes, gentle reader. Well, forget it. I won't tell you my story because I don't want you to know what it is. "My advice is, stay clear of danger," I told you. I put on war paint and brushed my hair while you watched, donning different disguises, finally choosing something appropriate but incomprehensible to you. I ignored you, but you were still there. "I'm going in like this," I said. "If you want to come along, keep to the rear and shut up. If you get lost, that's your own problem. I don't take stragglers."

I walked into September 1983, and it was just the way I remember leaving it. Little Tom was there, lying down, listening with apprehension to the sound of approaching footsteps. Plaid carpeting blazed red, gold, and brown on the floor. "We're in the attic," I told you. "Little Tom lives up there. Little Father has never come up here before." Three beds covered in cheap scarlet bedspreads thinner than crepe sagged in the middle like frowns. They had been placed randomly in the large room, one near a window, another along a wall in a cubbyhole, the third jutting out. The fluorescent light and the air conditioner hummed their separate frequencies.

Little Father walked up the stairs into the room, worrying the noise into more noise, the bedspreads into a deeper shade of red. My face burned as I watched Little Tom, lifeless on the bed. Little Father was bloated to six times his normal size, his face contorted in fear, his cheeks and forehead red with fear, his hair, brows, chin, eyes, black with the fear of death. He was here to reprimand, to do his fatherly duty: making sure his children obeyed the laws of decency. He began his inquiry. *"God damn it! Do you know what this is? Do you know what all this filth is?"*

I was ready for a fight, knowing exactly what this filth was, having explored it, tested it, viewed it, analyzed it, and shared it with others: nudie pictures. Naked men and naked women together, alone, or with others like themselves. Men and men. Men and women. Women and women. Little Tom had fifteen or twenty pornographic magazines stored carelessly under the depressed mattresses. He had *Playboy* and *Hustler* under there, and *Playgirl,* and hard-core pornographic magazines whose names no one knows. There were women holding their labia open and licking each other and touching their own breasts. There were men fucking women, and, under the farthest mattress, hidden by itself near the air conditioner, *The Joy of Gay Sex,* with a story in it that begins, "You've gone to the far end of the beach (where you know men in pairs and groups hang out) just because…well, just for fun. You don't really give it much thought, wanting to sun with these guys, but you do notice your mounting excitement."

At fifteen years old Little Tom was lanky and awkward, and his whole body slumped inward. His hair, which needed to be cut and brushed and cared for, hung down unevenly, covering his eyes. He didn't know that he was queer, because he didn't know what queer was. He did not know that his world, the queer world, the one that he owned and that owned him, was created by this dark threshing machine that came to visit him tonight, and that this machine, which made him awkward, which threatened to destroy him, also hid his world from him. Even though his ears were filled with the endless clanging in his pants, he thought he was heterosexual, like everyone else, a normal part of a strict, clean world.

They hid what he was from him, made a nugget of him, condensed him and told him no. Who did? He cannot even remember. Not a single name can be brought in front of us and charged with this crime. This deception was pervasive, was everywhere, was hummed out of the air conditioner. The hinged door on the window that swung out into the room hated him. It sneered and said queer. Nothing was his. The neighbors, the school bus, the children's museum down the street said queer. It said, you will visit here but you will never belong. The women who worked there were not queer, nor were the objects they sold or the exhibits on display. There was nothing queer in this town except this one little boy, this fifteen-year-old with thin arms and a stack of porn under his bed, about to be discovered, and this angry threshing machine in the room with him, filling the air with noise and hot dust.

Why did he have these things? He was too frightened to be curious and yet too curious, too lonely, too horny not to express, to be expressed somehow. What was pornography to him? Those who have been outlawed or called indecent or denied have no choice but to reach out to other outlaws. Like seeks like, and secret hope seeks fulfillment in whatever form it can find. What did he hope? He wanted to believe that men were kind, sexy, physical, that they touched each other. He could not touch any men, and each attempt, each yearning, each denial, was painful. Instead he touched his desire and, cut off from it, told that it was wrong, he transformed it, made a compact nugget out of it, something easily hidden. His desire became that pornography: dirty, under the mattress, pressed between pages, flattened. He was that hard lust, was only that. He had nothing else, no other expression. He had accepted this, with its dirtiness and its absolute silence, its ridiculous illustration of his life, and now it was about to be wiped out.

Little Tom was terrified. Standing now, because Little Father seemed to demand it, he wavered in the room, as if he were not pinned into the scene anywhere. He threatened to blink and go out at any moment. He did not know where he was, and the question lay in front of them, panting with Little Father's hot, rancid breath: *Do you know what this filth is?* Little Tom's desire was something he had never talked about before, something for which there were no words. Anyone could say the words "faggot" or "homosexual" but not "I am a faggot." These words were not used for self-description, just as the word *inquisition* was not used to describe a conversation between a father and son.

*"Do you know what this filth is?"* All of us in the room knew: me, you, Little Father, and Little Tom. Little Tom said, "Pornography?" His voice rose at the end, as if by sounding unsure of what it was, he could deny knowledge of its existence. He wanted out of the room, thinking that through logic or trickery he could escape the reality *The Joy of Gay Sex* and the other magazines in the room presented him with. It never occurred to him to say, "Wait. Slow down. This is not right," or to cry, touch him, say, "I don't know why I did it. Don't hate me for it. I love you, and I don't understand who I am." Little Father was not a lump of flesh that could be reached. He was a tack, a sharp voice, a robe, a gavel. The pornography stayed under the mattress through this whole discussion.

When Little Tom said the word "pornography," it was not enough. Father wanted Little Tom to tell him what kind of pornography it was, but Little Tom refused to answer. He could not believe Father wanted him to say it out loud. Or maybe Little Tom didn't know how to say it. He did not understand this new semantic game: Never had there been a verbal category "pornography," let alone a subset. Like a perverse hunter, Little Father was trying to draw him out of hiding, but he would not budge. He would not break the rules. Certain things must stay under the mattress. Finally Little Father said it himself: *"Homosexual pornography."*

I sighed, having seen it all before. I knew that soon he'd ask where Little Tom got such stuff. "It all belongs to Matt," he'd say, panicked. "I'm keeping it for him while his uncle is in town." His fear was this great: He had to remove himself from this situation by whatever means, so he sacrificed his best friend. He threw Matt between him and Little Father, a fact that sends darts through my spine even now. Oh, Matt, forgive him! He loved you, but he was so young and fragile. You were the fighter, Matt, which must have been why he invoked you here. You would have known what to do. Little Tom felt the very light in the room attacking him, felt his own destruction in the exposure of his secret shame. Perhaps he thought, *Later I can rectify this. I can take back what I said about Matt.* He did not know that Little Father was about to forbid him from ever talking to Matt again or that he would so easily obey, that he would turn his back and never look at you again. How could he know that three days later, you, Matt, would approach him at school, try to say hello, and he would ignore you, not look up? How could he know fifteen years and more would pass before he even had the nerve to speak of you again?

I decided not to watch this painful part again. I could not let the ultimatum be delivered, the shock be relived, without intervening. That's why I came anyway, to bust Little Father's chops. As he was saying, *"Once you get a reputation for being that, you'll never get rid of it,"* I pulled a tranquilizer gun out of my bag. I could see he was pleading with Little Tom under his aggressive posturing, begging him not to be gay, and I realized how small he was if you got rid of the belly. For the first time, it made sense to me: Only a small dog would bark so loudly, afraid of being ignored. I saw in the instant I switched the gun's safety off and checked to make sure I hadn't loaded too many darts that Little Father's world was full of danger he was constantly trying to push away.

He yelled because life for him was a battle against ever-encroaching evil, and I saw that this is where we were the same. We both felt the blackness and chaos in the universe, believed in its unending meaninglessness, but we responded in different ways. The small dog makes a ruckus, tries to keep it at bay as best he can. The large dog takes creatures on his back, wades into the stream with them, lets the void embrace his heart, enter his lungs; he rides the charge of fear, carries those he loves into it safely. I fired the dart into his calf, and he slumped immediately to the floor. He looked uncomfortable, so I stretched his legs out and propped him up against the bed, amazed at how light he felt. Little Tom was watching me now for the first time, and I sat down beside him on the bed.

"Hi, sweetheart. How are you doing?" I touched his arm, and he lowered his head, his face clouded with confusion. "It's going to be OK. Father is taking a rest after all that yelling. He got a little too upset about these nudie mags, so I thought I would give you a break. You're going to be OK, I promise." I put my arm around his shoulders and pulled him closer to me. He leaned in and started crying silent tears. Pains and strange joy shot through my heart as I sat on the bed holding my younger self. I let him know that he would survive this time and that he would turn out fine, that he would travel across the country, study literature, meet wonderful people, learn the beauty of his own life and of those around him.

He was voiceless. The area in his throat that catches wind and disturbance and turns it into sound had gone smooth from disuse. All input and output passed without a noise. He clung to my side like a baby chimp, and I wondered what was to be done. Little Father snored on the floor, and I knew I had one last thing to do before he woke, but what was it? What did I have to do? I opened my bag for advice from tools to find that all the knives and weapons were gone. A single item remained at the bottom, a yellow cylinder about four inches long, like a thick, short pen. I pulled off the cap: a seam ripper.

I kissed Little Tom's head and said, "Help me here. Grab his head." We stretched Little Father taut. He had wilted and flattened like a raft with the air let out, and we stared and stared at this man. This single creature, who was a powerful symbol for both of us, had starred in and represented so much of our anger, our desire for redemption, our despair. Only like this, deflated and inanimate, did he seem safe—

small and pudgy, his fine black hair falling around the coarse wrinkles of disappointment in his face.

Unable to look any longer, I placed the seam ripper at his feet, stabbed in gently, and—*rip!*—pulled up through the length of his body and beyond, rending the scene through its middle. My arm and the seam ripper groaned under the weight, bending, threatening to break. I worked my jaw as if going through an altitude change. Screeching sounds like the noise of bent metal assaulted my ears. The pieces of his body became tiny, weightless, and I put them carefully under my tongue so I would not lose them in the ensuing chaos. The scene spun, and an enormous gray-black void, the color of a slate chalkboard, appeared behind the attic scene. I grabbed Little Tom's hand and yours, dear reader, in mine, and we walked forward into that void, finding our feet, making up our own reference points and footholds with each step forward.

The air was full of that chalkboard feel, and coming from the left and right, I could hear the men's voices as they argued and laughed and held out their arms to one another. Little Tom's face was puffy, but his tears had dried and he was chattering continuously, asking questions about where we were and where we were going. He had gotten younger since the ripping, looked eight or nine years old. He seemed to have forgotten all about the pornography and the scene with Little Father. I sighed pleasantly and held his hand tighter, and as we walked he shrunk smaller and smaller, until he was the size of Little Father. I put him under my tongue.

At home I got in the bathtub to wash the sweat and dust off myself. I was going to meet some new friends to go dancing later on, and I pictured myself spinning and moving on the dance floor, being silly, sexual, free, but each time I saw myself this way, I burned with embarrassment and ran over to my friends. *Soon,* I thought, *I will know them well enough. I will not be embarrassed in front of them.* But why not now? Why wasn't I worthy of enjoyment, why couldn't I show them my happiness now? It was dark in the room, a single candle lighting the high bathroom walls, and it seemed that an epiphany should come in this dramatic setting, that all the work I had done should condense and reveal something here in the bath with the flickering candle beside me. I looked at my arms, lightly hairy, browned by the sun. They were a child's arms, so thin, and at once a warrior's arms—I knew how to make a fist. The arms of a queer? I could not tell. I slid down into the tub, and as the warm water swirled around my neck, I suddenly remembered the two cloth buttons under my tongue.

## Ms. Strangelove, or, How I Stopped Worrying and Learned to Love Gay Male Porn by Kris Franklin and Sarah E. Chinn

### Our Dirty Little Secret

Over the years, lesbians have become almost shameless about announcing our sexual desires. Dildos, butch-femme, S/M, piercing, and female ejaculation have all been analyzed, dissected, anatomized in the pages of various dyke publications. If there's one thing that we twenty-something dykes have learned from the infamous sex wars of the 1980s, it's that if it's about sex, it's worth saying. But slacker lesbos have a secret that's rarely aired in feminist journals, with or without glossy photo spreads. Surprise—it's about sex. And it's more scandalous than any tame branding scene from *On Our Backs*.

Boys. Buck-nekkid, oiled-up, pec-a-rific queer boys, rapturously plunging their throbbing man roots into one another. No kidding. An informal survey of our lesbian friends' pornographic predilections has, over the past few years, yielded this information (however sheepishly). On those woozy female-bonding evenings, late at night, surrounded by half-empty bottles of beer, we conducted our almost scientific research. "What kind of erotic material do you think is the hottest?" we asked. And hands down, the twenty-something urban activist dykes' response was "gay men's porn." And not just videos—photographs, dime novels, the endless *Meatmen* comic book series, phone-sex ads, the works. There's something about men boffing each other that gets us hot.

# MS. STRANGELOVE

## An Illustrative Fable

It's 1987. August. It's miserable, and we don't have air-conditioning or the money to go to a movie theater. So the small community of queer college students who hang around for the summer have all gathered at someone's off-campus apartment to watch porn movies. There's air-conditioning and a VCR. We've rented an ecumenical assortment: some straight porn, a "girl-girl" flick (made for straight men), *Erotic in Nature*—the only lesbian-made pornography you could find then—and a fag movie called something like *The Pizza Boy—He Delivers!*

As it turns out, each movie is more numbing than the last. We had high hopes for the lesbian feature, but no such luck. Yawns all around. After the abject failure of the last "girl-girl" movie, the dykes pack up to leave. The gay men seize their chance to pop in *The Pizza Boy*. Curiosity gets the better of the lesbians, even those who are halfway out the door. We're glued to the screen for the rest of the afternoon.

The men laugh at our interest, but after a while they get uncomfortable. In part they want us to leave them to their own devices, but that's not the whole story. They're also embarrassed, self-conscious. They feel like we're objectifying them.

And we are. Ha.

## Makin' Whoopee

When we came of political age, the sex wars were just winding down. The books that came out of the bitterly fought conflicts over pornography, censorship, and sexual practice—*Powers of Desire, Pleasure and Danger, Men Confront Pornography*—were on the required-reading lists of our introductory women's studies classes. It was clear to us that porn was more than just pictures of naked people arrayed for our entertainment. Rather, the stories that pornography told, the centrality of male pleasure and the come shot were part of a larger system of male dominance that limited women's sexuality even as it portrayed it on-screen.

We knew that we were against censorship, if only because we didn't want anyone telling us what we could or couldn't watch or read or write. But we had some serious reservations about the kind of erotic material that was out there. Straight porn was peopled by flaccid, disinterested men and shaved, Kewpie-doll women whose genitalia looked too, well, pink. The lesbian porn available to us was either filmed almost entirely in slow motion with a Vaseline-smeared lens or too concerned with technical displays of toys and latex. More to the point, even if we could have watched our own sexual lives on film, we didn't necessarily want to. It probably wouldn't be very exciting. And the sex we had with each other was not the same kind of sex we wanted to have represented in pornography. We wanted to see something that was hot, fast, sweaty, and had no political ramifications—fantasies that assured us that no women were oppressed in the making of this film.

### Privates on Parade

It is 1991, a spring evening. We're sitting around reading *The Village Voice* and *OutWeek*. Every other ad features glistening male bodies with tight, tanned muscles. They could be advertising a gym or a diner or a delivery service. It doesn't really matter—they're everywhere. Even as gay men throughout New York waste away, the male bodies in the queer and queer-friendly press are buff and fully functional.

We never thought we could be so turned-on by an ad for a dentist.

### Loving the Fag Within

It is a truism that AIDS activism brought lesbians and gay men back into political and social contact with one another. Young lesbians were surrounded by one of the most distinctive aspects of gay male culture: the intense eroticization of gay male bodies. Given the troubled history of lesbian political thinking about sex, gay male sexuality seemed—if only nostalgically—spontaneous, powerful, elemental. We looked at pictures of naked men, and we learned how to understand erotic images. We enjoyed them in ways we could never have enjoyed the pictures of half-naked women that were plastered onto every bill-board—as feminists we couldn't buy into a fantasy that rendered us at best invisible and at worst despicable, and as lesbians we found that the aesthetic was too straight for our lesbian tastes. Looking at images of gay men, we could for the first time appreciate sexual imagery without feeling judged or (and here's the irony) excluded.

At the same time, lesbian sexual politics were twisting and turning in all kinds of directions. We were talking openly and proudly about butch-femme as an erotic statement, playing with identifications of top and bottom. Out of this came a renewed appreciation of butch dykes—their toughness, their resilience, their sharp dress sense. Our politics of direct action were the politics of butchness to a certain extent, full of bravado and tough resolve, light on processing and theory. And we started talking about gay men in the same terms we used for ourselves, dividing them up into femme tops, butch bottoms, and everything in between. Some of the more adventurous among us talked about our straight friends in those terms too.

Somehow this felt different from accepting conventional codes of masculinity and femininity. To eroticize the butch in dykes and fags, to appreciate the hypermasculinity of women and men, didn't seem the same as the tired old macho shit we'd grown up with. But we had our doubts too. Why wasn't femmeness getting the same spring cleaning? While we had no trouble getting hot over those superbutch numbers in the Chelsea Gym ads, our queeny friends and acquaintances didn't provide quite the same effect. And as much as the direct-action dykes might pay lip service to a femme aesthetic, they never seemed to trust the girls in skirts.

### A Kiss Is Still a Kiss

It's 1995, August again, blisteringly hot and appallingly humid. We're in an arctically air-conditioned cinema watching *Jeffrey*, the gay male flick du jour. Jeffrey, the AIDS-phobic (anti)hero is at the gym (we like this movie already) when he meets Steve. Steve, a butch top if ever we saw one, puts some major moves on Jeffrey, and they kiss there and then.

The movie cuts to a supposed audience—two young straight white couples. The men grimace, groan, and throw popcorn. The women, sitting next to each other, sigh moonily at the cuteness and romance of the scene. Back in our real-life audience, we lesbians are left wondering where we fit in.

### Boys on the Side

The answer is, pretty much nowhere. Lesbians are just not envisioned as an audience for anything that isn't explicitly about—and usually made by—us. We have to comb mainstream media for satisfying, if submerged, lesbian content. This isn't easy, given the paucity of movies that actually feature women interacting with one another in meaningful ways (how long ago was *Thelma & Louise*?). But more important, lesbians aren't considered to have a stake as audiences of movies that don't represent us in any real way.

Not that movies for and about gay men should necessarily cater to lesbians. Rather, it was striking that a movie as self-conscious about audience as *Jeffrey* didn't even consider the possibility of lesbians as potential consumers. But consume it we did, rooting for Steve, dissing Jeffrey, loving the fabulously queeny Sterling. The movie proved once again that since dykes can't count on seeing ourselves represented, we can just hook on to other people's images.

As lesbian viewers, we're both aroused by and excluded from the kiss between Jeffrey and Steve. *Jeffrey* speaks immediately to a gay male audience and presumes a straight audience, as the cutaway to the straight "viewers" indicates. Sitting in that movie theater, we were turned-on by the sight of two men kissing passionately, but we were fully aware that that moment was judged off-limits to us as dykes.

## I Know What Boys Like

When we see men being sexual together on-screen, whether in a film like *Jeffrey* or, more often, in a porn movie, we're put in a peculiar position. It's comparable to the classic scenario in "girl-girl" porn movies in which the two women are having sex for the clandestine enjoyment of the male viewer; their sexuality is exciting because it is theoretically unavailable to him. The straight male viewer is often represented in the movie itself—a man intervenes in the scene, and the women are convinced to lavish their attention on him. He's so irresistible, they'd rather pleasure him than each other. Like all lesbians, all they need is a good fuck. But unlike the straight men watching girl-girl movies, we're not the major audience for this action. In fact, the possibility of a lesbian viewer isn't even considered.

But although we're not the intended audience, we feel as if we have at least partial ownership over gay male porn, for a couple of reasons. For one thing, all you need is two dollars and a dream to rent a queer boy video. It's one of the few forms of entertainment impoverished urban dykes can comfortably afford. More important, as a lesbian hero of ours once said, anything can be appropriated. We can take the unrestricted freedom presupposed in gay male porn, its status as pure fantasy, the unabashed pleasure taken in fucking, and immerse ourselves in it without having to identify with it or be implicated in it. And despite all the problems we have with the essentially femme-hating politics of gay male pornography, it doesn't differentiate between fuckers and fuckees: Actors in porn movies switch around, take turns, suck and fuck alternately. In some ways their sex is a lot like vanilla lesbian sex.

Of course, there are hitches to this dyke sex utopia. We feel nervous if the actors in gay male porn aren't visibly wearing condoms, although we don't practice "safer sex" together or expect that our lesbian friends necessarily do. We don't always identify with the men in the flick—sometimes we just care about them as gay men who live with the threat of HIV. And our gay male friends often use porn as a safety valve instead of engaging in unsafe sex. We see it as a symbol of unfettered raunch; for them it can be a tool for self-imposed sexual limitation. In one powerful respect, though, gay male porn brings twenty-something dykes and fags together—it's an emblem of an unattainable limitlessness of sexual freedom that none of us has experienced, the ability to shuck your clothes and fuck at the drop of a hat just because you want to and your partner's ready and willing.

### Girls Just Wanna Have...

So we're not quite sure what to do with the thought of thousands of under-thirty lesbians salivating at the idea of men fucking. Certainly we can understand why gay men might feel uncomfortable at the possibility. After all, if the situation were reversed, could gay men ever eroticize lesbian sexuality in a way that didn't feel prurient to us but instead felt celebratory of us, our sexuality, and our sensibilities? We seriously doubt it. But that scenario is almost unimaginable: Women are taught to view the world from a masculinist point of view, to identify power and sexual desire as male, weakness and sexual manipulation as female. That is, boys are cool, girls are gross.

More to the point, would we ever want gay men to look at our sexuality the way we look at theirs? In a word, no. We have to put up with that shit from straight men already—we want to think that our gay male comrades are better than that, that they value us as friends, political allies, and all-around superheroes, not babes.

Ultimately, we may not have the answers to our apprehensions about our pervy desires, but that's OK. Our fixation with queer-boy porn might not always be nice to them or us, but we think we can work with it. Dykes can claim so little in the sexual landscape that diving into someone else's swimming hole on a hot August day doesn't really seem so bad, and we're having a lot of fun splashing around.

*A Hand Curls Into a Fist*

## Alarming Transformations
by Eric C. Waldemar

L ast fall I was in Adams-Morgan, the culturally diverse mecca of
Washington, D.C., where blacks, Latinos, and whites all meet and
live in perfect harmony. At least that's what all the brochures say.
I was on the streets that afternoon in drag. From my wig down to my
hot pants, I was an extravaganza! As I neared the end of the block, I turned
around and saw a black girl. She couldn't have been older than fifteen or
sixteen. She had her schoolbooks in one hand and her son in the other. The
child was squawking and carrying on. "Let me go! Let me walk, Mama!"

The kid must have been about three years old, and at that age he
still had enough sense to admire someone like me: a black drag queen
in the heart of D.C. His eyes lit up when they walked past me.
Lovingly, he reached out to touch my clothes.

I crossed the street. When I looked back, I saw the child's arms still
reaching for me. "Mama let me go! Let me see her!" The girl figured
she would settle his curiosity right then and there. She dropped him
to the ground and let him fly into traffic.

My eyes lost their glow. I didn't give a damn what I looked like. I
wasn't even thinking about my own life. Everyone else on that block
just closed their eyes; cars slowed down, swerved, and nearly collided.
But I ran into traffic, picked up that girl's child, and rescued him.

I expected the girl to come running up to me with thanks or God
bless yous or just, "My baby!" That's all I wanted. But she didn't do
any of that. Instead she slapped me across the face.

"Faggot, take your hands off my kid, 'fore I kill you and all your kind."

I stood there with shock running through and through my bones. I was going to give up, take the abuse. But I couldn't do it. I held the kid tighter; my mind wouldn't let him go. My "faggot-ass hands" had taken control. Seconds later the girl pushed me to the ground. The kid was set free, and he stood there crying, "Mama, Mama…no!"

There were no cops around, but I knew my brothers and sisters would come to my defense. But they just stood there and laughed as the queen got her face punched in.

Now I carry a knife wherever I go.

# Breaking More Than Silence
## by Kimberly Scrafano

The first time was the hardest to ignore—to cover with soft words and maybe a thick bunch of fresh flowers. But after the first time, it got easier. I learned to live with the uncertainty of another's rage. I learned to live with my skin first red then pale and later deep purple, like the skin of an eggplant.

With her it was different. She wasn't like the men I hear about when I counsel battered women. She was my best friend, then my lover for two years. She was usually soft and kind, running her long fingers through my hair or maybe just looking at me with warm brown eyes. So when it did happen, she pretended it didn't, and I went along with it. If she left a mark, she would hug me and say it was just a slip of a hand, an angry flailing arm. It just happened to hit me in the face or leg or maybe on the sharp edge of my clavicle. And it wouldn't happen again because, really, it didn't happen.

It was manageable, see, and supposed to be getting better, already better. The truth was, though, it didn't disappear or fade like my black eye eventually did. Instead I spent too much time not going to class and missing dinner with friends and being late for my basketball game. No one could know or see or notice because she was an important person in different lesbian and Jewish communities. She reminded me of this often, saying that I had to respect that, that I must not let on that everything wasn't as perfect as the marriage she had planned or the babies—one boy just so we could raise one well—and perhaps a house in the country, close to the ocean. Besides, she said, we were different. And although we loved crazy sometimes, it was always better than anyone else could love. It was an accident, and she was really sorry this time. It wouldn't happen again, and she would kiss the tip of each of my fingers.

* * *

It took a long time for me to actually hear my friends and other people who care about me when they tried to explain that what was happening was not my responsibility. Although I knew that part of my ex-lover's violence stemmed from her own history of abuse, I still believed that I could "fix" our relationship. And despite the fact that she had expressed her violence since the beginning of our relationship—I once had to get thirteen stitches in my leg and another time actually feared my life—I believed that it wasn't a permanent part of us.

But it wasn't just the hitting and throwing a mug or a glass jar at me, although she usually missed. More often than not it was the dishonesty, the manipulation, the way she even found words to blame me for her suicide attempts. Though these aspects of her personality and behavior were detrimental to our relationship, I wasn't able to connect them to the physical violence and see her actions as part of the control she attempted to maintain over most aspects of my life. I saw only physical violence as abuse.

I ignored the emotional violence partially because I had grown up with violence and was accustomed to thinking that only the worst forms were really abuse. I denied, or rather didn't see, the different forms of violence because I didn't have the language I now have with which to speak about it. Having come from a working-class background, I had very little knowledge of feminist theory or anything even resembling it. This sort of linguistic "awakening" I experienced echoes my process as a survivor. I was first able to speak about being a survivor of sexual abuse when I reached college and met other women who had had similar experiences and were involved with rape crisis-center work.

My ex-lover, on the other hand, came from a well-educated, upper-middle-class background where her mother had been involved in the feminist movements of the 1970s. Although I don't believe that class and privilege completely dictated the dynamics of our relationship, they were prominent factors. While my lover would use feminist jargon and theory to negate her violence or attempt to prove that we could overcome it together, I often felt like I couldn't maintain that dialogue. It wasn't until the end of the relationship that I could use the same theory for my own self-preservation.

Even after I began listening to other people more and started thawing from the emotional vacuum I was in, it was not a simple situation to negotiate. It took a long time for me to be able to stay away from my ex-lover completely. Even after I read battery theory and found counseling and support, I would agree to try again, to do it right this time. I still believed in the kind parts of her and was sometimes willing to forget the rest. Although I had a support network during this time, I still found it difficult to find spaces in communities we had shared—political, religious, and social. Much of my process over the past couple of years has focused on finding new spaces and strengthening familiar ones.

I have also been negotiating what I see as the differences between lesbian domestic violence and the heterosexual paradigms which govern battery theory. Despite everything else, I do believe that lesbian domestic violence isn't the same as men smashing their fists into walls and cheekbones. There are definite problems with merely superimposing heterosexual theory about domestic violence onto lesbians. Still, women's fists often do strike the same as men's, no matter how much I wanted not to believe this. And no matter how much I wish it weren't true, I never feel like I wasn't a battered woman.

Although there hasn't been a proliferation of recent theory surrounding the issue of lesbian domestic violence, it does seem to be the latest hot topic. Perhaps this is because of the interest kindled in domestic violence as the newest political and social rage, the made-for-television movies about battered women, their eyes swollen and purple. Even the subways are loaded with images of women wearing dark sunglasses, the messages in English and Spanish and sometimes even Chinese. Shelters and other agencies are now offering support for lesbians.

Despite the visibility of domestic violence and the limited resources for lesbian survivors, however, some agencies that do offer support services seem to subscribe to a somewhat linear vision of the dynamics in lesbian relationships. Although most of these organizations wouldn't verbalize such stereotypes as the butch batterer and femme survivor or that only the batterers hit (which negates acts of self-defense), some of the support groups I looked into aligned themselves with these notions. Even though I hardly fought back against the violence of my ex-lover—an abstinence for which I am sometimes grateful and other times regretful—I declined a particular support group for survivors of lesbian domestic violence because I felt that there was no space to talk honestly about anger. I felt that the women in the group were too concerned with proving their innocence. Not that survivors are to blame on any level, but I needed the space to say without judgment that I did have violent thoughts as a reaction to the violence inflicted on me. I wanted to be able to scream about how I had torn my ex-lover's favorite silk blouse into a hundred pieces following an episode in which she was extremely violent. I wanted to be able to express my anger as it was, not to curb it so it sounded safe.

I don't believe in violence, not even as a reaction to violence; yet I think we need to be able to speak about our lives as they really are, not as we want them to be. Honesty is the only way to create a real safe space for women—not the self-declared safe spaces at the survivor's group. We need to stop being afraid that we will be seen as bad feminists or lesbians if we say, "I really wanted to kill her the last time she hit me," without feeling as if we'd committed the actual violence of this act. Perhaps some people do believe that fantasy and action are too closely linked for this sort of dialogue, but this concept of minimizing the space between these two realms works only in theory, not in practice. Although it would frighten me if a woman told me she wanted to hit me, it would not by any means be the same as what my ex-lover did. Thinking and acting out thoughts need to remain separate, even if this negotiation is delicate.

If we don't deal with the real issues of anger, then the violence we experience will transform and extend into other realms. Speaking about being angry and actually working through it are two very different things. I know. My ex-girlfriend was an incest survivor who, although aware of her issues, was not working on them in a space free from acting out against me. When she was violent she would say that she was having a flashback and didn't really remember or that she thought I was someone else, someone who had hurt her in the past.

\* \* \*

Aside from the practice of supporting lesbian survivors, women seem to finally be writing theories of lesbian domestic violence, however scarce. While lesbian battery theory is progressing, however, we cannot wait for it, nor can we allow it to be the sole site of change. First and foremost, practice must change. We need groups that explore the differences between heterosexual and lesbian domestic violence without negating the seriousness of either set of atrocities. As someone who has developed and implemented groups that address issues of HIV/AIDS and safer sex in relation to women's experiences of sexual assault, domestic violence, survival sex, and substance abuse, I found that younger women are more open to discussing the fundamentals of these issues and that facilitating these sorts of rap sessions isn't as difficult as I first thought. We battered lesbians need to demand a more sophisticated approach to support.

\* \* \*

My senior year in college, I spoke at a "Take Back the Night" rally about the violence I experienced at the hands of my ex-girlfriend. Before standing on stage, I was torn as to whether this was the space in which to speak about lesbian domestic violence, since it labeled itself as "woman-positive." In the end I did speak, especially since my ex-lover had still been lingering around campus despite the fact that I didn't get a restraining order because of her solemn promise that she would stay away from me completely. I also spoke because my ex-lover's violence stemmed from her experiences of sexual abuse: She claimed her actions were not violence because she was having a flashback or because of other survivor-related difficulties. I talked about how my ex-girlfriend's acting out created the violence I experienced. I said that survivors of sexual assault and incest need not only to break silences but also to break cycles of violence.

A few months later my ex-lover hunted me down. She confronted me about "Take Back the Night," which she had heard about from an acquaintance. I felt angry that although what is said at the "Take Back the Night" rally is supposed to remain in that space and anonymous, another woman went and told my ex-lover everything I had said.

My ex-lover harassed me about my reasons for speaking even though by this point she had finally admitted to her violence and claimed to be seeking help as a batterer. My ex-lover claimed enormous changes, but she was not able to treat me with respect despite the fact that we hadn't spoken in almost a year. The battery theory I read rang true for me—the violence was still present despite promises of reform. Often, unless there is intense counseling coupled with other programmatic activities, batterers will batter or act abusively in other ways, no matter how much they claim not to. And no matter how much we want them not to.

My speaking at "Take Back the Night" also affected the rape crisis center on campus, which called a number of emergency meetings because I had described how my ex-lover had been a counselor there years before. Instead of seeking ways in which to open the center to other forms of crisis counseling, however, the meetings focused on whether or not women were going to want to use the center now. I had revealed my ex-lover's involvement with the center to illustrate that politically conscious women also act out and hurt other women and that we as survivors of rape and sexual assault need to take personal responsibility for our own actions. I did not include this information to suggest any shortcomings at the rape crisis center.

The center's response to my speaking reflects some of the issues within lesbian and feminist communities that hinder real dialogue about lesbian domestic violence or other issues not clearly marked as "patriarchal" (a word I have come to despise). There seems to be a belief that if we blame women—even for actions that are clearly their responsibility—we will undermine some feminist causes, just as naming a counselor as a batterer undermines the respectability of a rape crisis center. Despite the fact that feminist theory layers itself on constant challenges and argumentative rhetoric, we seem less willing to allow this freedom of movement within our daily lives. Indicating our problems seems to threaten communities, while it should strengthen them. Because of this I've found far more strength and support from straight women than I have from lesbians. One friend of mine actually said that she knew what had happened to me was wrong but that she just couldn't blame women. She blamed men for making women this way. But how long can we continue this? How long can women abused by lovers and mothers and other women survive by not directing their anger where it should go—toward the perpetrators?

I have seen too many women hurt by women lovers or abused by mothers to be able to say that I can't blame women. In truth part of me didn't blame my ex-lover, because much of her violence came from what other people—including women—had done to her. This was why I tolerated her battering for so long. As feminists and lesbians and survivors, we need to stop this cycle of violence, not by chalking it up to some unnamed patriarchy but by taking responsibility for our own violence.

Although I survived this sort of violence and found little nonjudgmental support in lesbian communities, I have not given up completely on these communities and their politics. Instead I have transformed these feelings of betrayal into an energy with which I can attempt to build my own community, taking bits and pieces from spaces I have been in. I sometimes do wish that I could find strength in particular groups of women, but I think self-labeled "communities" are often just large cliques. If our goal is to maintain the status quo, protect our privilege, and deter self-criticism, then present lesbian communities are sufficient. If we want more diversity and real interaction, then we need to start questioning the foundations and stop worrying that we won't be able to rebuild if the house falls down on us.

# Life After Howard
## by Michael Olom Mennonno

### Howard and Me

When we were very young, my beautiful, wicked brother Howard and I used to have vicious staring contests. Beyond contests, really, these earnest attempts at mutual annihilation were routinely initiated by one of us without warning. To engage in the hostilities, one of us simply locked his gaze on the other, searing flesh, exposing fried ligaments and muscles and scorched skulls. Blood vessels burst, bones shattered like glass, eyes oozed from their sockets. Each contest was a little apocalypse.

I, with my melancholy disposition, possessed the patience and resoluteness of a chiliastic saint. I consistently vanquished Howard with my X-ray vision, a faculty I'd discovered with the aid of Shazam!, the first-ever white-trash Saturday-morning superhero who, if I remember correctly, lived in a mobile home much like the one in which we grew up.

X-ray vision, as I practiced it, consisted of a kind of hypersight, augmenting the opponent's pores, which then served as portals through which I could enter the opponent's body. A visual Rolfing, very intrusive and often painful. In our staring contests I sailed through Howard's pores and into his bloodstream like the crew in *Fantastic Voyage*, piloting a scorn-powered corpuscle.

I became invisible in this act of looking, and Howard, likewise, became invisible as an object seen in extreme close-up. This dissolution of subject and object is what allowed me a kind of second sight, and I could stare for hours into the spectacular diffused light.

This was really the only game I excelled at as a kid. Howard, on the other hand, excelled at all games that dramatized his incessant visibility, baseball especially. Baseball is a unique team sport in that each player is at some point in the game utterly alone and utterly exposed, forced to show the world what he's made of.

I wanted nothing to do with it.

I wanted to be invisible.

**\* \* \***

Howard was a Little League prodigy. He demonstrated a special talent for throwing sliders and curveballs, switch-hitting, and playing all positions. Everybody cheered for Howard, brought him red, white, and blue snow cones at the end of each inning. For me, the consequence of all this talent and adulation was summer after endless summer wasted at the ballpark. My childhood was sacrificed to baseball for Howard. The whole family piled into my dad's crappy '74 Camaro and trekked to the diamonds three and four times a week. I was forced to play, relegated to left field, where I spent three miserable eternal innings several games a week praying to all the gods of heaven and earth to protect me from grounders and pop flies. I daydreamed constantly about waking up from the nightmare of my life to find myself in another country speaking another language in which *baseball* was just a funny little nonsensical word in English that I'd never heard.

Worse than the half innings in the field, of course, were the half innings at bat. Depending on the pace of the game and how well we were doing, I might be required to bat two or three times. No one wanted to see me standing in the batter's box, but out of some twisted egalitarian ethic (or, more likely, a barely concealed sadism) the coach tossed me to the lions game after game, claiming he was doing it to bolster my self-esteem. But every at bat was a little death: the false encouragement of the parents in the bleachers, the sardonic voices of the kids in the dugout, who could not conceal their disgust in close games, where the only hope for victory hinged on my willingness to thrust myself before a fastball and limp to first with my thigh or hip stinging.

After several years of Little League misery, the indignities of which I suffered in silence, I came to welcome the sting of the fastball on my shoulder or thigh, as it was the easiest way out of the batter's box. I didn't care about honor as the seasons wore on and summer after summer was wasted. I learned to smile as I took the direct hit. Smile and wave at my folks sitting shamefaced in the bleachers. I ceased even to fake a limp on my way to first base. I sauntered up the baseline or skipped when I felt especially brave. Pitchers began aiming for vital parts. Umpires chastised me for leaning too far over the plate. I came to be universally despised.

I wanted to be invisible.

I did not want to live my brother's triumphal dream.

* * *

Howard and I are very close in age (he's a year and a half older). We're rivals by dint of this fact, and because of the physical disparity between us in childhood, I hated Howard for his looks and he feared me on account of mine. He looked like the lithe animalistic kid in the movie *The Blue Lagoon*, had the same svelte soft-core child-porn figure, cocoa-colored skin, and curly blond hair. His prized golden mane was maintained at great cost, regularly permed by a woman named Effie who worked out of a paneled salon in what used to be her garage. She looked like a strung-out Stevie Nicks, spoke with what must have been a contrived British accent, chain-smoked slender brown cigarettes, and was really into Paul McCartney and Wings. For a time my mother took me along with her and Howard to Effie's exotic boutique but never suggested I get a perm. I wasn't blond, and I didn't look like the kid from *The Blue Lagoon*, and my hair was already unruly. So while Howard got to carry a Black Power pick—the one with the fist for a handle—in his back pocket, I didn't even carry a comb, as combs had no effect on me. I was soon enough relegated to the strip-mall barbershop.

While Howard took after our father in the best of his traits, I resembled Dad in the worst of them; that is, Howard *looked* my father, while I *felt* like the old man (and looked like what he felt like through most of the seventies: displaced, disoriented, discouraged, and just generally dissed). Like my dad, a retired USMC badass, I was born angry and brooding. From an early age I demonstrated an unsettling proclivity for psychic brutality and a tendency toward megalomania. While my dad used the military to focus and hone these traits into tools deemed meritorious by society, the only thing that saved me from actualizing this brutality in adulthood was the sanctuary of the melancholy temperament that houses my wickedness.

I was very serious and mostly a good boy through the earliest years of childhood, but I was very sad because, as is the case with all serious children, I had nothing, really, to be serious about and so latched on to all manner of absurd and comical things about which to feel melancholy. This presented a deep ethical dilemma at a very young age. I realized my temperament required I seek out some truly wicked things about which to feel sadness and regret or else be relegated to a life of unbearable absurdity. Thus, I engaged in fantasies of evil.

Once I realized my potential for evil, I became a silent scourge—foraging like a wild animal under beds and in desk drawers and closets for the materials necessary for the perpetration of unspeakably, undetectably, unknowably dirty deeds. I became a relentless snoop and an unrepentant thief, but only, it seemed to me at the time, because my parents and brothers were secretive, incurable paranoiacs who hid their most glorious artifacts out of sight. Curiosity was generally considered illicit around our house, but it wasn't mere curiosity that motivated me in these constant incursions; rather, it was the anticipation of opportunities for revenge.

I pilfered my dad's medals from Korea and Vietnam, for example, lifting them from a shoe box in the back of his closet and placing them in a shoe box in the back of my closet as punishment for his silence about his wartime experiences.

My brothers' goods were less pilferable but no less exotic. My big brother Russell, five years my senior (and actually my mother's bastard son), was an outlaw among outlaws, dating a black girl named Gayle while hanging out with a gang of skinheads. I never saw much of Russell, but his closet was fantastic: a shrine to Gayle, whom he called "Old Girl." Her name, which was considered a sacrilegious utterance by my parents, was emblazoned in big bubble letters in red Magic Marker on the walls inside his closet (which always smelled like latex rubbers and Froot Loops) along with a clumsy reproduction of the rainbow and prism from the album cover of Pink Floyd's *Dark Side of the Moon*. While this was a truly impressive tribute to star-crossed lovers, Speedway, Indiana's own secret Taj Mahal, I wasn't really interested in Russell's well-known secrets or his teenage rebellion. It was Howard I was after. His closet was the holiest of holies as far as I was concerned. My forays into his territory played a major role in my most elaborate and far-reaching scheme of vengeance, precisely because his closet contained no secrets at all—only baseball equipment, evidence of Howard's single, impossible vision of immanent superstardom. Not a day went by without Howard smashing Wiffle balls or bouncing tennis balls against the aluminum siding of the mobile home for hours while commentating aloud on the game going on in his head.

My plan was to bide my time, to wait in silence (all my greatest revenge schemes were exacted in silence—proof that the universe was working according to my unholy designs), to wait until the seeds of failure that had been sown in abundance all around me came to fruition. Howard's eventual abandonment of his all-consuming dream would be my revenge for Howard's existence. I would someday, I fantasized, be justified in alone having doubted his talents, vindicated for the childhood I'd sacrificed to his rotten dream.

\* \* \*

Howard was a bilious demon with an angel's face (although in late adolescence this placidity would be ruined by zits too numerous to count; his face would widen and flatten, and his fruity, red lips would crack and peel), and, sensing my growing cache of indictments against him, he intensified his attacks on me in the first years of puberty.

Puberty provided Howard with the perfect tool, the one he'd been using to get me all along without knowing it: his body. I was late to develop and only a little younger than Howard, and so I found his daily confrontations intolerable. Seemingly through no effort of his own, Howard was becoming a man, and I was not. This was unacceptable to me. No matter how avidly I petitioned the gods to acquire the mysterious, lush attributes of masculinity, the gods saw fit to grant Howard all I desired and to dangle him before me as an image of sweet, hard, hot sublimity beyond my grasp.

In a wickedly conceived continuation of our childhood staring contests, Howard took to sauntering around the mobile home naked on hot summer days, lounging like the Barberini Faun on the sofa across from my perch in the window seat while I fought the urge to peer over my book at the hated vision of sublimity before me. As a natural athlete and exhibitionist, he quite naturally sought out his complement, a natural aesthete and voyeur, which he conveniently found in me.

Although perhaps a part of me felt that the shame Howard was expecting would accompany my unnameable desire, I was finally less ashamed of looking (which, as I've said, is my nature) than of convincing him that I felt what he intended me to feel so that he would continue to indulge me in my desire to see him indulge in his own delicious vice.

Of course, when it finally occurred to Howard that his act of exhibitionism was as illicit and as bald a function of desire as the act of voyeurism he demanded of me, he resented me terribly for having repeatedly obliged him in what he'd conceived as exercises in my debasement.

The transgression that caused the lapse into silence—which has characterized my relationship with Howard ever since these first years of puberty—was not explicitly sexual. Rather, it was the unexpected and frightening revelation of the fluidity of the self that caused Howard to retract and build impenetrable defenses against me. For me, the introduction of erotic desire into our familiar, hostile staring game was initially unsettling. But I got used to having desire define the contours of my being and my apprehension of the world.

Silence, in the end, was a fitting response to all our mixed desires. In my adolescence desire would cease to be a category separate from being; I would come to recognize in it a strange truth of totality, a dissolution of all distinctions, and a resonating silence.

This silence is what marks my childhood. This silence would become a language in itself.

## Life After Howard (Girls)

Angie was the prototype for all the girls who followed: tenacious to the point of being bitchy, with a pugilist's ability to take a punch and to give it as good as she got it. Edgy and easily drawn into sparring. Outrageously curvaceous. (By hooking up with girls whose breasts and buttocks were somewhat exaggerated, I was perhaps compensating for my own lack of interest in these parts—as though I wouldn't notice them unless it were impossible not to. The less interested in female breasts and buttocks I became, the larger the size of the breasts and buttocks on the girls I dated.)

I dated girls because I could not consider the alternative. Although I was born twelve days after Stonewall, news of the riots didn't reach Speedway in time for my adolescence, and I quite doubt many folks showed up for last year's twenty-fifth anniversary parade. I grew up without a spoken language, without a network such as the World Wide Web, without CNN or MTV (at least until junior high school), with nothing but the absence of an example to shape my concept of what I knew was present in me.

The most vivid depiction of something *like* homosexuality in my youth was in the character of Jack Tripper on *Three's Company*. On the sitcom, a stereotyped homosexuality was used as the foil for a variety of zany sexcapades. In the topsy-turvy world of polymorphous perversity, Jack adapted by adopting the persona of a stereotypical homosexual. The show's hook, in an age of sexual liberation, was that Jack was actually a *closeted heterosexual.* Though his heterosexuality was subversive, Jack was not quite the mirror image of the homosexual. The depiction of a man viewers know to be straight who's being forced by a perverse, repulsive landlord to play at being gay was nowhere matched by the depiction of a man known to be homosexual who's being forced by a perverse, repulsive landlord to play at being straight, which seems to me a very different thing and not so rife with opportunities for uproarious laughter. It was intuitively obvious to me, the adolescent viewer, that this contrivance of a homosexual person was derisive. The humor was in the idea that such aberrant behavior could be considered normal.

So television provided, at best, mixed messages. On the rare occasions gay men and lesbians were present on television, they were absently present, as objects of discourse, denied as participants, denied depiction in human form, denied a voice of their own. I didn't pay close attention to the so-called depictions of gays in the media because I'd grown used to seeing not actual depictions of gays in the media but depictions of depictions of gays by natives of the straight world.

\* \* \*

In adolescence my longing manifested itself not in a direct apprehension of sexual desire but through a sense of "outsider vision." It was obvious to me that I did not conceive of my self-identity and masculinity in the same terms as other boys but that I was, nonetheless, a boy. I was shaped like a boy, I had boy parts, and I believe I essentially thought boy thoughts, but I was not quite A Boy. Initially, in the hope of obtaining their secrets, I (alien spy fitted with the skin of a boy) watched real boys ceaselessly.

I cataloged their secrets in my mind.

How is it, I wondered, that real boys effortlessly maintain such graceful musculature and tense their jaws when they take drags off their cigarettes? What is the secret of the hard glare and the unrepentant naked smile? How is the innocent, lascivious curve of the torso resting on the hip achieved? Where do they obtain the proliferation of ultrafine blond hairs that covers their soft-hard bodies? Where does the lush dark hair filling the furrow of the linea alba come from, and the dense bristles on the chin? How do these boys come to swagger and spit, to bellow their beautiful, brutal profanity and gently construct their lewd discourses?

These were things I could not understand and would not master if I could. The body has its own language, unique to each body but universal. It's a brazen, impenetrable language, one that tenaciously resists translation.

**\* \* \***

I dated girls because I wanted to be a Real Boy, and dating girls is one of the things Real Boys do. Although Angie was not my first steady girlfriend, she was the first girl I ever really wanted to love. I wanted my love for her to be as illicit and dangerous as Russell's love for Gayle had been. I wanted to love Angie enough to keep my love in the closet, like Russell had done. I wanted an outlaw love.

We lived out of the backseat of Angie's '78 Malibu Classic for most of our junior and senior years in high school. Of all the tastes we had in common and the intimacies we shared, our favorites came to be shoving and slugging one another. We engaged in rough exchanges several times a day, daring each other constantly to push our brutal theatrics beyond drama. Although real pain resulted from our brutal slugfests, neither of us was willing to either renegotiate the terms of our union or dissolve it altogether. I don't know about Angie, but my excuse for complicity in our mutual degradation was my furtive desire to avoid sexual intimacy, and physical brutality seemed an effective substitute.

Eventually our slugfests fell into a pattern. Invariably, Angie, doubled over in spasms of pain, would concede victory to me. When her pain persisted, Angie saw a doctor who diagnosed her spasms as petit mal seizures, which I discovered I could induce at will. Because I blamed her for what I could not or would not name, Angie became subject to the brutality of my silence.

**\* \* \***

A couple years after we graduated from high school and went our separate ways, Angie called to tell me she'd had a miscarriage shortly after our breakup. She said she knew it was mine and that she had been determined to have it. She was going to have it because she loved me. And she just wanted me to know.

I told her it wasn't mine. I was sure of it.

She insisted, with a word I could not fathom and did not want to, that it was "ours."

I didn't care at this point, and it didn't matter, because as far as I was concerned, nothing had happened. I told her that if something goes in and nothing comes out then it's just the same as nothing going in in the first place.

She responded that *something* came out.

She told me over and over that she would have had the baby.

I grew indignant. It seemed absurd to me. What a stupid thing to call something: The Baby. *I was going to have The Baby.* So have the damned baby, I told her. You might as well say you're going to have a million dollars. It'd mean the same thing.

I remember she cried into the phone. I listened to her, thinking about what I'd do with a million bucks.

### Life After Howard (Boys)

Rudy and I are staring. We're not cruising. We're merely looking, experiencing all the benefits of seeing, the instantaneous dissolution and reformulation of the self and the other.

Rudy and I sit at a booth in a restaurant popular with the students in the sleepy college town in Southern Indiana where I live at the moment, checking out the short-order cook working at the grill. He's a clean-cut young guy in a tight white T-shirt, with tattoos on his biceps.

Occasionally he looks out at us from under his brow with the intense, complicated mixture of bravado, apprehension, and annoyance so typical of straight boys used to tolerating (and perhaps pretending not to enjoy) the indiscreet, hopeful stares of gay men.

We stare. He stares back. Someone relents. He returns to his work. We return to our conversation.

I make an effort to concentrate on Rudy while waiting for a look from the kid at the grill. I'm a little worried that in paying attention to Rudy, I'll miss it when Grill Boy gives me The Look, the go-ahead. I also don't want to appear too attached to Rudy. Rudy is somewhat effeminate, sleek like a feline, with smooth, fair skin; a soft voice; and slightly too-graceful mannerisms. I'm a different kind of man altogether: harder, tougher, uglier, and meaner than Rudy. I've worked at it.

Rudy's teasing me about the cook. "It's you he wants," he says. "He's looking at you."

The mere suggestion that the grill cook might entertain the thought causes me to become agitated. I don't want his capitulation. I don't want a consummation. I simply want to look at him and look at him looking at me until I've seen all I can stand.

Rudy leans over the table, gestures toward the grill cook, and whispers, "His name is Sean."

I lean in to him and demand to know where he's obtained this information—if it's true, this name is a revelation, containing within it the very meaning and fulfillment of a vast, unnameable desire.

"I heard the waitress call him Sean," Rudy says matter-of-factly. "He could be in pornos, for Chrissake."

Rudy smiles at me because he has seen me ache like this before at the mere mention of a boy's name. He knows all I need is a name to build a religion on, to house my longing.

*Sean:* It sounds like waves rolling up on a beach under a fat, bright moon. "I wonder if it's *-E-A-N* or *-A-U-N?*"

"Or *-A-W-N?*"

We agree it must be capital *S-E-A-N.*

*Sean.*

**\* \* \***

This is the language of desire. In the names Sean, Rudy, Brian, Marcus, James, Luis, Nathan, Ben, Peter, Felix, Jeremy, Curt, Anthony, Doug, Timothy, Chris, and on and on. In each name I see the body moving, clothed and naked. Each name brings to mind the tint of the flesh, the tautness of muscle. Each name describes the smell of him in the morning, the way his eyes betray his tongue, the way his body quivers just slightly while he rests on top of me or grips me solidly from below without a trace of trepidation.

All sacred things are in the name. All eternal things. The only proper means of addressing desire from the vantage point of the mind (desire is, after all, the domain of the senses and can't really be made sense of) is through the names of the beloved, each unique and all the same. I too have a name.

# More Like Myself
## by Lacy Silberman

I didn't really come out until ninth grade when my English teacher, Mrs. Fleishman, told us we had to write a five-paragraph essay and deliver it in front of the class. We could choose our own topic, so I chose gay marriage. I told people what I was going to do, and a lot of people laughed at the topic like it wasn't serious enough. Sometimes I'd come out to people when I talked about my paper. I just kinda told Christy one day in art class, and she was cool. We talked about the girls I liked and stuff. I usually didn't tell other people—I mean, it's kinda dumb to walk up to someone and say, "I'm gay"—but I started acting more like myself. I'd say that that girl was cute or something, and they would be like, "Oh, I didn't know. Blah blah blah…"

I did tell a few more people, though. The first was Nettie, during math class. I knew she had a big mouth, so I knew it would get around. But I didn't expect her reaction. She scrunched up her face, said "E-e-ew!" and pushed her desk away from mine. She didn't wait to tell anyone. She whispered it to Fayola, and Fayola whispered it to Jorge, and so on. Jorge came up to me, asking, "Do you like sucking titties?" and told me that I was going to catch AIDS. He said, "It's Adam and Eve, not Adam and Steve." When someone told Joai, who's pregnant and almost due, she turned to look at me, gave me this cheesy shit smile, and waved. Soon other people came up to me and told me I was sinning and that I was going to hell.

When Wayne and Casey found out—they're like Beavis and Butt-head when they're together—Wayne asked in his Beavis voice, "You're kidding, right?" When I said no he said, "You're a lezzie!" Since my name is not too far away from *lezzie,* they kept saying, "Hey, lezzie—oh, I mean Lacy."

I also told Justin. At first, he thought I was kidding, but now we scope girls together in the lunchroom. Most times I think he has bad taste in girls. He pointed out one girl he went out with, and I was like, "Mistake, Justin. Mistake."

What surprised me the most about the whole coming-out-at-school thing was that Charles, my lab partner in Science, accepts me. Charles is basically a Florida "cracker" who has made anti-Semitic jokes, racist jokes, and basically I-hate-everybody jokes all semester. To my surprise, when he found out I was gay, he didn't call me "lezzie" like the other people. He even said, "I won't call you 'lezzie.' " This coming from Charles was almost unbelievable. He doesn't bother me, and I don't bother him. We don't really talk about girls much. But I did tell him to rent *Dressed to Kill* because it has lots of tits in it. I know he'll thank me.

# Moral Fabrics
## by Jennifer DiMarco

There is a difference between what I know and what I am taught. There is a difference between what I see and what I am told to see. There is *no* difference between hate and cowardice. These are the first things I learn.

I am a round, warm, no-haired baby. Pale skin, giant eyes. Blue eyes like great-grandma Nanna, who was the first in my family to come to America. Small head like a cue ball. Four pounds at birth. I am the first grandchild on either side.

They call me Number One, Cue Ball, Big Eyes, Owl Head, and three thousand renditions of darling, in three different languages.

I am born into a world of pasta, potato pancakes, red wine, and honeyed ham. I am born into the world by my mother, who gave up everything and married in black just to have me. She writes children's stories instead of novels.

My father helped too, I suppose. He gave up nothing, except his life.

### Flannel

Him. Father.

I sit on a still lap. I am two. He is silent. He. I know that. He is not Mama. I never learn to say Daddy. I have one hand in his long hair. He is smiling, but it's hard to tell what's real. Sometimes people smile and pretend they're happy when they want to cry. I know that too. No one told me. I found out myself.

I sit on one knee; the musty cigar box full of bullets sits on the other. The bullets are cold and slick. There are so many of them. I reach out and wrap a tiny hand around a 158-grain hollow point. My fingers just reach around it. He looks at my hand. He looks at me. He isn't smiling. His tears are the first I ever see.

His long hair covers his soft face. He is crying in Mama's arms. He's shaking, he's so scared. I am scared. We live in a one-room apartment, the floors and walls bare, the refrigerator empty. Mama has two jobs, and he is too frightened to work, even to leave the house. I know what all this means. I am four years old, and I have to know. Because the rest of the world must never find out. This secret: his fear, Mama's strength. I have to be perfect so no one sees the rest.

IT IS BETTER TO HAVE A GUN AND NOT NEED ONE THAN TO NEED ONE AND NOT HAVE ONE. These are the words scrawled on the back of our door. I can read them, but I don't know what they mean. He wrote them. He also drew the gun beside them. I know what guns are.

Mama is at her night job. I am in a fourth-hand high-chair. He should be cooking dinner. The smell of grease and chicken slink from the minuscule kitchen. But there is also a new smell in the apartment. Sour, sharp, strong. It comes from him, asleep on the couch, and the spilled bottle that has soaked his flannel shirt, one cuff dripping onto the floor.
    When he sleeps he is not afraid, and so I am silent. I am a good baby. There comes another smell, quickly overwhelming all others, but I remember it as a smoke. Thick, dark, black smoke. Then the smoke parts like an opening mouth and I scream, because there is fire behind it.

Mama saved us from that fire. She picked me up first, high chair and all, and then dragged him out as well. I sat outside in my chair, watching the red, red sun rise above the mountains and drown the world in liquid fire while Mama, in the apartment, was silent as the flames ate the flesh off her hands.

That is the last memory I have of him. Asleep there, on the couch, his flannel shirt dripping alcohol. I do not remember him ever talking to me. I cannot place his voice or his gestures. He was like a little boy, though; I think I knew that even then.

Mama and I moved away. I never saw him again. I never asked for him. I did not miss him until I was nineteen. No one saw him. His parents told me he had gone on a long business trip. They showed me where he had gone on their big map. I knew they were lying. I was four, almost five, and I knew they were lying.

Angel, my baby sister, was born. I had asked for her. She never knew her father.

Mama's parents told me he had something wrong with him. There was something terribly wrong. He was too scared, and it got him in trouble.

The FBI told me to go to my room.

Mama told me the truth ten years later. That day I learned that no one knows where he went. Because no one knows where you go when someone kills you.

Perhaps that young man with the long brown hair and the eyes full of tears was correct all along. Perhaps my father was right to be afraid.

### Denim

Her. Mama.

Smiling. Loving. Strong. Muscles and wisdom and tenderness and knowledge.

Mama has black curly hair with wisps of auburn like mine and hazel like Angel's. She has blue eyes like mine and Nanna's. She has olive skin like Angel's. She is twenty years old when I am born. Twenty-four when Angel is. She lives for us. We adore her.

Mama is always smiling a brave-tough smile. She has only one rule: *Don't lie to me.* We never do. She works double jobs, but somehow she's always there to drive us to school in the morning and tuck us in at night. We don't know where she works, but she sells something to someone. She makes something. She makes do. She is always her own boss.

Mama knows everything. Mama can do anything. She can answer every question and build things and lift things. She can also be quiet and read to us or just sit and hold us when we have nothing to eat.

Mama dresses in sweaters or T-shirts and coveralls, boots that have hard toes, and worn denim jackets. She doesn't care if what she wears matches or if it's old. We dress like her. We're clean children, but our hair is scraggly, tangled, and uncut for years. We don't know what

"school shopping" is or what it's like to have a man in the house. We know words like *food bank, work-for-it, slumlord.*
We take nothing for granted. We have each other and nothing else.

I sit in the circle of her arms. She is the best mama in the world. There is nothing wrong with her, and she can do no wrong. She is my mama. Mine. I am proud of her.

I have nightmares, and she makes me a special pillow that will take them away. She reads me a story about how love is strength and shows me her byline. She pulls a quarter from behind my ear and an egg out of a hat.

Mama is magic.

We are out walking. We have to go to the store, but the motorcycle is broken. The sky is dark with no moon. We buy eggs. Mama is holding Angel on her shoulder, and I am holding Mama's hand.

Mama's hand is the strongest in the world. It is warm and smooth and can do everything. I think about this and smile. I hold her hand tighter. When I grow up I want to have my mama's hands.

A man steps out from behind a willow tree. I jump. He calls my mama a word I have never heard before. He calls her "dyke."

She is very still, and she says something back, "Wha'z it ta you, prick?" Her New York accent shows, and I can tell what is going to happen. She is still because she is ready. The man says "dyke" again, and he comes forward. Mama hands me Angel and stops the man from coming any closer.

We leave him there on the sidewalk. I don't hear his moans because I don't care. Mama takes Angel again. She had never let go of the eggs. None of them are broken. She hasn't broken one to this day.

I learned to tell time. I learned to make tea. At six a.m. I would slip off the mattress Angel and I shared. I would kiss Angel on the head. I would boil water. In my long T-shirt I would stand by the front door. The bare floor was always cold. At six-thirty Mama would come home. Her eyes would almost be shut. She was exhausted. It hurt me to see her so tried. She was not smiling. I would take her coat, help her off with her boots, and bring her tea. I was almost six. She needed me.

But somehow, one early morning as I walked back to my and Angel's mattress, somehow I knew Mama needed more. She needed someone else. Mama needed a partner.

## Silk

Her. Mumu.

Courage. Soul. Smarts. Responsible and spiritual and feminine and serious.

The first thing I know about the woman who will become my mumu is her perfume. The scent to me means nobility and luxury and the exotic. Before her I had never known anyone who wore perfume. Everyone I know smells like hair and skin and clothes. But this new scent lingers in every room, like dancing spices and flowers. It's strongest in the corner of the living room where Mama's mattress is. Strongest when Angel and I come home from school after being gone all day.

Angel says it first. I don't know how she knew; I didn't. "It's a mumu," she says. She is almost three; I am six and a half. For a long while we play only inside, quietly hidden, all the time hoping that the mumu will appear.

Other changes begin to happen. The house is cleaner. There are new cups and bowls. A big bright green plant appears in the hall. New toothbrushes. And food. Cereal and oatmeal and fruit and bread and just-for-kids vitamins find their way into our big open cupboard. I hold Angel up so she can see in, and her green eyes grow as big as the navel oranges.

Then Mama tells us. She has fallen in love with a woman. She has found us a mumu. A certain kind of joy seeps up through me. I hug Mama tight. Her happiness makes my world shine. I know something incredible has happened.

Mumu has ginger hair and green eyes. Her face is softer than Mama's, but her body is the same small toughness. She wears simple glasses. She works at a large company and takes classes to become a therapist. She drives a car, not a motorcycle. She works in her garden with gloves over her hands and clean, oval nails. She wears slacks and silk blouses, all in bright colors. She is not the same type of woman Mama is—she does not fix cars, swear at injustice, or fight with strangers four or five times a week. She mediates, she frowns, she talks about human behavior.

Mumu is the type of woman who does not hesitate to fall in love with a twenty-six year old widow and her two young children who live on the receiving end of poverty. Mumu is strong.

Mumu smiles at us. She takes out her keys and opens her front door. Angel and I walk into her house holding hands. Our mouths are open in amazement. Mumu has a fireplace. Mumu has a washing machine, a dryer, a toilet that doesn't leak, a bathtub without cracks. Mumu has carpets, curtains, cupboards full of rice and cereal and soup, and glass jars full of pasta.

Mumu shows us a staircase. The house has two floors! We climb the steps, and she shows us two rooms, two beds, two dressers, two desks, two toy chests. One room has wood paneling on the walls and a shelf full of books. The other room is painted pink and white with a pillowed window seat. We stare up at Mumu. "Would you like to come live here with me?" she asks.

Angel nods vigorously but then looks at me for approval. I meet Mumu's gaze. "Can Mama come too?"

Sack lunches. Mumu makes us sack lunches so we don't have to wait at the end of the line at school to get ours for free.

Paper, rulers, and pencils. Mumu never buys us silly things. Books, games to play together, craft kits. Mumu likes it that we don't watch television—we'd never had one.

Mumu asks us what kind of clothes we'd like. And our hair too. We get to choose how we want it cut. It takes Angel and me two weeks to come up with any answers. We'd never had choices before.

Once a month Mumu cooks a thanksgiving dinner. The turkey is always so big, Mama helps me carry it to the table. Angel carries the cranberry sauce or the mashed potatoes or peas. We gather together, and Mumu says a prayer: "Dear Goddess, thank you for bringing us together, for letting us find each other in the world. Thank you for making us a family."

Mumu has many rules, not just one, like Mama's, but we don't mind. Her rules are good rules. There are no drugs. No alcohol. No guns.

Mumu tells us if someone breaks into the house to be quiet and let them take anything. Things can be replaced, people can't. And even your own gun can be used against you.

I think of him...and I know Mumu is right.

Our family is complete. I love my parents with all that I am. I would die for them. I would live for them. I would survive for them.

## Skin

As it seems to do, time passes. My parents are my balance; Angel is my little sister to protect, my friend to laugh with and my coconspirator against the world that is against our mothers. We learn so early that difference is feared, difference is hated. We believe in our hearts, there is no choice but to stand up and fight, stand up and yell, "Enough!"

We survive ridicule, rock throwing, and rumbles. We survive job losses, car wrecks, and revisiting the food bank.

Angel survives being behind the other students at school because of the poor education offered to us before Mumu came. Angel survives to graduate as her class's valedictorian.

I survive kidnapping and rape. I survive to escape and write my first novel at age ten.

Eight years and thirteen novels later, after a dozen interviews on the radio and in the papers, after being called a whiz kid and a prodigy, after never having sent a letter or a manuscript, a New York publisher asks to see all of my work.

I send them sixty-five pounds of manuscripts. They send me a contract.

Four months later I leave home for the first time in my eighteen years to embark on a national book tour.

Everything in my childhood prepared me for this first of many tours. Everything my parents ever said or did or taught. Mama gave me her fists, and Mumu gave me her voice.

## Cotton

Childhood and career...

A boy at school insults my parents. He calls them dirty, he calls them freaks. I grab him by the hair and wrestle him into the wood chips. He starts to cry. There is blood on my white T-shirt and on my fist. I hear Angel cheering from the gathered crowd of children. He screams that it doesn't matter that I can fight because his daddy says girls aren't worth spit because they don't have balls. I have no idea what he's talking about, but when I tell my parents, they give me a huge pickle jar filled with rubber balls.

The interviewer says to me, "The KKK says you're recruiting. That you make being queer look too good. They've made threats that if you speak tomorrow at the queer pride rally, they'll shoot you."

I nod my head once.

The interviewer asks, "Will you wear a bulletproof vest? Will you be accompanied by bodyguards?"

"No," I reply, my voice very steady. "Nothing will stop me from getting onstage tomorrow. If it's my time to die, so be it. I'll die doing what I believe in."

The next morning I march in the pride parade under the bright California sun. In my black jeans and boots, with a sleeveless cotton shirt open down the front, I smile as I walk. I smile at the robed Klan members as they holler from behind police barricades. "Don't be ashamed!" I shout to them, "It's OK to be in drag—take off your hoods! Don't hide your faces, you will be accepted—robes and all!"

I give my speech. Five thousand people cheer.

## Wool

Wisdom and wit…

A long shadow falls across my friends, Angel, and me; it blocks out the thin winter sun. I look up from the game of jacks on the playground asphalt, my favorite red ball poised in my hand. Jill stands so tall and smug above me that I rise to my feet with a growl. She is still a head and a half taller than I, her arms and legs lean and lanky compared to my small, stocky build. Not even my thick wool sweater gives me enough bulk to make up for my lack of height.

"I saw your parents," she sneers. "You have two girl parents with weird short hair like boys. They're just trying to be men for each other!"

"If they wanted men," I answer, "they'd get some."

Jill screws up her face. "Your parents are gross!"

My friends are silent. My hand curls into a fist around my ball. Angel starts to clean up the jacks to make more room for the fight. I look up, way up, at Jill. Her shirtsleeves are too short on her arms and her pant cuffs ride up. We are the same age, but she's taller than anyone else at school. She has no friends.

I hold up my fist, and she tenses. I open it, revealing my red ball, offering it so she can take a turn. "It's hard to be different," I say. "It's very hard."

I smooth my wool suit jacket and straighten my tie. My boots make a steady thunk, thunk, thunk across the cold parking lot of the large bookstore, but the sound is unheard beneath the hollered protests of the gathered crowd as they wave Bibles and curse homosexuals. They've all awaited my arrival for an hour. My reading and autograph party begins in fifteen minutes, and I don't want to have to yell above the chanting.

I lock eyes with the ringleader. I reach into my jacket. He tenses. I pull out my special pen and snatch the Bible from his flailing hand. "Before I was sixteen I had read the Bible from cover to cover three times and taught Bible school classes for four months." I smile, opening the Good Book. "So since I know these words better than you, why don't I autograph it for you?"

## Leather

Passion and pride...

I walk down a midnight city street with Mickie. We're laughing loudly, slapping each other on the back, exchanging tales of love won and lost. We both wear 501s—though his fit a bit differently in the front— white T-shirts, and leather jackets. We both wear pink triangle buttons.

We reach Mickie's house. He waves good-bye as I turn and go, and he starts up his steps. I have walked ten feet when I hear him cry my name.

There are two of them. Their hair is shaved, their studded gloves catch the streetlight and their faces are hideous with hate. I am running to him even as I see Mickie thrown down the flight of steps he had just climbed. Will it always be like this?

I take him into my arms. I murmur to him. He opens his eyes. He moves. Something somewhere is broken, but his eyes tell me to run. To run away. But he knows I don't do that. He knows.

I look up. I stand up. I place myself between the two bashers and my friend. They stand above me on the stairs, but they are moving closer.

"What are you, another fag?" one of them spits.

I shake my head, my body ready. "No, a soft butch," I say. "But I can see how an idiot would confuse the two."

Mumu taught me that fists—even backed with three black belts— cannot solve everything. But fists combined with pressing assault charges come pretty close.

"Yes, Officer, my *brother* and I were just walking along when..."

It has been a long day. New York City buzzes around me with its constant din, even at four in the morning. My last interview was twenty minutes ago, and I sit in the back of a taxi, sipping root beer from a bottle and wishing I were already in bed. Over my dress shirt I have shrugged into my leather jacket with the roaring tiger on the back.

I barely know the city, but after having come and gone from the same hotel for over three weeks, I know the set of wrong turns when they happen. I open my mouth to ask when I see the driver's eyes blazing into me from the rearview mirror. I reach for the door handle. We are traveling at forty miles an hour. I open the door.

The taxi squeals into a narrow alleyway and jerks to a stop. My door hits the alley wall, only open an inch. The driver swivels in his seat. Does he think he'll climb over? He grabs my collar, slamming me toward him and against the jammed door. His breath is stale and thick. His fingers are working themselves to my shirt. He rips it.

I remember the bottle in my hand.

The feeling, the sound of the half-full thick glass bottle connecting with his head is something I will never forget. It is a powerful sound of freedom.

I am six blocks away, the broken bottle still clenched in my hand, when the taxi cuts me off in the road, accompanied by a police car. The driver, blood running down his face, insists that I got out of his cab without paying the six-dollar fee.

The officer looks from the man's face to the broken bottle to my torn shirt to the taxi meter. He asks, "Can I take you home, Miss?"

I look at him. "I'd rather walk, but thank you."

**\* \* \***

There is a difference between what I know and what I am taught. There is a difference between what I see and what I am told to see. There is *no* difference between hate and cowardice.

These are the first things I learned.

I am a daughter. A mother's daughter. The daughter of a writer, a builder, a street fighter. The daughter of a photographer, a counselor, a word warrior. A daughter of poverty, of freedom, of sorrow. A daughter of courage. Strength. Victory. Survival. A daughter of mothers.

The radio show is broadcast live in Omaha, and the long-distance crackle of the phone-line sounds like fire. The receiver in my hand is the only thing connecting me to the onslaught of questions, accusations, and damnations of the call-in bigots.

Even the radio-show host has to throw in, "Jennifer, don't you think you're ruining the moral fabric of America?"

"Ruining it?" My voice is brave and incredulous. "Why, sir, I'm the best part."

*A Fag, a Dyke,*
*a Gender-Switch Queer*

## Significant Others: A Queer Autobiography
## by Anna Myers-Parrelli

*I was twenty. You remember twenty?*
*I was alienated—and damn proud of it!*
—Ferron

### May 13, 1988: Blastoff

My parents' eyes are as wide as saucers. They sit, wooden in their cheap kitchen chairs as my nervous eyes dart from mother to father and back again. I wonder silently, *How long have we been sitting here? How long since any of us blinked? How long has it been since I announced, in one breath, "Mom-and-Dad-I'm-a-lesbian"?*

At last my father swallows. "So?" he says and resumes eating his lunch.

This scene was not what I had expected, not the scenario I had prepared for. I wandered off in a daze, unnecessary adrenaline surging through my body. I was disturbed; coming out to my parents had not followed the scripts I had studied in the history books—*our* history books, the ones I had relied upon to guide me through my closet doors. When a lesbian comes out, the books read, parents are supposed to faint/cry/scream/disown you/deny/argue. But all my parents said was, "So?" If my coming out was not following the course that other lesbians before me had charted, I wondered, then how much of the rest of my life would their experiences apply to?

Uneasy, I leafed again through my copy of *The Coming Out Stories*. This book had so far been my "travel planner" in the coming-out process. At college three months earlier, I had waved good-bye to my boyfriend as he left for the weekend and then used his absence as a time to study lesbianism. I had read continually, comparing my childhood experience to each of the women's stories recorded in this lesbian primer. Mentally I had checked off the ingredients of queerness that I could glean from the book: a) I had always felt "different"; b) I had been a tomboy; c) I did not wear dresses or play with dolls; and finally, d) I was not attracted to boys. I decided I met all the basic requirements. Unlike most of the women in *The Coming Out Stories*, though, I did not "wake up" to my sexuality after falling in love. Instead I sought out and chose this identity in a single weekend, without ever having slept with a woman. My first and only boyfriend left his lover on a Friday and came home that Sunday to a lesbian.

It was March when I came out. By May of that year, I had already served as a peacekeeper in the local lesbian and gay pride march. I had already promised to help coordinate the campus lesbian alliance the next semester. I came out to my parents one week later—an event I considered a "bridge-burning" since I could not imagine losing face by changing my mind at some point in the future. Still, as I sat queasily in my bedroom that May afternoon, I wondered if I really were gay. It had never occurred to me to wait until I was sure before coming out. I had run toward and embraced this expression of my "differentness." And like the women in *The Coming Out Stories*, coming out had filled a hollow place within me; my need was not simply a sexual one.

## June 1973: T Minus 16 and Counting...

I was three years old when my family moved to the small, white, Republican town in Connecticut where I grew up. In this rarefied environment it did not take long for my feelings of differentness to develop.

I sit on the carpet, playing Barbies with my sister and our best friend, Martha. My sister and Martha always play Barbie or Skipper. I always play Ken or Bob or sometimes the horse. Today they joke and call me an "it." I do not get it. Above us our parents remark on the strange pattern they observe, using big words. The words—*it, androgynous, tomboy, he/she*—haunt me. None of the parents tries to change me, but underneath their words I sense something to fear. I resolve to try harder to squeeze into the Barbie-doll mold.

As I grew I did my best to hide. As a teenager, along with the rest of my overprivileged peers, I adopted the junior-high dress code: Farrah Fawcett "wings" hairstyle, a Bermuda bag purse with covers that can be changed to match one's outfit, and my choice of oxford or Izod shirts and Fair Isle sweaters. Even as my anxious teenage self strove to feather her hair in the required manner, though, another side of me rebelled. When other girls started dating in high school, that other side of me stayed home, doing homework and writing poetry. When I was offered admission to Brown University, that other side of me chose instead to attend Hampshire College—an experimental, almost unheard-of college in western Massachusetts.

Attending Hampshire was my first attempt to break out of the Barbie mold that my life had been in up to age eighteen. Coming out as a lesbian reaffirmed my commitment to the rebellious stranger within. Suddenly I viewed the world with new eyes. I developed my "gaydar," learning to spot a lesbian at twenty paces. I returned home after that first college year proudly displaying my pink triangle T-shirt and buttons for all to see. Strangely, though, the entire town reacted just as my parents had. No one seemed to notice or care.

I needed to find a more receptive audience.

### December 24, 1989: T Plus 1.5

My father is drunk. I sit on the couch next to him, my growing awareness of his alcoholism a barrier to true conversation. Still, on this night we have somehow managed to engage each other. I mention casually that it scares me not to know any "old" gay people. I wonder aloud what happens to gays when they age.

"I suppose it's time you knew," he said. "I'm gay."

*What?*

Listening to my father as he soaks himself in alcohol, I realize that my queer roots go deeper than I ever imagined. I sit next to my gay father, stunned and speechless.

He is surprised by my surprise. Had I not guessed that he was gay? he wanted to know. After a lifetime of watching him cook, clean, launder, and raise children, had I not concluded that my father was, in his words, "a flaming faggot"? I had not.

## June 1976: T Minus 12 and Counting...

My father comes home from work wearing a white carnation and carrying a papier-mâché jackass that he has been given as a gift. "Your father has retired early," I am told. I am six years old. From that day forward Dad became a househusband. I grew up in a home that he cleaned, wore clothes that he washed, and ate gourmet dinners that he cooked and bread that he baked. He scrupulously copied his recipes from magazines, newspapers, and other housewives. When I was in first grade, he served as my class's "room mother"—the adult helper who assisted our teacher with parties and field trips. My friends loved his brownies, and no one ever asked why my father stayed at home while my mother worked. My father told me later, though, that nobody ever talked to him at the PTA.

In my early years I did not question these strange developments. I was not disturbed by the gender-bending term *room mother* applied to my dad. After all, I had my own, inner, experience of gender-bending. And I was used to my parents' unconventional life. For example, there were the strange parties they dragged me to at my enormous, loud godmother's home. "Aunt" Gloria lived alone, but her parties filled the house and overflowed into surrounding yards. I remember hiding under her blue and green seventies-style furniture and watching people mill about. Often I could not tell which were women and which were men.

Sometimes we would visit my father's friends, Bruce and Alistair. Their house was as large and inviting as Gloria's was small and overwhelming. Their walls were graced by hunting trophies of all species; the glass-eyed animals befriended me while the grown-ups spoke of dull things outside. I remember one day when the animal heads began to bore me. I went out to the patio, crawled up over the rim of the aboveground pool, and fell in. The next thing I remember is Bruce fishing me out, wrapping me in a sweater that was bigger than I was, and letting me sit on his lap until I got warm. Years later I learned that Alistair killed himself when Bruce left him for another man.

The same-sex partnership did not strike me as odd. After all, two of my mother's best friends were a female couple: "the Nancys." These two women had different surnames, but both were called Nancy. I speculated in my child's mind that if a man and a woman got married and took the same last name, perhaps when two women got married, they took the same first name. I never got up the courage to ask.

My childhood dragged on, and there were more dinner parties. But in all of the strange houses that my parents dragged us to, there lived as many same-gender couples as mixed couples. I never thought to question these arrangements until, sitting next to my gay, drunk father on our couch at home, I finally realized that most of my parents' friends were queer.

### January 1990: T Plus 1.5 and Counting...

Regrettably, I never pursued my father's abbreviated coming-out to me. I left home after Christmas break, bewildered by my discoveries and unsure how they applied to my life. Besides, there were other matters of importance to occupy my attention. It was my third year at college, and I still had not acquired a girlfriend. My doubts about my sexuality had diminished, though, and there were several women to whom I was attracted. I moved in with all of them.

My three apartment mates and I were leaders in the campus gay and lesbian community. Together we formed the major organizing force behind the politically powerful lesbian-gay-bisexual alliance on campus. In negotiations with college administrators, we acted as moderators—the "reasonable" queers who tempered the fire of the supposedly "radical" younger members. What the administrators never knew, though, is that we three *were* those more radical members. Frustrated by the slow pace of daytime diplomacy, my friends and I formed the fly-by-night secret organization Campus Lesbian Terrorists (CLT). Together we would attack bathroom walls, painting slogans such as LESBIANISM—WHO COULD ASK FOR ANYTHING MORE? or LESBIANISM—THE ONLY ALTERNATIVE. We cherished our secret identities, meeting for bonding rituals that included bloodletting and shaving labyrises into our pubic hair. Other students started to refer to CLT as "the clit cult."

I turned twenty-one that year. Rebellion still flowed hot through my veins. I still felt I had to prove I was not the winged, Bermuda bag-bearing teenager who had attended middle school so many years before. Perhaps it was for this reason that I chose to ignore my father's coming-out. Likewise, I chose to ignore his and my mother's friends—the gay men and lesbians who were already adults, ordinary men and women who might have taught me much about our history. I also began to ignore much of what I had read in our history books. As with *The Coming Out Stories*, I had devoured other works by gay and lesbian writers. While I found them powerful and inspiring, they nevertheless did not seem relevant to the future that was unfolding before me. Like others my age, I felt that we were creating our own future, taking for granted our ancestors' accomplishments and concentrating our energies on expanding what the world allowed us to say and do. All things appeared to be possible, and "No limits!" was our rallying cry. *How could the Daughters of Bilitis ever compare to CLT or the Lesbian Avengers?* I wondered.

But then I left college. My personal activist network disbanded, and I watched from afar as the powerful political organization I had built on campus became once again a loose social circle. I moved to Northampton, Massachusetts, which the *National Enquirer* had recently dubbed "Lesbianville, USA." There, within the local community, lesbians who had built the town into a haven for "womyn" during the seventies and eighties were in an uproar. They claimed that "students, sadomasochists, and bisexuals" were "taking over" their community, draining its power.

Like many students and recent graduates, I ignored these Northampton women's lament. I did not mourn what they called their community. Like others my age, I felt I was creating my own history and my own future. The community they described—a group of flannel- and work boot-wearing androgynes—was ancient history to me. The vivid descriptions of how things "used to be" in Northampton did not entice me. Even as I cried over the embers of the political force I had built at Hampshire College, I had no compassion for the older lesbians, who were, I now realize, mourning a similar transformation.

In Northampton I abandoned my activism for a time. I became more concerned with establishing myself, building a career, and becoming a professional. And then I met *her.*

### June 23, 1991: T Plus 3 and Counting...

The striking Italian butch strides into my hangout one evening and announces to all present that she is newly single. She sports a leather jacket and a rebellious flair. My friends warn me away, saying she is "dangerous." We flirt. We date: once? twice? We fall in love. Jo and Anna disappear from the local lesbian community. It is rumored that they go to bed at eight p.m., yet neither of them ever seems to sleep...

Two years pass, full of queer harmony—followed by a wedding on Lammas Eve, July 31, 1993.

My courting over at last, I crawled sleepily back into the local lesbian community. Things had changed, I saw. LGBAs on college campuses had become "queer alliances." The dyke debates no longer raged about bisexuals and S/M. Now lesbians argued about the place of transsexuals in "women's" space. My friends had moved. The historic on-campus lesbian apartment that I had once inhabited now housed gay men and "pansexuals." And somehow I found that in two years I had changed from a hot new threatening radical to a croaking crone of yesteryear.

### May 13, 1995: T Plus 7 and Counting...

They say the body re-creates itself every seven years. It has now been seven years since I came out. I have re-created myself, indeed. Now I use the tools of conformity from my Connecticut upbringing in order to be more successful in my career. I use the tools of activism from my college days in order to reshape my profession toward a less oppressive future. I invent new tools in order to succeed in my marriage, now two years old. From the ashes of a winged, Bermuda bag-bearing teen has risen a fiery dyke activist/Ph.D. candidate/wife. Sometimes I wonder if I am reinventing myself or simply shedding my skin—growing ever closer to the true me at my core.

It seems the curse of our oppression that our community feels the need to make itself anew every decade or so. In the 1950s being a lesbian meant being butch or femme. In the 1970s lesbianism meant androgyny. In the 1980s and since, being a lesbian increasingly comes to mean anything that each individual woman wants it to mean. In the 1990s some of us have even thrown off the title "lesbian" and claimed the labels "queer" and "transgendered" in order to show that we do not bow down to society's gender roles. Since the Stonewall riots our communities continue to reinvent themselves—fueled by the energy of the young and alienated. Our people change too quickly for any of us to keep up.

Perhaps the instability of our communities reflects the instability of our status in the world. Now I enjoy free medical and dental benefits because I am "married" to another woman who is employed by the local university. Today gay and lesbian weddings are almost commonplace. But I realize that a few years ago none of these privileges existed. And today still, the wrong president, a conservative Congress, a hateful group of local citizens, or any of a thousand dangers can take this freedom from us. If I move to another state, I will have to check myself before even acknowledging my wife in public. Our communities may be strong, but our gains are fragile.

And so perhaps it is this very fragility that causes our groups to be always in flux. So little time has passed since Stonewall, and yet we have accomplished so much. Our activists work feverishly to preserve our gains as our youngest members work to expand our territory. I feel as though I have been out for centuries, and it has only been seven years.

I am twenty-six years old now. Rebellion and alienation are not as evident in my daily life as they once were. Still, I cherish my rebelliousness as a weapon that has served me well and will again. But now there is time in my life for contemplation too. My parents' friends are dead, mostly, and I regret that I never asked them about their stories, about the communities into which they came out. Too late I begin to appreciate their history, for it is also my own.

Now I teach at a college campus. I watch the younger queers, and I wish I could instill in them the need to value their history: our own frenetic past. At the same time, I respect the need to rebel, the frantic energy with which we attack the limits that have been placed upon our lives. Even as I worry that they will forget their roots, I silently encourage these younger ones onward—toward victories and gains that today I cannot imagine.

As we grow and change in our shifting, twisting rhythms, are we really reinventing ourselves? Or is our community simply shedding its skin, moving us ever closer to our core?

# Me and My Gender(s)
## by Nadya Arnaoot

My gender identity is as fluid as the rest of me. I am an Arab-American, born to a American woman from the South and a man from Huffa, Syria. I was born in Texas and have lived all over the place, but I currently make my home in the outskirts of Washington, D.C., right on the shifting border between North and South. And I am a 24-year-old woman who also identifies as a teenage boy.

I learned how to be a boy from my father. He has told me that in Islamic thought the sun is female and the moon is male. I think of that whenever I see my parents at a party. My mother tells loud stories and demands attention with her voice and her hands. He stands to the side with a drink in his hand, observing everyone, talking to the people who come to tell him their problems.

I take after my father.

The men on his side of the family are all soft-spoken intellectuals; they don't like football, and they can't fix cars. The women have a lot in common with my mother—they are loud, macho, and fiercely good with their hands. If I acted like one of my Arab aunts (or like my mother), people would say I was butch. But I act like my dad, so I am called femme.

My grandmother on my father's side used to ride around her small town on horseback, carrying a gun and scaring her neighbors to death. One of my aunts went to Kuwait during the Gulf War, intimidated a banker into giving her all of her and her parents' money, and got out again. My uncle Azzize was a judge; he spoke quietly and listened well. At my age my dad was a Communist artfag. His stories of the passionate intellectual conversation and intense ideological debate in the Arab Commie community at the University of Texas in the sixties remind me of my time in dyke activism.

Photos of my dad at my age show an earnest young scholar/art geek. He's darker-skinned than I am, and the rims of his glasses are made of huge plastic as opposed to little round wires. Still, the similarities are obvious.

Both of us attract confidences to the point that it sometimes becomes annoying. I think people go to my father with their problems for the same reasons they come to me: our detached empathy. They sense that I am a little bit apart from ordinary affairs, outside of the usual. Most people do not connect this difference to my androgyny, but I do. The same quality that kept me ostracized for years also makes people confess their sins, stories, and problems to me.

I've also been very much influenced by Vamp, my queer role model in the goth scene. For about a year we were inseparable, dressing up together and going out to clubs. He knows how to bleach hair and dye it purple, dance, and put on stunning eyeliner. I learned to flirt and gossip from guys like Vamp, which makes me campier than the average dyke. Running around with Vamp, I also learned how to put on makeup, whiteface, eyeliner, and black or dried-blood lipstick. I started doing goth-industrial boy drag: cutoffs, fishnets, combat boots, and a ripped black T-shirt. Or a more formal look: vest and coat. Both of us will wear the occasional long skirt, but with my build people assume that I'm a woman when I'm wearing a skirt, which can be annoying. Dabbing on some facial hair, giving myself a monobrow, or wearing something a little bit too drag-queeny for a woman are ways to get around that. My favorite queer sticker reads, FUCK YOUR GENDER. I like making people wonder when they look at me.

I have found more gender play within the goth-industrial culture than in my circle of dyke friends. My current male lover, despite identifying as straight, is more comfortable with my being a boy and a girl and a woman and various combinations thereof than any of the women I've dated. Being with someone who accepts—actually enjoys—my androgyny is making me realize how damaging it was for me to be with people who couldn't handle it. My first lover was constantly telling me how much butch girls turned her off, and the trans-gendered girl I dated recently kept telling me how she liked only femmes. That was particularly depressing because I was so into her as a boy and a woman—delighted by her intelligence, her boyish good looks, and her complications—but she just wasn't into my in-betweenness in the same way.

I've resolved never again to date someone who doesn't enjoy my mixed genders.

Like many goths, I was a bit of an outcast in high school, a depressed, shy kid generally dismissed with amused contempt. I think much of the angst came from my transgendered and queer nature; I was always ashamed when somebody thought I was a boy. Clamping down on emotions, avoiding people, and trying to be an abstract mind, I became somehow sexless, both asexual and genderless, a bit of a monk. I figure I lost about six years, from ages twelve through eigh-teen. My desert-island years.

Now I claim my androgyny with pride. I delight in being called "sir...um...ma'am...um..." I just bought wings for my black leather jacket; I want to be a radical fairy. I like playing dress-up; I like being a boy, a grrrl, a woman, a fag, a dyke, a gender-switch queer. And I love talking to people who have as complicated genders as I do. I fig-ure I'm making up for lost time—I have six years of exploration to catch up on. Most recently I have been developing a fifteen-year-old boy persona, Alec. He's cynical, shy, eager to please—a lot like me at his age but more able to connect with other people. I'm just starting to introduce him to my friends, and every time he gets a compliment, it heals an old bruise.

# With a Chorus of Naked Queers
## by J. Keiko Lane

For James Carroll Pickett and W. Wayne Karr

2 yu hu n the fuchur dwel
Judj uz not 2 much harshilee
Nor pitee pleez the lz hu fel
Atemptun rowlz heerowuklee
The un b luvud az yu c
Reveel thayr dreems imodustlee
May yurz be baythd n evurgreen
Godspeed 2 yu owr projunee
N sum sumurz deep deelyt
Neeth munlez skyz with starz ubuv
Win feerful pashunz burn 2 bryt
Tayk hart frum thowz hu dayrd 2 luv
If thiz we mask sum way ofendz
Danz flawluzlee. Mak owr amenz.
— *James Carroll Pickett,*
Queen of Angels

## I

So it happened again. Talking about my AIDS literature thesis, my academic advisor said, "Well, you have to narrow your focus, isolate some of the texts. I assume you're only going to write about a few people." So I sat in her office and tried to think of a way to tell her about connections. The way obscurity became outrageous artistic license. Like the way *AIDS! The Musical* put our queer family onstage—not only as writers, director, and cast but also as characters and context. We watched ourselves onstage laughing at ourselves, and we laughed too and forgot who was writing and who was listening.

## II

Wayne introduced me to James Carroll Pickett at the opening of *AIDS! The Musical.* Jim's lover, an old friend of ours, was in the cast. "Girl, he's brilliant," Wayne had said to me in a stage whisper as he introduced us. Six months earlier Wayne and I had run into each other in that same theater, at the opening of *Queen of Angels,* Jim's last play.

## III

So I sat in my advisor's office and started listing authors, however the connections led me to each one.

## IV

The first time I saw W. Wayne Karr was at the very first Queer Nation meeting that I was brave enough to drag myself to. One dark Saturday night in February 1991, out of frustration—perhaps desperation—the need for tribe overtook my fear and propelled me into an unfamiliar part of town to get lost, driving around in circles for what seemed like hours, looking for Plummer Park. Walking into a room of a hundred queers in various drag—high camp, full leather, four-inch platforms, men in skirts and lipstick, women in leather and piercings. Some of the faces looked familiar from a winter of antiwar demonstrations. Almost everyone wore fluorescent crack-and-peel stickers. It made sense, I remember thinking—every army has its uniform. When the issue of how Queer Nation as a group dealt with gender hit the floor, Wayne was steadfast in his claim that the fags in the room needed to take responsibility for their sexism just as the dykes in the room needed to take responsibility for AIDS-phobia. He knew that if we all took responsibility for all the issues on the floor, no one subgroup of us would be relegated to the role of teacher all the time. If we were indeed a community, then each of us had an equal responsibility to

everyone else. The sticker on Wayne's black skirt read PAZ CON JUSTI-
CIA AHORA. At the end of the meeting, I watched him stand in fishnet
stockings and combat boots to kiss another man good-bye.

The response to the gender disparity in Queer Nation became a ritual Saturday-afternoon gathering called "Gender Que(e)ries." Each
week we drank thick coffee and tackled a new topic. The familiar site
for battle between Wayne and me was ageism, as he, once an ambitious young peace activist himself, admitted to a skeptical fear that the
decadence of youth would overtake the effectiveness of action.

Sometime at the end of that first summer, we called a happy truce
and declared ourselves a chosen family. Many evenings and weekends
were spent in the house, dubbed "Queer Acres," that Wayne was sharing with his two lovers and a dyke buddy. We would spend evenings
bickering over whose turn it was to make coffee, reading each other
poetry and memoirs, determined to document our world.

## V

I bring my advisor Sarah Schulman's novel *People in Trouble,* which
fictionalizes ACT UP. One of her characters says defiantly from his
hospital bed, "Not everyone dies. Michael Callen is still alive."

Michael Callen died in December 1993.

## VI

Pulling into a grocery-store parking lot, I see that the paper bags of the
store have red ribbons imprinted on them. The cover of *People* magazine shows a Hollywood diva of the month in a formal gown wearing
a sequined red ribbon.

Wayne was arrested at the Oscars the year Queer Nation got it into
our heads to take on Hollywood. I got to the action three hours after
getting my first college acceptance letter. Walking up the street toward
the demo, I passed the paddy wagon and heard my name. I looked up
to see Wayne and several other Queer Nationals in plastic handcuffs.
"I thought you weren't planning on getting arrested today," I chastised
Wayne. "Just get us out of here, girl," he hissed back at me. Several
hours later Wayne was released from downtown's Parker Center, the
home of Daryl Gates, on his own recognizance and on the grounds
that I take him home immediately. Hauling me out the door so that
he could have a cigarette and plot the release of the rest of the

arrestees, Wayne glared at me when I told him to get into my car, that our legal team was already on the way to deal with the rest of the affinity group. "I'm not bailing your glamorous ass out of jail twice in one day, girl," I warned, holding open the car door. "Madam, your vehicle. Get in."

## VII

One summer Jim coproduced a show called *AIDS/Us/Women,* which put several of the women we knew onstage to tell their stories of living during the plague years. Every evening before the show went up in a different theater or church, traveling through the war zones of Los Angeles, our city of angels and demons, Jim would pace the back of the room, worrying about how this particular audience would internalize the testimonies. During every show I sat in the back of the room with Jim and watched him watching the audience and the stage, judging the interactions, catching his breath before different lines were spoken, then seeing if others heard them the way he did. Every night of that show, Roxy, a playwright and dear friend of ours, told her story of her husband's dying, then sang to her daughter a few days later as she died: *"You are my sunshine / My only sunshine / You make me happy / When skies are gray / You'll never know, dear / How much I love you / Just don't take my sunshine away."* Every night as she sang, I watched Jim sit with one hand clenched, white-knuckled, the other hand leaning up against it, opening and closing around it. His eyes were closed.

## VIII

Rereading Schulman's novel with my advisor, I find a lovely, wise character named James Carroll. This character is a survivor and a visionary. In the beginning of the novel, he feels hopeful for some form of change. By the close his lover has died and he is waiting to get sick, feeling that perhaps humanity cannot be redirected from this course.

I think of James Carroll Pickett. This is part of the contradiction of AIDS and the arts. Jim Pickett played basketball in his Southern high school and married his high school girlfriend. He became a beautiful L.A. fag playwright-poet.

In the age of the modern plague, we are artists screaming one another's stories into the four winds as the stories become our own, as we become a part of one another's stories. We become our own archetypes. The outcasts of the plague become the models and visions of hope. James Carroll Pickett. 1949-1994.

## IX

One evening, sitting around Queer Acres, several of us found ourselves near Wayne, listening to him tell stories about the preplague years of his own decadent youth. Wayne spun tales of disappearing for days into underground dungeons and S/M clubs in New York. We kept begging for more stories, like children before bed, and Wayne kept telling them, trying to breathe them back to life. We sat in candlelight in the lengthening night. Someone pulled out a bag of clothespins and scarves and handcuffs as Wayne talked. One at a time a few members of that family stood against the doorway into the hall, trusting familiar hands that cuffed wrists and manipulated the pins, forming patterns of reddening and blanching skin. Wayne kept telling stories, peeling off layers of his masks. The stories are ancient. So are the masks. Every story revealed a little bit more of his truth, just as with every story he spun, more skin was revealed by the queers in front of the altar. Trying to hold on to his truths, Wayne discarded the masks. And we tried them on.

## X

In a fiction workshop a student tells me that my characters are too self-conscious about being gay and lesbian. They are too self-conscious about AIDS. They think too much and don't have enough fun. The professor, known for long, rambling diatribes in favor of violence in short stories as a method of holding an audience, agrees with her. Someone else in the workshop tells me that there are too many "issues" in the story, that it is too complicated.

I laugh out loud.

It is all true. It is all true. It is all true. It is all true.

## XI

One of Wayne's professors once tried to kick him out of a class because, over a decade into the plague, this professor still believed that he could "catch AIDS" from touching Wayne's papers. Wayne worked hard in school, determined to get his degree. He was admitted to

Hollywood Community Hospital soon after the confrontation. I think that was yet another bout of pneumonia. We all planned our retaliation from his hospital room. It culminated in an action called "Educate the Educators" and a press conference. Wayne graduated that spring. Second in his class. He wore a Queer Nation INFECTED FAGGOT sticker with his cap and gown. He was sure that if we speak our truths, there is nothing left for them to hurt us with. As long as we claim our lives.

### XII

The night I finally made my decision to travel a thousand miles away to college in the fall, I arrived at Plummer Park late for the evening's long-awaited and tediously planned feast and ritual. It was the weekend Harry Hay turned eighty. The ritual began in a circle. I looked around at all of the faces in the room. We had kept true to so many promises. As candles were passed around the circle, I looked into every face lit by the motion of the light. Several generations of queers. The father of the modern movement turning eighty. And outliving most of his children.

We are one another's points of reference. What do we do when those points of reference are dying or, rather, are dead? On a good day I think denial leaves us reluctant to fill in the gaps, as though it might appear that we are trying to replace one another. On more cynical days I think there just aren't replacements out there waiting to inherit this.

### XIII

Soon after I began my thesis on AIDS literature as a signifier of queer culture and queer culture as a signifier of the social construction of AIDS, a professor asked me if I was going to look at AIDS as a moral issue in the gay community. She was eager to know whether I was going to be discussing the "moral appropriateness of flagrant sexuality in the midst of the epidemic." Clearly she had her doubts. "No," I told her, not wanting to believe that she had even asked. No.

### XIV

One February evening something made me stop at the phone outside the computer center in the basement of the library. I'd had a long day, but I stopped at the phone and punched in the code for my answering machine. I held my breath as the first of two messages began. "Hi, sweetie, this is Richard. It's Tuesday. Call me tonight, it doesn't matter how late. I'll be home after nine. I love you." Immediately my familiar mantra started: *No, no, no, not yet...* Message number two: "Hello, darling, it's Judy. I have bad news. Wayne died early this morning. Call me when you get this."

## XV

In 1992 when the governor vetoed our antidiscrimination bill for housing and employment, I was at home, sick in bed, watching the demonstrations unfold on the news, playing phone tag as part of a legal-team network to keep track of everyone in case of arrests. Richard called me from work. "Turn on the news and stay by a phone," he said. I turned on the news in time to see the demo hit the California state building downtown. Denied entrance and access by security, protesters crushed against the plate-glass doors. One of the doors' handles simply came off in Wayne's hand. Without a second thought he lifted the handle, brought it over his shoulder like every baseball bat that had ever crushed a queer body on a late-night street corner or park, and hurled it through the door. The news replayed over and over the image of glass shattering—Wayne's face twisted in rage and hurt, his fist raised in fury.

## XVI

The last celebration I went to at Wayne's house was a birthday party for one of his housemates. Wayne played hostess for a while, then retreated into his bedroom. One by one, beckoned by the music or laughter or simply following one another, the guests ended up in his room, listening to him tell stories and hold court from his bed, the throne for an old queen. I curled up on the edge of the bed and draped my arm across his legs. They were thinner than I remembered. He was playing Sondheim collections and telling stories of seeing Broadway shows. "Listen to this," he'd say, or "Have you ever heard this one?" or "Just one more, isn't it fabulous?" As people drifted in and out of his room, I cozied myself at the foot of his bed. "Tired of this yet?" he asked. "Of course not." One more. He'd close his eyes and listen to the music of fairy tales, and he could have been anywhere he wanted. And I imagined that he was.

### XVII

One month and four days later, Richard called again. This time he was only calling to check on me, to see how I was coping. "Fine," I told him, "nothing new. These days that constitutes 'wonderful.' " Richard knows this as well as anyone. A year ago he watched his lover die. Richard spends his time taking care of us. He is always fighting for us and rescuing us. He used to be a part of the "Welcoming Committee" of Queer Nation. He wanted all of the members of the tribe to find one another. He loved watching us file in the door on Saturday nights. He liked being able to say hello. But in the end he watched Rob die. And he said good-bye.

### XVIII

The last time I went to see Wayne in the hospital, I was home for winter break. He was asleep. He never woke up while Richard and I were there that day. He never knew I was there. Or maybe he did. Richard and I retreated back to his apartment to talk and catch up on the news of the tribe. We put on *Into the Woods*. We laughed until tears ran down our cheeks, remembering Wayne dressed up as a demented Kimberly Bergalis to amuse Richard's partner, who was on a hunger strike for that bill the governor vetoed anyway. We laughed until I cried, and the ghost of the Baker's wife sang, *"Sometimes people leave you / Halfway through the wood / Do not let it grieve you / No one leaves for good..."*

### XIX

Sitting in a Portland café, I am talking with a friend about my thesis. We are talking about life in a queer chosen family and about what it means for that family to die. I am trying to explain that somehow it must be possible to understand how a person can be transformed by something without entirely understanding the thing that is causing the transformation.

Two men walk into the café and sit down at a table near us. One of the men is a little bit too thin and leans a little too heavily on the table. His friend looks concerned but is trying hard not to look worried. The man coughs, then breathes heavily for a moment, looks at his watch, then reaches into the pocket of his jacket and pulls out a vial of pills and shakes two into his hand. He asks the waitress for a glass of water, smiling bravely at her and at his breakfast companion. I look back at my friend, who is watching me expectantly. "Bactrim or fluconazole?" I ask, taking a swig of my coffee. "Excuse me?" She looks confused. "Guess the opportunistic infections." She is stunned. "After a while you do anything you can to keep busy and amuse yourself, to keep yourself in constant motion." I look down into my coffee and smile. Wayne would have found it much too weak.

# Fuck Your Healthy Gay Lifestyle (The FRINGE Manifesto—Freaks, Radicals, and Inverts Nail Gay Elite!)
## by Christy Calame and Robbie Scott Phillips

Gays and lesbians do not exist—there are only queers and straights. Those known as "gay and lesbian people" are essentially straight assholes who sleep with members of their same sex and have nothing to do with queerness except their fear and rape of it. Queers are twisted and disgusting, beautiful and glamorous, extreme and alive. We live outside the margin and move to keep working edges, surviving co-optation, decimation, and attack by those so-called gay and lesbian people. We are everywhere things are truly happening. Ass-kissing "gay and lesbian" bores scramble on their knees to give blow jobs to the straight power brokers and earn favor as their subservient underlings while simultaneously trying to steal the excitement of the queer life force. They masquerade in both straight and queer camps as it suits their fancy, but the truth is, they don't exist anywhere and aren't anything, because they don't know who they are.

One of the most dismal manifestations of those "gay and lesbian" specimens is their desire to breed and replicate the noxious straight nuclear family to prove their existence and fit in. Lesbian breeder bags and their designer third-world babies are the worst form of living genocide. Postterm fetuses are used as entrée into polite normal society and are showcased at "gay and lesbian" validation events known as "pride."

During this sniveling event "gays and lesbians" spend one afternoon out of the year tokenizing the vital queerness of drag as though it were part of their "culture." In the midst of this celebration of essential straightness (healthy sexless muscle boys and mommy lesbian drones), a few unsuspecting and therefore tokenized queers can be found. All disenfranchised queers have been led to believe that this is their one glorious day, but it is actually a ridiculous genuflection to nothing. This "pride" event is both queer baiting and queer hating. It is a prime example of the complex system of closeted/closeting symbols that allows "gays and lesbians" to recognize one another without getting dirty or offending the Master Race (straights). Even the truly fabulous drag queens who parade down the dirty "gay and lesbian" backstreets are being used. The "gay and lesbian" vision of drag queens is that they are quaint anomalies offered to straight society like silly enslaved creatures trapped in a petting zoo. "Pride day" is the one day real queers of all stripes are embraced, and then only to spice up the homogenized, boring "gay and lesbian" death march.

"Gays and lesbians" rely on safe, discreet imagery such as the insipid rainbow flag (which symbolizes nothing, certainly not diversity), the lambda symbol (arcane!), the red ribbon (ooh, pretty!) and "freedom" rings. All of these items can conveniently be made into tacky jewelry that "gays and lesbians" adore. This insider code is a product of what "gay and lesbian" people refer to as the closet—and the code perpetuates it.

While sucking the life out of anything queer they can get their hands on, "gay and lesbian" people worship and adore any straight person who would deign to be seen with them and thus validate their alleged measly existence. This collaboration is greatly beneficial to the straights as it feeds their already engorged egos with proof of the inherent superiority of heterosexuals and their benevolence in being seen with an inferior "gay" or "lesbian" person. All current "gay and lesbian" "politics" is corporate-sponsored power sharing with mainstream culture and is designed to maintain the status quo at all costs. Mainstream organizations solicit "gay and lesbian" consumers via elaborate public relations campaigns for profit and profit only. Thankfully queers and hets never have and never will have such a contract. Queer people do not mirror, celebrate, or tolerate het-ness. "Gays and lesbians" are the carriers who co-opt queer culture and barter it in the marketplace for points with the powers that be.

"Gay and lesbian" people are not real; they are lacking in queer qualities such as intensity, rage, provocativeness, and intelligence. They posture with synthetic affect; most notably, sentimentality and self-pity. When reality strikes them in the face, they respond with whiny, Christian, peaceful candlelight vigils and deferential speeches free of anger. "Gay and lesbian" people appear to be incapable of rage, of breaking out of the mindless conformity and fucking with their oppressors. They need stagnancy to maintain the myth of "gay and lesbian"-ism. Queer rage scares the shit out of them and sends them running hysterically back to their straight role models.

Since "gay and lesbian" people are completely aligned with straight culture but are attracted to the allure of queerness, they assume a victim mentality and both deny and abuse their privilege. Their "activism" is about getting more power, money, and straight approval. Their "activism" leaves behind nonwhites, S/M fetishists, fat dykes, transsexual/transgendered people, poor people, etc.—in other words, true queer agendas. They believe in Clinton, democracy, AIDS profiteering organizations, walkathons, liberal guilt disguised as "political correctness," and babies.

However, the most egregious crime of "gays and lesbians" is Bad Fashion. The boys adopt a repulsively sterile aesthetic of health reminiscent of a mythical germ-free adolescence to stave off death from AIDS: clones parading around in Bugle Boy jeans, displaying designer muscles, reeking of cK one, and dancing idiotically to boring "house" music with their peroxide and their fake tans. The girls "work" an outmoded bowl cut with a nonwardrobe intended to be as lackluster and sexless as possible. The boys look the same, the girls look the same. They suffer from a massive dose of self-imposed fascist gender policing. This bland homogeneity is their flock mentality, their way of feeling safety in numbers and recognizing their "family" without alerting their het superiors. They fabricate a concept of clone-family-tribe, which really just means they are begging for a collective cattle prod.

It is our duty as queers to expose the lie of "gay and lesbian" identity, to humiliate them with otherness. We must puke on their shoes, shit in their faces, and *kick their asses*. But first and foremost we must *refuse* to allow them entrance into queer culture. We must force them to be totally absorbed into the straight mainstream from which they spring. We must make queer clubs, music, and art for us and not let them, in their pathetic quest for an identity, come near it. We cannot afford to settle for their bogus "gay and lesbian" culture or to believe their lies—it is killing us, drowning us in pabulum, and numbing us to the point of invisibility. *We are the true culture. These parasites exist only as they feed off both queer and straight culture.*

*They are dead.* Now let's remind them of it.

# Q-Punk Grammar
## by Justin Chin

Once, I did a radio interview with a journalist who was doing this mondo piece about the twenty-fifth anniversary of Stonewall. He needed an Asian (any ethnicity), and I thought it might be an interesting experience. The interview went fine until I used the phrase, "black and Puerto Rican drag queens." That's when the entire interview went sloshing downhill.

"No!" Mr. Journalist declared. "That's a myth, and I want to debunk the myth, I want to tell the *truth!*" He whipped out pie charts and little flowcharts that illustrated his point. He said that he had interviewed at least six different people who claimed they threw the first brick. "Besides, the Stonewall bar did not allow nonwhites or drag queens into it, so they couldn't have been there. They came the second night." Mr. Journalist beamed triumphantly; he had done this before. Then came the icing on his cupcake. "Knowing that, how does this change your opinions about Stonewall?" he asked smugly.

In retrospect my answer was quite lame. "History is a matter of opinion," I said. "Different people will view history differently. I don't think who started it makes any difference, and I don't think it changes what was achieved and what was lost."

\* \* \*

Thinking back now, I realize that I never understood Stonewall at all; I was told it was important (is it?) and that I had to be suitably thankful for it (am I?). But that's what history is all about, isn't it? (Thank god for that London fire, otherwise we'd all be dead of bubonic plague—phew.)

We know something of where and how we were, but where the hell are we going? Certainly gays and lesbians existed and were organized before Stonewall. I was way queer—and agreeably practicing it— before I had even heard of Stonewall. But those June nights in 1969, when I was a mere queer fetus, did something irrevocable and incredible that cannot be denied. Still, time goes on—history is made, and history is lost. The line from a song by San Francisco performer David Johnston says it best: "You fought at Stonewall? Get over it, queen!"

The gay community is experiencing a great generational gap. It's a vicious cycle; each generation feels it has cornered the market on what it's like to be gay. The older generation tells us about being really gay *back then,* when they had

- Donna Summer when she meant something;
- Bette Midler when she meant something;
- good punk music and mosh pits that were mosh pits;
- real bell-bottoms, not retro fashion shit;
- sex without condoms;
- venerial diseases that didn't kill you outright; and
- those insidious little homosexual mustaches.

My generation tells the younger queer brats what it was like to be queer *back then.* And how they will never know what it was like

- to sit in a room of sixty people on a Wednesday night and try to reach consensus on something;
- to wear black leather jackets with fluorescent queer-positive stickers;
- to be at a kiss-in when a kiss-in meant something;
- to be so filled with anger and a strange hope at an AIDS demo;
- to have to defend using the word *queer;*
- when piercing our bodies meant something beyond fashion; and
- to make those damn zines.

It's hard to live in the past, but still some people persist. Nostalgia bites hard. The old refuse to grow old, the young refuse to grow up. Maybe it's understandable. We don't want to grow old in a culture that doesn't value age, we don't want to be less than what we feel we're worth, and we cling to the best days of our lives. For some it's the sixties or the seventies. I find myself watching eighties music videos on

MTV and tearing up. We want to forever be nubile young brown bodies lying in the sun, glorious as a Whitman ode, succulent enough to make the boys we secretly loved forget to say their prayers.

I look in my closet, and I see that I have inherited a gaggle of multicolored drag queens (though some would still disagree as to their color) tossing bricks at cops who look suspiciously like uniformed queens in a leather bar then or twenty years later. Torrid stories of poppers and nights of unsafe sex in bathhouse upon bathhouse, each successive one more fanciful, more sleazy, and more capable of fulfilling every homosexual fantasy: *But you will never know what it's like to have fifty men stick their dicks in all your orifices every day of your life, will you, sonny boy?* I have inherited a virus, a wrecked community, memorials, the NAMES Quilt, clinical trials, and the AIDS industry as a viable and "noble" career choice.

But here I shall make a break: Let the younger ones be queer the way they want to be queer, as long as they are queer, as long as they find among themselves one another to love. I've given up the dream of Queer Nation. Race, class, gender, ideology, and values will always divide us. It is ludicrous to think that since we share a common passion, we should all want the same things out of this life. We are one another's angels, and we are one another's demons. Beyond ourselves there will always be those who wish for nothing more than to see us dead; for centuries they have been wishing and acting on it, but we are not vanishing. Call it sheer luck, call it divine intervention, call it tenacity. The fundamentalist Christians will call it a symptom of the end of the world as prophesied.

I have no idea what it is to be gay or queer anymore, nor do I care. I am so over being queer, and I don't care what I call myself or what anyone else calls me; it's all a matter of convenience these days. I believe in being unapologetic for my desires. All I know is that when I wake in the night to find my lover's body next to mine, no history—real or imagined, myth or fact, inherited or created—can make me feel any less than brilliant in his arms.

# Contributors

**Nadya Arnaoot** is an artdyke/fag living in the suburbs of Washington, D.C. She does a zine, *more fragments from sappho's island*, is sporadically involved in riot grrrl, and spends more time than she'd care to admit on the Internet. She graduated with honors in English from the University of Chicago but is working as a secretary while she tries to figure out what to do with her life. **Alec** is her current name when she is a boy.

**Robin Bernstein** was born on April 15, 1969, in New York City. Her writing appears in many anthologies (most recently Roz Warren's *Dyke Strippers: Lesbian Cartoonists A to Z* and Lesléa Newman's *Eating Our Hearts Out: Women and Food*) and over twenty periodicals including *Belles Lettres, The Harvard Gay and Lesbian Review, Deneuve, 10 Percent, The Baltimore Jewish Times, Lambda Book Report, The Lesbian Review of Books, Sojourner, Bay Windows, The Philadelphia Gay News,* and *The Washington Blade,* for which she served as associate editor. She holds a B.A. in creative writing from Bryn Mawr College and an M.A. in history of theater from the University of Maryland.

**K. Burdette** was born in Washington, D.C., in 1970. She received her B.A. in radio, television, and film and is currently pursuing a graduate degree. Her previous writings have been published in *The Washington Review, Link: A Critical Journal on the Arts in Baltimore and the World,* and her friends' feminist zines. Ms. Burdette has worked as a photojournalist, a teacher of film theory, and an Internet database coordinator in the recent past. She is now working on an

CONTRIBUTORS

E-zine titled *Mouchette: For Alienated Girls and Bresson Fans,* which may or may not ever make it on-line. Her recent video work has been screened in local and international festivals in Washington, D.C.; New York; Los Angeles; and San Francisco.

**Christy Calame** is a hospice social worker and therapist living in Boston by day and a queer bi femme all the time. Since the death of direct-action groups such as Queer Nation, she has practiced her activism by coauthoring the antigay zine *Her Posse* and engaging in gender fucking and fetishism of all kinds.

**Justin Chin** is a writer and performance artist. His writings have appeared in *Men on Men 5: Best New Gay Fiction, Premonitions: The Kaya Anthology of New Asian American Poetry, Blue Mesa Review, Puerto Del Sol, Dissident Song: A Contemporary Asian American Anthology, Modern Words,* and *The James White Review,* among others. His performance works include *Attack of the Man-Eating Lotus Blossoms; Go, or, the Approximate Infinite Universe of Mrs. Robert Lomax;* and *Advice for Tragic Queens at Home and Abroad.* He was born in 1969.

**Charlotte Cooper** was born on October 26th, 1968, and recalls reading in the *National Enquirer* that she shares her birthday with Burt Reynolds. She is a fat activist and writer living on the dole in the East End of London. Her book, *Fat & Proud,* will be published in 1996 by the Women's Press, but you may know her from a cute write-up in *Seventeen* magazine and from her contributions to *Fat Girl.*

**Emily Cotlier,** born in 1970, is a perverse femme who has been involved in the East Coast leather scene for five and a half years. She is currently working on a book, *Laying It Down: Queer Bottoms Speak Out,* which should be published in 1997.

**Bree Coven** was born in New York City on October 19, 1972. She was first published at age sixteen, came out at eighteen, and is currently a writing student at Sarah Lawrence College. Bree originated the baby dyke column, "Hey, Baby!" for *Deneuve* magazine (now *Curve*), where she continues as a regular contributor. Her poetry, essays, and short fiction also appear in *Princess* magazine and the anthologies *The Femme Mystique* and *Motherlies.*

**Jim Davis-Rosenthal** and the accompanying multiple-celebrity personalities have recently completed a degree and are known collectively as Dr. goGo. "He" is a poet and visual artist as well as an editor for the on-line journal *Standards.*

**Jennifer DiMarco** was born during an incredible thunderstorm in September, 1973, in Seattle. A daughter of mothers, Jennifer has worked construction, taught martial arts, and is the author of almost two dozen novels, children's books, and screen and stage plays. Currently Jennifer is the president of Pride Publications, a national publishing and production company, and a lecturer on creative writing and queer/queer-youth empowerment.

**Michael Thomas Ford** is the author of several books, including *100 Questions & Answers About AIDS, The Voices of AIDS,* and *In a Different Light: Thoughts on Growing Up Queer.* His articles and reviews have appeared in *The Advocate, Music Alive, Current Biography, QW, The Washington Blade, Lambda Book Report,* and *Publishers Weekly.* His monthly humor column, "My Queer Life," appears in newspapers across the country. He was born on the first day of October, 1968.

**Kris Franklin,** born May 20, 1967, and **Sarah E. Chinn,** born October 25, 1967, have managed to stay together for almost ten years despite the fact that their signs are not compatible. Sarah is a doctoral candidate with a cow fixation, and Kris is a poverty lawyer who dreams of having her every whim indulged.

**M. Paz Galupo,** born August 14, 1968, resides in Fayetteville, Arkansas, with her three-year-old daughter, Isabel. She attends the University of Arkansas, where she is pursuing a doctorate in physiological psychology.

**Nels P. Highberg** was born on September 20, 1969. He holds a B.A. in English from the University of Houston and an M.A. in women's studies from Ohio State University and has had two poems published in *A Loving Testimony: Remembering Loved Ones Lost to AIDS,* edited by Lesléa Newman.

**Wayne Hoffman** was born on December 8, 1970, and grew up in an unusually functional Jewish family in Silver Spring, Maryland. After surviving high school and endless years of Hebrew school, he earned a B.A. in social politics from Tufts University. He is currently enmeshed in a doctoral program at New York University, focusing on gay popular culture through the American Studies department. As a journalist, Hoffman writes a media column, "Public Image," which is syndicated in a dozen gay newspapers nationally. Additionally, his freelance articles and interviews have appeared in over two dozen publications, including *The Washington Blade, Deneuve, Frontiers, 50/50 Magazine,* and *The Boston Phoenix.* As part of the Dangerous Bedfellows collective, he is coediting an anthology called *Policing Public Sex,* due out from South End Press in fall 1996. He lives in New York City.

**Surina A. Khan** is an associate analyst at Political Research Associates, a progressive think tank that monitors and researches the right wing. She has contributed to *The Harvard Gay and Lesbian Review, The Boston Phoenix, The Washington Blade, Deneuve, Girlfriends, Windy City Times, Southern Voice,* and was the former copublisher of *Metroline.* She lives in Boston.

**Erika Kleinman** was born on February 1, 1974, exactly one month after the U.S. surgeon general declared that homosexuality is not a mental illness. Her parents, Ronald and Victorine, have been domestic partners for twenty-four years. She has a baby brother (he hates it when she calls him that) named Ronald Wayne Kleinman Jr. She learned about AIDS in 1987 as it applied to Rock Hudson. She was thirteen. She came out to herself as a lesbian when she was fourteen, to her family when she was fifteen, and to the world from then on. She is blissfully married to Sam, her domestic partner of two years. They share a house in the suburbs and plan on having children in a few years. Sam has been incredibly patient and supportive of Erika's political life. She's cute too. Erika is very active with gay youth organizations and Bigot Busters. Besides being a gay rights activist, she is also a writer.

**J. Keiko Lane** is a Japanese-American Jewish queer from Los Angeles. A long-term survivor of Queer Nation and the Los Angeles chapter of ACT UP, she was guest editor for issue fifteen of *Infected Faggot Perspectives.* Currently she is finishing her AIDS literature thesis in Portland, Oregon.

**Hedda Lettuce** has been in this business called drag since 1992. She is an accomplished performer, with MTV, major motion pictures, sold-out solo performances, and *The Hedda Lettuce Show,* Hedda's very own cable sitcom, which airs every Wednesday on channel thirty-five in New York City at 9:30 p.m., all under her sequined belt. Hedda is also an avid spokesperson for MADD, Mothers Against Drunk Drag Queens, and speaks out against dragging and drinking whenever possible.

**Tom Maroney** lives in San Francisco.

**Doug Mattis**, born in 1967, is a six-time member of the U.S. international ice skating team.

**Pete McDade** lives in Atlanta. He writes fiction and is the drummer for 57 Records/550 Music recording artist 3 Lb. Thrill.

**Kelly McQuain**, an artist and writer living in Philadelphia, is a graduate of the Temple University Creative Writing Program. His stories and poetry have appeared in *The Philadelphia Inquirer Sunday Magazine, The James White Review, American Writing, The Sycamore Review, Wilde,* and the Alyson anthology *Certain Voices.* In 1994 he was named a Fiction Discipline Winner by the Pew Fellowships in the Arts. A native of West Virginia, he was born on February 5, 1967. He is currently working on a novel.

**Dolissa Medina,** born on February 6, 1971, is a second-generation "Aqueerian" who thanks all the hippie homos who came before her. Her work has appeared in *ConMocion: A Magazine for Latina Lesbians* as well as in numerous San Francisco publications. This is her first published piece in an anthology.

## CONTRIBUTORS

**Michael Olom Mennonno** was born on July 10, 1969, twelve days after Stonewall, in the naval hospital at Camp Lejeune, North Carolina, the youngest of three boys. He grew up in Speedway, Indiana, on Delores Drive, just two blocks from the Indy 500 racetrack and across the street from the Coca-Cola plant. He received a B.A. in U.S. history from Indiana University at Bloomington in 1993. He lives in New Hampshire with his dogs Reuben, Isabel, and Petie and a fat gray cat named Misha.

**Tom Musbach** received his B.A. in English from Yale University in 1988 and is working as an editor for Gay.Net, an on-line service for the gay community. Currently a resident of San Francisco, he grew up in Cleveland, where he was born on October 3, 1965.

**Anna Myers-Parrelli** is a writer who lives with her wife, Jo Myers-Parrelli, in Burlington, Vermont. Anna was born on Martin Luther King Jr.'s birthday, January 15, 1969. She graduated from Hampshire College in 1991 with a B.A. in psychology and feminist studies. Afterward she served for a time as program director in a residential mental-health program for adults with chronic psychiatric disabilities. She is currently in her second year in the University of Vermont's clinical psychology Ph.D. program, where she studies women and body-image, eating disorders, and issues of oppression.

**A. Rey Pamatmat** was born in Royal Oak, Michigan, on March 20, 1976, the second son in a growing Filipino family. The first story he wrote as a first-grade boy was about a young squirrel afraid to be ridiculed by his friends should they see him wearing his new glasses. He currently attends New York University as an aspiring actor/writer/performance artist/Lord-knows-what-else. He would like to thank his dearest friends as well as Micah, Joel, Tim, Dan, and Scott, the five men who have inspired his work most.

**Robbie Scott Phillips**, a romantic and modernist, publishes the visionary antigay and -lesbian zine *Her Posse*. He runs a record store in Boston and finds new reasons to despise the gay and lesbian drones on a daily basis. Recently single and known to many as King Johnny Comet or Miss Tracy Been Husky, Robbie believes Kate Moss and

Courtney Love are queer-punk icons. Rock and roll has saved his soul. Write to *Her Posse* at P.O. Box 15137, Boston, MA 02215.

**Catherine Saalfield** is a videomaker, writer, educator, and activist. Her video work concentrates on issues of HIV/AIDS, the religious right, homophobia, multiculturalism, and other lesbian and gay issues. Her production credits include *Positive: Life With HIV, Sacred Lies Civil Truths, Not Just Passing Through, Cuz It's Boy, Keep Your Laws Off My Body,* and *I'm You You're Me: Women Surviving Prison Living With AIDS,* all of which have been screened nationally and internationally. Saalfield currently teaches video to gay, lesbian, bisexual, and trans-gendered youth at the Hetrick-Martin Institute in New York City, where she established BENT TV, a monthly public-access show. She would like to thank John Greyson, who is also a very close friend of Ray Navarro's, for reading through her essay and for remembering.

**Kimberly Scrafano** spends most of her free time writing poetry and fiction. She currently works as a writer and editor in an incarceration-alternative program. She also counsels battered women at a shelter. Before this she did extensive HIV/AIDS prevention work for young lesbians and women sleeping with women and has experience in rape-crisis hot line counseling. She was born on December 18, 1972; grew up working-class in a small town in eastern Pennsylvania; and now lives in New York City.

**Ricco V. Siasoco** was born in Iowa in 1972 into a family of immigrant parents, six siblings and their spouses, fourteen nieces and nephews, two great-nieces, and two great-nephews. He received a degree in broadcasting and film from Boston University. He lives in Boston, where he is completing his first novel.

**Lacy Silberman**, born December 26, 1981, lives in Florida, where she recently pierced her eyebrow. She passes the time praying to her shrine of Jodie Foster and E-mailing her brother Seth.

**Seth Clark Silberman**, born June 17, 1968, is a Ph.D. student in the Program of Comparative Literature at the University of Maryland, where he teaches lesbian and gay studies, film, and postcolonial literatures. He also teaches at the Maryland College of Art and Design. His writing has been included in *The Gay and Lesbian Literary Heritage: A Reader's Companion to the Writers and Their Works, From Antiquity to the Present; Contemporary Gay American Novelists: A Bio-Bibliographical Critical Sourcebook;* and the journal *In Process.* While editing this book, Seth ran the 1995 Marine Corps Marathon (his first) in four hours, one minute, and thirty-eight seconds.

Born on the 13th of July, 1966, on San Bernardino Air Force Base near Albuquerque, **Forrest Tyler Stevens** currently lives in Durham, North Carolina, with his boyfriend. He has degrees in computer science and English literature from the University of Colorado at Boulder.

**Cianna P. Stewart** is a Mestiza Filipina British Islander American mutt, 1.5 generation and DAR. She currently lives in San Francisco but is prone to wandering. She works as an HIV-prevention educator and freelance theater director. She is a columnist for *Anything That Moves: The Magazine for the Uncompromising Bisexual,* and collaborates on slut-style outreach to transgendered and disabled folks and the Asian and Pacific Islander communities. She is obsessed with the consumption and regurgitation of words and images. She has frequently been caught performing her own work and is noted for disregarding advice in reference to high caffeine-intake levels.

**Sarah Pemberton Strong** has just finished writing a novel set in the Dominican Republic. She works as a teaching assistant in the public school system, where, to her dismay, they don't take many field trips. She is still friends with her eighth-grade teacher.

**Denise Tuggle** was born on January 21, 1965, in Chicago. When she was a junior at Bryn Mawr College, her work on the relationship between race and the Ivy League was published in issue twenty-five of *Heresies.* She lives in Oakland, California, where she divides her time between the emergency shelter where she works, Hand to Hand Kajukenbo Kung Fu School, and her life partner, Daphne.

**Eric C. Waldemar** is a published playwright, poet, and essayist. In 1995 his semiautobiographical one-act play, *Make-Up Stories,* placed first in the Kennedy Center/American College Theatre Festival Lorraine Hansberry Playwriting Award competition. The award is presented annually for the best student-written play on the African-American experience. Eric is also the recipient of the Shenandoah International Playwright's Retreat Fellowship and the Black History Makers of Tomorrow Award. His other dramatic works include *Splitting Images, Revelations, A Legend in My Dressing Room, Transformations,* and *Freeing Zoey.* Eric is a graduate of the University of Maryland, where he studied theater and practiced playwriting.

Other books of interest from
# ALYSON PUBLICATIONS

**These books and other Alyson titles are available at your local bookstore. If you can't find a book listed below or would like more information, please call us directly at 1-800-5-ALYSON.**

❏ **BETTER ANGEL,** by Forman Brown. Written in 1933, this classic, touching story focuses on a young man's gay awakening in the years between the world wars. Kurt Gray is a shy, bookish boy growing up in small-town Michigan. Even at the age of thirteen he knows that somehow he is different. Gradually he recognizes his desire for a man's companionship and love. As a talented composer breaking into New York's musical world, he finds the love he has sought. This new edition contains an updated epilogue and black-and-white photographs from the author's life.

❏ **BI ANY OTHER NAME: BISEXUAL PEOPLE SPEAK OUT,** edited by Loraine Hutchins and Lani Kaahumanu. Hear their voices as more than seventy women and men from all walks of life describe their lives as bisexuals. They tell their stories — personal, political, spiritual, historical — in prose, poetry, art, and essays. These are individuals who have fought prejudice from both the gay and straight communities and who have begun only recently to share their experiences. This groundbreaking anthology is an important step in the process of forming a new bisexual community.

❏ **BROTHER TO BROTHER: NEW WRITINGS BY BLACK GAY MEN,** edited by Essex Hemphill. The late black activist and poet Essex Hemphill followed in the footsteps of Joseph Beam with this anthology of fiction, essays, and poetry by black gay men. Contributors include Assoto Saint, Craig G. Harris, Melvin Dixon, Marlon Riggs, and many newer writers.

❏ **CAPTAIN SWING,** by Larry Duplechan. Johnnie Ray Rousseau's life is at its lowest ebb. The love of his life was killed in a hit-and-run accident, and now he's been called to the deathbed of his hateful, homophobic father. There he meets Nigel, his second cousin, who looks like mortal sin in Levi's and a tank top and who offers a love that Johnnie is none too sure he ought to accept.

❏ **CHARLEYHORSE,** by Cecil Dawkins. Charley was born wanting things she was not supposed to want: horses, flying planes, and driving combine harvesters. Charley runs a ranch half the size of a township, but it's not enough. When Juna, a new schoolteacher from New York, moves in, Charley finally has a chance at what she wants — but first she has to deal with her eccentric and manipulative mother.

**a**

❑ **CODY,** by Keith Hale. Steven Trottingham Taylor, "Trotsky" to his friends, is new in Little Rock. Washington Damon Cody has lived there all his life. Yet when they meet, there's a familiarity — a sense that they've known each other before. Their friendship grows and develops a rare intensity, although one of them is gay and the other is straight.

❑ **CRUSH,** by Jane Futcher. It wasn't easy fitting in at an exclusive girls' school like Huntington Hill. But in her senior year, Jinx finally felt as if she belonged. Lexie — beautiful, popular Lexie — wanted her for a friend. Jinx knew she had a big crush on Lexie, and she knew she had to do something to make it go away. But Lexie had other plans. And Lexie always got her way.

❑ **DEATH BY DENIAL: STUDIES OF SUICIDE IN GAY AND LESBIAN TEENAGERS,** edited by Gary Remafedi. A federal study found in 1989 that teenagers struggling with issues of sexual orientation were three times more likely than their peers to attempt suicide. The report was swept aside by the Bush administration, yet the problem didn't go away. Here are the full findings of that report and of several other studies; they document the difficulties faced by teenagers who are coming out and propose ways to ease that process.

❑ **EYES OF DESIRE: A DEAF GAY AND LESBIAN READER,** edited by Raymond Luczak. Coming out is hard enough already. But it becomes a new challenge altogether when one can't take communication itself for granted. Here, for the first time, lesbians and gay men who are deaf tell about their lives: discovering their sexual identities; overcoming barriers to communication in a sound-based world; and, finally, creating a deaf gay and lesbian culture in a world that is too often afraid of differences.

❑ **HAPPY ENDINGS ARE ALL ALIKE,** by Sandra Scoppettone. It was their last summer before college, and Jaret and Peggy were in love. But as Jaret said: "It always seems as if when something great happens, then something lousy happens soon after." Soon her worst fears turned into brute reality.

❑ **A LOTUS OF ANOTHER COLOR: AN UNFOLDING OF THE SOUTH ASIAN GAY AND LESBIAN EXPERIENCE,** edited by Rakesh Ratti. For the first time gay men and lesbians from India, Pakistan, and other South Asian countries relate their coming-out stories. In essays and poetry they tell of challenging prejudice from both the South Asian and gay cultures and express the exhilaration of finally finding a sense of community.

❑ **NOT THE ONLY ONE: LESBIAN AND GAY FICTION FOR TEENS,** by Tony Grima. Many lesbians and gay men remember their teen years as a time of isolation and anxiety, when exploring sexuality meant facing possible rejection by family and

**a**

friends. But it can also be a time of exciting discovery and of hope for the future. These stories capture all the fears, joys, confusion, and energy of teenagers coming face-to-face with gay issues, either as they themselves come out or as they learn that a friend or family member is gay.

❑ **ONE TEACHER IN TEN: GAY AND LESBIAN EDUCATORS TELL THEIR STORIES,** edited by Kevin Jennings. Gay and lesbian teachers have traditionally dwelt in the deepest of closets. But increasing numbers of young people are now served by teachers who are out and proud. Here, for the first time, educators from all regions of the country tell about their struggles and victories as they have put their own careers at risk in their fight for justice.

❑ **THE PRESIDENT'S SON,** by Krandall Kraus. D.J. Marshall is the handsome, gay son of a popular president. But as the reelection campaign begins, D.J. finds himself cut off from his father by ambitious advisers who are determined that no scandal should threaten their power. Soon D.J. realizes that he has no one to trust. No one except Parker, the beefy Secret Service agent who is taking an unusual interest in D.J.'s personal life. But just how far can Parker be trusted?

❑ **REFLECTIONS OF A ROCK LOBSTER,** by Aaron Fricke. Guess who's coming to the prom! Aaron Fricke made national news by taking a male date to his high school prom. Here, told with rare insight and humor, is Aaron's story about growing up gay, realizing that he is different, and ultimately developing a positive gay identity in spite of the prejudice around him.

❑ **REVELATIONS,** edited by Adrien Saks and Wayne Curtis. For most gay men, one critical moment stands out as a special time in the coming-out process. It may be a special friendship or a sexual episode or a book or movie that communicates the right message at the right time. In this collection, twenty-two men of varying ages and backgrounds give an account of this moment of truth. These tales of self-discovery will strike a chord of recognition in every gay reader.

❑ **SCHOOL'S OUT: THE IMPACT OF GAY AND LESBIAN ISSUES ON AMERICA'S SCHOOLS,** by Dan Woog. America's schools are filled with gay men and lesbians: students, teachers, principals, coaches, and counselors. Author Dan Woog interviewed nearly 300 people in this exploration of the impact of gay and lesbian issues and people on the U.S. educational system. From the scared teenager who doesn't want his teammates to know he's gay to the straight teacher who wants to honor diversity by teaching gay issues in the classroom, Woog puts a human face on the people who truly are fighting for "liberty and justice for all."

❑ **SOCIETY AND THE HEALTHY HOMOSEXUAL,** by George Weinberg. Rarely has anyone communicated so much, in a single word, as Dr. George Weinberg did when he introduced the term "homophobia." With a single stroke of the pen, he turned the tables on centuries of prejudice. Homosexuality is healthy, said Weinberg: Homophobia is a sickness. In this pioneering book, Weinberg examines the causes of homophobia. He shows how gay people can overcome its pervasive influence to lead happy and fulfilling lives.

❏ **TESTIMONIES,** edited by Karen Barber and Sarah Holmes. More than twenty women of widely varying backgrounds and ages give accounts of their journeys toward self-discovery. The stories portray the women's efforts to develop a lesbian identity, explore their sexuality, and build a community with other lesbians.

❏ **TOMBOYS! TALES OF DYKE DERRING-DO,** edited by Lynne Yamaguchi Fletcher and Karen Barber. For many people, "tomboy" is virtually a synonym for "lesbian," and there is, in fact, considerable overlap between the two categories. This collection of stories, essays, and photographs examines and celebrates tomboyhood and its meaning for those tomboys who grew up to be lesbians. Readers will delight in both the commonalities and the varieties of experience revealed in these tales told with humor, attitude, nostalgia, longing, and, above all, love.

❏ **TWO TEENAGERS IN 20: WRITINGS BY GAY AND LESBIAN YOUTH,** edited by Ann Heron. Twelve years after compiling *One Teenager In Ten,* the first book ever to allow dozens of teenagers to describe what it's like to be gay or lesbian, Ann Heron asked for stories from a new generation. She found that their sense of isolation and despair runs every bit as deep as a decade ago. *Two Teenagers in 20* combines these new voices with many essays from her first book. This book will greatly ease the way for teenagers just now coming out and will help the adults who seek to support them.

❏ **UNLIVED AFFECTIONS,** by George Shannon. After the grandmother who raised him dies, eighteen-year-old Willie is eager to leave everything behind as he clears out her house for auction. His tenuous sense of family and self is shaken to the core as he reads a hidden box of letters written to his long-dead mother from the father he'd never known. A father who he'd been told was dead. A father who'd never been told he had a son. A father who'd been searching for his own sense of self and family as a gay man eighteen years before.

❏ **YOUNG, GAY, & PROUD!** edited by Don Romesburg. One high school student in ten is gay. When *Young, Gay, & Proud!* first appeared in 1980, it was the first book to address the needs of this often-invisible minority. In this revised edition the editor has reworked the book to make it newly relevant to the issues faced by gay teens in the mid '90s, issues such as: Am I really gay? What would my friends think if I told them? Should I tell my parents? Other sections discuss health concerns, sexuality, and suggestions for further reading.

**a**